LESSONS

FROM

ABOVE

Lessons from Above

Ahaleaiah

Spirit Healings Publishing

Table of Contents

Dedicated to my husband,

Keith.

Every day with you is all I ever need.

Thank you for the love, the lessons, the

support, and most of all,

For being, You.

Acknowledgements

I am eternally thankful to everyone who supported me over the years in helping me write this book. It has been a long journey, and it is far from being over.

First and foremost, this book would not have been possible without Reverend Bob Copeland and his guide, Ashlem. Bob dedicated his life to serving the Brotherhood of Light by allowing Ashlem to share his body, enabling Ashlem to teach, guide, and share his wisdom with humankind.

Bob dedicated over fifty years of his life to this journey of service. He was always available to those of us who needed him as we continued our journey and mission on Earth. Ashlem taught thousands of people on Earth, from his New Year's Eve meditations to his Wednesday night classes and personal Akashic readings for people worldwide. Bob traveled to Texas, Colorado Springs, and other places for years so that Ashlem could reach out to Lightworkers for guidance as we enter this highly anticipated time in human existence. Bob transitioned to the Spirit World two years ago, and I know he was welcomed with open arms. Thank you, Bob and Ashlem; your patience, kindness, and love have changed my life. I hope to continue spreading the knowledge and wisdom you began here on Earth.

I want to thank my husband, Keith. I can't thank him enough for all the love, support, dedication, patience, and comfort he's given me over the years. He understood what I needed to do and gave me all the freedom I needed to accomplish what I came back to Earth to do. I am blessed you chose me. You are eternally in my heart, and I will love you forever.

The list of people who believed in me to write this book is long. I am forever grateful to everyone. No one is more or less important to me.

Granddaughter Crow for her guidance from the realms. Sonya Shannon for her beautiful cover work and for bringing the vision I couldn't put into words. Tisha Smith, for being my right-hand; I couldn't do what I do without you. Stephanie Sufian, for the cajoling, laughter, support, and messages that I wasn't listening to. Tisha Benoit, my mentor, my friend, my confidante. Chris Rossie, to my oldest and dearest friend. You watched me wrestle through every step of my life and supported me in ways I could never fully express. Reverend Jim Campbell, you poked, prodded, and asked a million questions to guide me on my journey. I'm forever thankful and blessed to have you in my life. And Martin Knife Chief, your kindness and compassion transcend time and space; I'm eternally grateful and honored to have met you.

To my dearest friends in heaven, Lynnette Bohannon and Julie Gray, who crossed over while I was writing this book, I miss you more than you'll ever know. I miss your faces, your laughter, your love for everyone, and your ability to stay positive through your final moments. I know you have your wings in heaven as you did on Earth. I love you both.

To my patients who stayed with me, taught me, believed in me, and honored me with your presence in my office, I am deeply grateful.

To those whom I have not mentioned, I thank you. You will always be in my heart.

Most of all, I give thanks and praise to the Blessed Virgin Mary, my Guides, my Angels, my Brothers and Sisters in the Brotherhood of Light, Confucius, Buddha, Quan Yin, the Great Spirit, and the Father/Mother/God/Creation. I am humbled and blessed by the opportunities you give and the life you help me create. Without you, nothing is possible; with you, everything is possible.

Preface

For many years, I knew I had to write this book and share my Akashic records and life story. I was asked to teach the people of Earth about our Oneness with God, the Lord, Mother/Father, the Universe, Source, Allah, Tao, and the Void. It is not for my own benefit, but to provide wisdom, knowledge, and understanding of our divine selves—not separate from God, Lord, Mother/Father, the Universe, Source, Allah, Tao, Void, or whatever name you use for Creation. We each have our own spiritual path; there is no single right or wrong way.

This book will help you understand the reasons behind your struggles and accept that everything happens for a reason. Sometimes, that reason is to learn a lesson, gain an experience, or guide you in a different direction. The stories I share about my journey and how I recognized people, places, and things will help you question and learn about your own path through life while gaining a deeper understanding of your own Akashics.

My story offers hope that things can get better and that life will become more meaningful and fulfilling. Sometimes, knowledge is hidden from us, along with answers that are meant to be accepted without question. I tell you, *"Listen to your heart. Your true heart. And you will know without doubt your destined path of happiness."*

Most importantly, I hope you realize your own Divinity. You are not separate from the Whole—EVER. You are a part of every atom in existence, beyond your own presence and being. I hope these words open the door to a deeper understanding of your true self, and that recognizing your authentic self helps you find love, peace, and understanding in this lifetime.

No matter where you are on your journey of life or how complex your path seems right now, it will change. Hope, understanding, love, patience, and forgiveness open the doors that lead you out of your current situation. You might be thinking, *"Easier said than done."* And my response is, *"I know exactly how you feel. I may not have walked the same path you are, but every struggle is real. And there is a reason for that struggle. Learn your lessons now, and the rest of your life becomes easier."*

This book is the first in a series of readings and lessons. When I transcribed my Akashic readings, I bold italicized The Blessed Virgin Mary's and Ashlem's words. When Bob or I spoke during the readings, those words were only italicized.

I share with you one of the most valuable lessons I learned from Ashlem:

I give to you the sign of peace. Of the Father and of the Son, and of thee and thy Holy Spirit, that the Circle of God is eternal. Never beginning, never ending, and never to be separated from the whole, and that is thee. And the force of Being be upon thee at this time. Amen.

I am honored to share my story with you, and I hope it helps you make better choices than I did.

Chapter One: In the Beginning

After many years of trials and tribulations, and without a clear understanding of when or how my life would unfold, I now have a life I cherish. It did not happen quickly, easily, magically, or in any distinct way. It was a long road filled with hardship, struggles, and lessons learned repeatedly.

After navigating many ups and downs in love, I have found an amazing husband who completes my world. He shows me daily how loved and respected I am, inspiring me to explore and embrace new experiences.

I proudly operate my own healing practice in Oriental Medicine, surrounded by wonderful and appreciative clients. I left the corporate world to start this medical practice. Helping my patients with their pain, health issues, and anxiety gives me a deep sense of satisfaction that I never felt in my previous jobs. Many of my patients seek spiritual counseling, and this part of my work is the most rewarding and uplifting moment of my day.

Additionally, I have completed the long and challenging initiation to become the spiritual teacher I was destined to be. I was asked to teach the life and spiritual lessons that Ashlem, an Ascended Master, imparted to me, which I spent over twenty years learning from him. Life is incredibly fulfilling.

My Childhood

In a sudden realization, I saw how different my life was from my humble beginnings. I grew up in a small, conservative farming community about forty miles northeast of Philadelphia. I was born into an Italian/Pennsylvania Dutch family, with my Pennsylvania Dutch ancestors being the thirteenth family to settle in Berks County, PA, in the early 1700s.

The Italian side of my family immigrated to the US in the 1910s as fascism was gaining power in Italy. Because of this meshing of two strong-willed races, I learned at an incredibly young age to respect my parents, elders, others, and other people's property. Respect for others was, first and foremost, the fundamental lesson I had to learn. I was reminded repeatedly that I did not own anything in this world when I came into it. I had to earn the money to afford the lifestyle I wanted, and I couldn't touch anything that didn't belong to me. If I wanted to look at an object a family member had in their home, I needed to ask for permission. Asking for permission and saying 'please' and 'thank you' were non-negotiable.

We were a WASP community (White Anglo-Saxon Protestants). Everyone believed in the importance of hard work and dedication to their families. Traditional values were taught to children and expected from each member. Women were expected to stay home with their children until they were at least in kindergarten. Divorce was uncommon and viewed suspiciously. There was extraordinarily little racial diversity, maybe three or four black families and one Asian family.

Much of the community attended church every Sunday, and children were expected to participate in Bible and confirmation classes until they were in their teens. There were always bake sales at the Churches and children's events at Easter and Christmas. Attendance at Church was mandatory for these two most important holidays of the year. Holidays such as New Year's, Memorial Day, Fourth of July, Labor Day, and Thanksgiving were just as important. On these holidays, few stores or restaurants were open, and you were expected to spend time with and honor your family. You were expected to honor those who lost their lives in combat. You were expected to celebrate the founding of our nation. And you were expected to honor the lives lost in the fight for fair and decent wages. Memorial Day, the Fourth of July, and Labor Day were marked by parades and family picnics that strengthened community and family bonds. Nothing else was ever as important.

The community was gracious and helpful. They looked out for each other but always kept a watchful eye on strangers. If you left for a few years and moved back, you had to prove yourself all over again. Anyone new to the community was suspect and not readily accepted. My elementary school was located on the road where I lived, and I would walk home from school every day. As I passed by the houses on my way home, older people would look out their windows to ensure I made it home safely. I never knew this was happening until my mother blurted it out one day.

Growing up outside Philadelphia gave me a keen sense of the area's history and its importance. In 1975, Elton John released Philadelphia Freedom, commemorating the 200th anniversary of our nation's Independence Day. It was my favorite song, and I was so happy when it came on the radio. I would sing it every day as I walked home from school. It had more significance to me than just the Bicentennial. I did not know it at the time, but the lines:

> *"'Cause I live and breathe this Philadelphia freedom,*
> *"From the day that I was born, I've waved the flag.*
> *"Some others choose the good old family home;*
> *"I like living easy without family ties."*

Little did I realize how significant this song would be to me later in life, and especially those lines. However, those moments live with me, even to this day.

This marked the beginning of a pivotal time in my life, during which I was completely unaware of the lasting impact it would have on my life today. I never understood why I was so different. I never understood why I knew things, could feel things, and heard things that were "shocking" to everyone else. I never understood why I didn't seem to fit in with those around me, including family, friends, and acquaintances. I saw the world differently. I felt it differently. I heard it differently. It didn't feel like I was a misfit at school or an outcast in my family; it felt like I was an alien who had come to Earth from outer space. When I talked to my family about what I felt and saw, I was told I was weird. This is a phrase I would often hear.

Throughout my life, I have been interested in growing food and using herbs to treat illnesses. My grandfather had a lovely family farm, where everyone helped sow the seeds, water the garden, harvest the crops, and prepare for the winter months ahead. Spring was my absolute favorite time of the year. I loved the planting season – I could not wait to see the seedlings poking out of the soil. I loved the Summer: seeing the plants grow to a few feet tall, and I loved climbing the apple and cherry trees. When Fall arrived, I was amazed at all the wonderful fruits, vegetables, flowers, and herbs we grew. I did not like winter and could not wait for Spring. My family always called me the little farmer – they could not keep me out of it!

As time passed and I entered my teenage years, my passion for nature and the seasons' cycles waned. The restlessness of puberty and becoming a young woman demanded more of my attention than the garden.

Many of my past life recollections occurred during my elementary school years. The most profound memories of my past lives were those I needed to recall in this lifetime. In sixth grade, the school took my class to Philadelphia to see the Liberty Bell, Independence Hall, Constitution Hall, the United States Mint, and Betsy Ross's house. I vividly remember that trip. When I arrived at Betsy's house and saw her Flag, I could not move. I was stuck; I almost fell to my knees. I didn't understand why I felt like a thunderbolt had hit me.

Another recollection I often had was seeing myself running across a desert under a full moon, hearing the call of *"Bedouin, Bedouin."* At other times, I would hear a noise while sleeping and wake up in a panic. I would say to myself, *"My father is coming to molest me!"* But after a few moments of quiet, I would say, *"It's not this father; it's a different father."* Then, I would fall sound asleep. I never questioned why I could separate this father from another father. I intuitively knew the answer; I had other lives and other fathers.

This last recollection is one that I will still experience. Sometimes, I fall asleep when, suddenly, severe fright overcomes me, and it feels like I am having an anxiety attack. My arms and hands shake; I am hyperventilating, and my heart is beating out of my chest. There was nothing I could do to stop it. Sometimes, I must leave my bed and walk around to settle in. After a few minutes, my breathing and heartbeat slowed, and I stopped shaking. It will take me another ten minutes to relax, and then I can go back to sleep. In the morning, I will learn that someone has passed away at the exact moment of my "episode." It is one of the scariest moments I have had because it feels like my soul is leaving my body with the person who is passing. This is my karma, and I must respect the process.

Fortunately, the other recollections I have are not as intense. Once, our class was taken to a nearby Native American Village. I remember sitting in that teepee and feeling completely at ease, as if I had returned home. I was at peace and happy for the first time in my short life.

I carried that feeling almost every day, and one day, in my school library, I came across a book in the sixth-grade section titled *"Custer's Last Stand."* I immediately despised Custer without knowing anything about him. Each time I walked by that book, I felt utterly repulsed. I could not wait to check out that book in sixth grade. Without even reading a sentence, I knew it was full of lies and mistruths. I remember feeling immense sadness for the Native Americans suffering at the hands of the white man. I admired their strength and their way of life. I cried when I saw in history books the enormous mounds of dead buffalo heads; what a terrible waste. Why did I feel so connected to the Native Americans? Another question that I could not answer.

I also remember defending them to anyone, including my family. I defended their rights to govern themselves on their reservations and build casinos so they could support themselves. However, I was dismissed because "*I had no idea what I was talking about.*" This is a phrase I often heard growing up.

One evening, around the age of eight, I was watching a TV show, which I believe was *"Wonder Woman,"* and there was an episode where she washed up on shore without drowning in the ocean. At that moment, I knew I had experienced the same thing in a different lifetime. Suddenly, I could see the water, the waves, and myself washing up on the beach. I felt the sting of the cold water, the exhaustion from nearly drowning, and then a deep feeling of loneliness followed.

I remember my maternal grandmother's funeral in May 1978 and asking my mother if I would ever see her again, and she told me, *"No."* I couldn't accept that answer; it didn't feel right. But her response sent shivers of fear through my body. Why would I never see her again? You see everyone again.

Another time, in 1980, I was listening to the radio when *"Ah! Leah!"* by Donnie Iris came on. I turned around because I thought someone was calling my name. I never understood why I felt that way. Every time I heard the song, I turned around. Why? It was another "weird" coincidence.

I remember a pivotal day, October 6, 1981. I was in fifth grade when the school turned on all the televisions in our classrooms to show the news: Anwar El-Sadat was assassinated during a victory parade. I felt profound sadness, so intense it was like losing a close family member or an uncle. I kept thinking, *"This is so bad. Nothing will ever be the same. He was a Savior for the Middle East."* I have come to realize that Sadat's death set in motion the disastrous war with Lebanon in 1982, the creation of Hezbollah, and the foundations of al-Qaida. My sadness was almost as overwhelming when I learned of Yitzhak Rabin's assassination on November 04, 1995. I felt the Middle East would never recover from these devastating losses.

Middle School

As I entered junior high and high school, the feeling of being an outcast only increased my loneliness. Every teenager endures the same feeling at some point, but mine felt different. Music has always had a profound impact on me, and in 1982, Rush released "*Subdivisions*." I don't know any song that has ever impacted me as much as that one did. Channel 17's Video Rock played its videos every Friday night. The lyrics reverberated in my mind repeatedly. They were singing about my life!

> *"Nowhere is the dreamer or the misfit so alone.*
> *"In the high school halls,*
> *"In the shopping malls, Conform or be cast out."*

Years went by, and I made a few friends, but those connections were not deep. They gave me an outlet for my teenage turmoil and some stability without empathy. But it wasn't just my schoolmates. My family and I had little in common. They often told me, "*I don't know where you came from*," and "*You are weird.*"

I often thought about running away from home. I made plans, but I never followed through. I heard stories about runaways who were never seen again. This was a time when missing children were featured on milk cartons, and I didn't want to end up there. Instead, I planned my escape in quieter ways: I kept my thoughts to myself, became an introvert, studied hard, took every class I could, and waited until I turned 18. Then, when I was finally on my own and living the life I wanted, I could do it without fear of judgment or being belittled. The world would be my stage, and I could play whatever role I chose.

Sadly, I had many more years to wait before I could do what I truly wanted.

As I entered 8th grade, I was very excited to attend my social studies class. We learned about ancient history, including Mesopotamia, the Tigris and Euphrates River basin, the Sumerians, King Hammurabi, Babylon, the Seven Wonders of the Ancient World, the Egyptians, the Greeks, the Romans, Ancient China, and the Silk Road. I was amazed because I already knew that information before Mrs. Carr taught it. I constantly asked questions about the history of those regions— questions that weren't covered in our textbook. I'm not sure if she knew the answers, but she fostered a very supportive environment that fueled my desire to learn.

On the social side of junior high school, I was extremely shy. Every day, a group of us seventh graders sat at the same long table, with some female ninth graders next to us. I remember them disliking me, putting me down, making fun of me, and being downright rude. I ignored them, but their behavior seemed to get worse. I honestly had no idea what I had done to become their target, but it continued every day all year. That was when I began to see cruelty in the world. As the days went on, I started to tease and mock other girls in my class— those who weren't pretty or smart. I was harsh to them, and no one stopped me. At that age, you learn to be resilient and take everything in stride. It makes you stronger and teaches you how to get through tough times that will come later. Looking back, I realize I only felt anger and loneliness, and those classmates became my outlet.

At some point in eighth grade, I experienced a spark of recognition and hope that I hadn't felt in a long time. There was a ninth-grade boy I absolutely fell in love with (at least the kind of love you feel in junior high). It was more than just teenage hormones. I felt like I knew him and recognized him, but I couldn't quite figure out where or how. I wanted him to see me and fall in love with me. Maybe someone will finally love me. So, I did all the silly, awkward things teenagers do and failed. He definitely knew me but never said a word to me. I was rejected again.

I remember my first day of high school. I was in 10th grade. The loneliness I felt throughout elementary and junior high school only grew worse. There was no one like me. No one I could connect with. I became very introverted. I dropped out of my extracurricular activities and focused on my studies.

My parents owned a collection of medical encyclopedias, and I read them nonstop. I wanted to learn as much as possible about known medical conditions. Was this my path in life? I knew I wanted to go to college; it was the escape from my small hometown that I needed and desired. I remember thinking, *"Just get through high school, and you can go anywhere and do anything you want to do. No one will tell you what to do. No one will ridicule you. No one will treat you less than you are."* My self-esteem was very low, like that of most high school students. It was something I hadn't realized: that most people felt just like me.

In 1986, I remember watching the news when the broadcaster announced that Chichen Itza had just been declared an archaeological monument, and he went on to share its history. I had never heard of Chichen Itza before, but an incredible sense of emptiness washed over me. It felt as though I was transported back in time, and hazy memories flooded my mind. I didn't understand what was happening, and I didn't try to understand. I just accepted it as another ordinary, "weird" experience. It contributed to my feeling of not fitting in anywhere.

Not only did my past lives come to me, but my intuition was also incredibly sharp and precise. I knew when my great-grandfather would pass away. He was born in June 1897, and for many years, I thought he would die in May 1987, which he did. I remember playing pinochle with my grandfather and father, and I could see their hands, although not always; many times, I could. I would get "strange" feelings when I saw an object, and later, it would turn out to be a crucial part of a situation that had happened. For example, in twelfth grade, my class was taken to Manhattan, and we visited the Twin Towers. I remember standing on the observation deck, feeling the building sway in the wind, and looking down at the street. I felt a deep sadness that it wouldn't be there for future generations and that another terror attack would bring the building down. Another time, I received some pictures of Mt. Rainer and Waikiki Beach. Those images captivated me; I didn't understand why at the time. The reasons became clearer later in life.

At times, I can read people's thoughts, listen to them, and sense what will happen. I know when their words don't match the reality of the situation. If they confided in me about choices they needed to make, I could tell which would benefit them the most; I felt wise beyond my years. All these things still happen to me, and I use this gift to guide friends and patients on their journeys. These gifts seem to be both a curse and a blessing: the knowledge of what's to come and the awareness that I still have a long way to go.

Off to College

After graduating from high school, I went to college in Western Pennsylvania, as far from Philadelphia as I could go without leaving the state. In college, I hoped to find someone who would understand me and like me for who I was, someone who could accept me and treat me with love and compassion. I was angry and needed a new environment to start fresh. I looked forward to freedom and independence. I was finally eighteen, and I felt like I could do whatever I wanted, whenever I wanted! FREEDOM! What I wanted most was freedom, but I soon realized I didn't understand the responsibilities that came with it. That lesson came at a steep price.

At the start of my freshman semester, I never went out drinking or partying like my other classmates. I had a boyfriend back home who didn't like the idea of me going out. However, in October, I grew tired of his overprotectiveness and ended our relationship. That weekend, I went out with my dorm friends and partied. And yes, I drank too much one night. My friend Kim met up with a guy she knew at the party because he lived in the same dorms as us. He agreed to walk us home.

Kim and I were highly intoxicated. I don't think we could have gotten back to my dorm without his help. I remember him walking Kim to her room and dropping her off, then walking me to mine. All I wanted was to lie down and sleep off this drunken fog. I don't remember him leaving, and I know I didn't invite him to stay the night. I had never been with a man before, and I wanted it to be a special experience. I wanted to decide when the time was right for me. Tonight wasn't the night, and he wasn't the right person. The gift I wanted to share with a man I loved and who loved me was taken away.

But it happened that way. At one point, I remember waking up, and he was inside of me. I didn't know what to do, so I froze. In my state, I couldn't understand what was happening, and I couldn't stop it. The words *"No"* and *"Stop"* were stuck in my throat.

Afterward, he left, and I got up and locked my dorm room. The click of the lock was a reminder that my life had been forever changed. I was so ashamed. What just happened, and how did I let this happen to me?

A few days after the incident, I lay in the grass in front of our dorms to soak up some sun. I was lost in thought when I saw a hand waving at me. It was him. He was about twenty feet away, talking with another woman. I realized then that he felt no remorse. I was just another notch in his belt, and he was working on adding another one in front of me. He had no idea what he had taken from me.

Over the next few days, which stretched into weeks and then months, I completely withdrew from my life. I stopped attending class, constantly went out, and partied. I never refused a man. I was nothing, and I behaved like it. I lacked self-esteem, self-respect, and hope for the future. My humiliation and shame intensified the anger I already felt before college. My rage fueled every action I took from then on. I already had a strong personality, and now I behaved with reckless desperation. I either lost friends or they barely tolerated me. I had changed, and it wasn't for the better.

After a few months, I decided to seek counseling at the school to help cope with the rape. The counselor was not empathetic; I was just another young woman assaulted because of the bad choices I made. My anger grew deeper. One more person who was supposed to help those in need judged me without compassion or love. After this terrible letdown, my anger drove me to test every limit I could, and I did not look back.

A few weeks after the semester ended and I returned home, I discovered I had failed out of college. My failures kept piling up. I graduated from high school with a 3.67 GPA, but in my first year of college, my GPA dropped to 1.87. College, which was five hours away from home, was supposed to be my ticket to a better life. How did I let this happen? At 19, how could I even have an answer? I thought I had done the right thing by reaching out for help from a professional, but I received none. I didn't have friends I could rely on during this incredibly tough time. I didn't think I would get my family's support. And I lacked the faith or confidence to believe in myself.

As expected, my family showed no support; they were only angry that I failed out of college. They believed I only partied and never studied. Yes, that was true and a result of my actions, but not the real reason. I couldn't tell them about the rape. They would blame me and make me feel like it was my fault. My self-confidence was already shattered, and I let them continue to exploit it. I had no one to turn to. Or at least, I thought I didn't.

My college gave me the chance to take summer classes to raise my GPA above 2.00. It was my only opportunity to turn my college career around, but I had no money and couldn't get a student loan. I also didn't have a car to get to campus. My parents decided not to help me at all. They told me this was my problem, and I needed to fix it. My life was falling apart faster than I could imagine.

A few days later, my grandfather approached me and said, "*I don't know what happened, and I don't want to know what happened, but I believe in you. I know you can do this. Let me help you.*" It felt like a hand from God reached out to me through my grandfather. At that moment, my love for this man deepened beyond what I had ever known. Someone believed in me! At my lowest point, there was someone who showed love and mercy. I will never forget that moment. I owe my life to him, and I promised myself I would never let him down.

During those six weeks of summer school, I started to change; I was still angry, especially at my family, but I realized I needed to refocus and prioritize myself. I made a promise to never let another man take advantage of me. My anger now had a purpose. I attended every class, studied hard, and consistently did well on every test. I wasn't going to let this opportunity slip away carelessly. I was given a second chance, and I wanted to make the most of it.

On my last night at summer school, one of the frat houses was playing Journey's "*Still They Ride.*" It felt magical in that moment. The night was warm outside with a gentle breeze, and the music wasn't loud. It was comforting. As I listened to the lyrics of the song, I felt like Jesse did: Times have changed, he keeps riding through the night, chasing thunder and knowing that only the strong will survive.

I didn't know my next steps or how I would survive another semester, but I believed I could. The song gave me hope, more than I had in the past twelve months. Even now, when I listen to that song, my memory takes me back to that night—

realizing I had lost my childhood innocence and that the future was approaching. Still, hope was always a choice, regardless of what situation I faced.

The Return to College

A few weeks after I returned home from summer school, my college sent me a letter informing me that I had increased my GPA enough to be re-admitted, so I returned for the fall semester. I chose not to go out and party with friends; I found refuge in the Catholic Church. It was a place of peace for me. I learned everything I could about the Catholic Church and its beliefs. I attended Mass at least three times a week, and I volunteered to light candles at Mass. I was hooked and took the classes to convert to Catholicism.

Why the Catholic Church? Because I loved the Blessed Virgin Mary. I admired her strength to step forward, declaring she was with child and facing the harsh judgments people made about her. I respected her love and care for humanity by appearing at Fatima, Portugal; Lourdes, France; Guadalupe, Mexico; and many other locations. I did not understand, and to this day, I still do not understand why other religions and religious people looked down on Mary. Their passionate reactions to her can be shocking. I felt a deep sense of peace while thinking and praying to Mary, and I continued to do so.

Because I spent a lot of time at church, my social life during my sophomore year was nonexistent. The friends I had in my freshman year went their separate ways. They continued to go to parties and finding boyfriends. They spent time together as a group, and I no longer felt like I fit in. I didn't know where to find friends at this point; I needed some time to heal from the trauma. Jumping back into the chaos of college life wasn't going to help me. However, I felt another spark and hope of love.

On the first day of my biology lab, I sat in the back corner, and I remember seeing a man come around the corner and sit beside me. He smiled, and I melted. He was beautiful; the Light shining from his eyes pierced right through me. I was hooked. I felt more than just young love; I felt as if I had known him in another lifetime. I couldn't explain it to anyone, and honestly, I couldn't fully understand it myself. All I knew was what I felt. I was crazy in love from that very first moment.

Gary was my lab partner throughout the entire semester. We talked, laughed, and joked, and I learned a lot about him. I felt very connected to him. I remember being in my dorm room and knowing that if I went for a walk out to Main Street right then, I would see him driving by in his yellow Ford Mustang Convertible. And I did. Every time I had that feeling, it turned out to be true. Throughout the semester, I became increasingly captivated by him.

Sadly, my feelings weren't returned. He was interested in someone else. Gary dropped out of college after his first year, and I heard through an acquaintance that he joined the Bureau of Police River Patrol for Three Rivers. I never saw him again. I knew our paths would never cross again. I was heartbroken and wanted to crawl into bed and never get out.

At the end of my second year of college, I still believed in and aligned with the teachings of the Catholic Church, but questions continued to arise. I started to feel that some of the teachings were flawed; the core was there, but not entirely authentic. Our relatable young priest left and was replaced by another who couldn't connect the Catholic teachings with our lives as college students. His sermons were overly critical and outdated. I soon stopped attending church, except for a few special occasions. I took the lessons I learned and moved forward. However, I never let go of Mary, Jesus, the Archangels, the Saints, or the mysticism I experienced during those dark days. The Church was the beginning of my healing. It gave me a cloak of peace and safety. A place to start over. The Church saved my life – literally.

While my fellow college students went out partying, I immersed myself in movies. When *The Seventh Sign* was released in 1988, I was completely captivated by the story. I had many questions. Did the producers and writers realize they were telling a story of reincarnation set against the end of time? Is the Guff a hall of souls not yet born? When it becomes empty, will the end of time arrive? Since Jesus was Jewish, why isn't this concept of the Guff part of the Catholic and Christian faiths? Will Jesus come back to life to break open the seven seals? Will he come through a womb, or will he appear to the world? And if he is born through a womb, how would he navigate today's world with so much hatred and little compassion?

I watched *The Name of the Rose* with Sean Connery, Christian Slater, and F. Murray Abraham. Why did the Inquisition scare me to my core? Why was I captivated by the mystery of the hidden scrolls and how they were kept away from the other monks? Why did the scenes of guilty men and the sorceress burning on a pole bother and sadden me so? Why did I feel like I had actually been there?

In 1992, *Thunderheart* was released, and as I watched the movie, I felt an overwhelming sense of sadness and pain. The massacre of women and children at Wounded Knee disturbed me in ways I could not understand or even explain. I saw the Sioux shot in the back as they ran away. How could men, especially American soldiers, fire on unarmed women and children? Once again, why did I feel like I had lived that life? These questions remained unanswered for many years.

Another movie released in 1992 was *Bram Stoker's Dracula*. Again, I was mesmerized and transported to another world. I thought, *"Why would this movie mean so much to me?"* As I analyzed it, I realized that all the characters came together in another lifetime to complete the karma or business that had begun hundreds of years earlier. Reincarnation. That was it.

As the years went by, I reached my senior year of college with no clear idea of what I wanted to do for a career or where I wanted to live. I was scared. Should I return to the homestead to settle down? Should I move out of state? What kind of work do I want to pursue? Yes, I was about to graduate with a Bachelor of Science in Business Administration, but that didn't mean I wanted to enter the business world. It was an easy degree, but I still needed to figure out what I was qualified to do and what I truly wanted to do.

I met a man, and he seemed to love me in every way. Did I love him? At first, I did. But not as much as I valued the comfort of belonging to someone who could and should protect me in this vast world. That was what I thought and hoped. I never felt the same connection to him that I had with Mike in junior high or Gary in college. I never felt the butterflies or the sensation of joy in my stomach that I experienced with others. Still, I needed someone to love me and take care of me. I had been through so much by then, and I hoped this would be my chance to "rest my heart." Unfortunately, there were signs before the wedding that it wouldn't work between us—indicators that he was selfish and disrespectful. I was in a no-win situation, but I went ahead with the marriage.

I remember the wedding day: it rained nonstop, an ominous sign. I felt no joy or happiness. I wanted to cancel it right then. I thought about all the time and money everyone had spent on my wedding, and I couldn't cancel it. I climbed into the back of the limousine to go to the church and get married. I remember walking down the aisle, and my body and mind screamed, *"Don't do it!"* Events were already set in motion, and I couldn't stop them. If someone had said to me, *"Are you sure? You can cancel at any time,"* I would have ended the whole thing right there. No one did, and I said, *"I do,"* but I didn't want to.

After we got married, we moved back to the town where I had attended college. My husband owned several businesses on campus, and I started working at one of them. Working in a restaurant wasn't exactly my dream. I wanted to support him, but it felt entirely unfamiliar for me. And to him.

The two businesses only lasted another six months. Little did I realize at the time that he had financed them using his credit card advances, and the debt was massive. We considered filing for bankruptcy. The landlord and the previous owner of the restaurant agreed to let us walk away without penalty. They understood that if we filed for bankruptcy, the property would be tied up in court for months, and it was easier for them to cancel our debt and regain ownership.

After transferring the businesses to their respective owners, we decided to change our scenery and moved to

Phoenix, AZ. His older brother lived there, and he could help us get back on our feet.

In March 1994, we traveled to Phoenix, leaving everything behind. We felt excited about the change and the new adventure ahead. The possibilities and opportunities seemed endless, and we were eager to make our mark on the world.

Looking back, I realized my husband wanted to escape his problems just as much as I was trying to escape mine. Our marriage could never survive with two people so emotionally and mentally unhealthy, and we weren't ready to admit or face our demons.

Chapter Two: Phoenix It Is

Phoenix was unlike anything I had ever seen—the desert, the mountains, the city. I had entered a completely different world and was excited for a new beginning. I got a job at a large, upscale retail store in the home department. I was happy working and learned a lot from my coworkers. I never saw Waterford Crystal, Royal Doulton China, or Towle Silver. They were stunning, and I was thrilled to work in such a beautiful environment. Life was moving along, but my marriage was unhappy. We just existed with each other. He treated me poorly, like a wife from the 1940s. My wishes and wants weren't considered in our decisions. Only his desires mattered, and I failed when I tried to please him. We lived and tolerated each other, but little did I know his eyes had already begun to wander.

I lost my retail job after a new store manager took over. He reorganized the store, and I was not the type of person he wanted on his team. At the time, I didn't realize it, but many of the other managers didn't like me. My East Coast bluntness and harsh way of speaking didn't fit in with the others. I never intended to hurt anyone I worked with; I was unaware of the impression I made. After I left, I joined a small company on the verge of success: Office Ergonomics. The owner was entrepreneurial and knowledgeable. Anyone familiar with workplace innovation knew this could have a big impact. By 1995, every office worker had used a computer, and many suffered from repetitive strain and occupational injuries. Unfortunately, my boss didn't manage the business well, and I was laid off.

I shifted my focus to real estate and secured a job as a leasing consultant at Tapatio Cliffs Resort, a large apartment complex. I met people from all walks of life. In the late 1970s, Gosnell Development built The Pointe at Tapatio Cliffs Resort. In 1982, it opened its doors to welcome a wide range of travelers, dignitaries, and celebrities. The press called it "the place to be and be seen." And it was. The Pointe was beautifully designed; if you drove to the top, you could see South Mountain. It was heaven.

I had no idea my life was about to fall apart again. My husband could no longer pay his credit card debts. He had to declare bankruptcy, and since I didn't realize Arizona was a community property state, I had to file as well. There was no way around it. If he had done this in Pennsylvania before we moved, I wouldn't have had to face this terrible outcome. I was angry. I was embarrassed. I blamed him for everything, and I hated being married to him.

During the bankruptcy proceedings, I discovered that my husband was having an affair. He professed his love for her and wanted her to have his children. He never said those words to me, and I felt devastated. Not because it was him, but because no one had ever told me that, and the one person who should have — my husband — did not. He reserved those words for someone else. I felt unworthy of any man, even one with such an unprincipled character. The pain caused by this amplified all the other pains and traumas I had experienced in my life so far: the unworthiness, the loneliness, the guilt, the shame. I felt like I was trapped in a pit of doom with walls as tall as twenty skyscrapers.

I left him in January 1996 and started rebuilding my life. I told my family about the divorce and his cheating, but I didn't feel much support. They were embarrassed by their divorced daughter. Things like that didn't happen in my small, conservative hometown. Luckily, since I work in the apartment community business, my company offered rental discounts to employees. I didn't make much money then —just barely over minimum wage —but I was determined to survive and thrive. After paying all my bills, I had only $30 a week for food and gas. I remember going to Burger King for their 99-cent cheeseburger, and that felt like a treat! Otherwise, I survived on pasta, potatoes, and whatever else was on sale that I could afford.

If life wasn't challenging enough, one night, while I was driving home, I got into a car accident. It was my fault; I didn't see the other car and turned left right in front of it. My vehicle was totaled, and I was lucky to survive that crash. Fortunately, no one was seriously hurt, but I lost the only real property I owned.

Unfortunately, I had only the minimum state insurance, which didn't cover all the medical and liability costs. The victims were threatening to sue me for the difference. One day, an insurance adjuster came to my apartment to check if I owned any valuable items. He left disappointed, and I was relieved there would be no further litigation. In my mind, I heard the Bob Dylan song, *"When you ain't got nothing, you got nothing to lose."* That's been my life so far. I had nothing, and there was nothing to take.

I faced one misfortune after another, and it felt like there was no end in sight. I barely made ends meet; I didn't have a car, I was estranged from my family, and the man I was dating didn't care much. He was seeing others, and I was just part of the rotation. Rock bottom—that's where I was. I often felt like I wanted to leave this Earth, but I couldn't even consider suicide. There were times I wanted to give up. However, very deep down inside of me, I knew that I couldn't give up. I didn't understand my drive to keep going. In the back of my mind, I heard, *"This is temporary."* It didn't feel temporary as the setbacks kept repeating themselves.

My thoughts drifted to the movie *Sliding Doors*, starring Gwyneth Paltrow and John Hannah. The film shows how a single moment can change your entire life. I believe that any moment—any second, minute, day, or week—can bring positive changes to your world. I was waiting for that change. I prayed for the moment my life would turn around.

I've always felt I had an important purpose in life. I didn't know what it was or what I needed to do to fulfill it. I could only hope that I went through what I did to reach that point, where I can do what I was meant to do. Although today was not the day of knowing. It was another day of struggle.

I lay in bed for days at a time, feeling sorry for myself, trying to figure out how I got here and how to escape this situation. I needed a break in at least one part of my life. I believed there had to be more to life than this, but life wasn't showing that to be true. Running away and living on a deserted island was a thought. But where in this world does such an island exist? I pulled myself together and went to work.

My Assistant Property Manager befriended me, and I thought we had a good relationship. Many days, it seemed like she was trying to prove herself to me. Maybe she lacked confidence, and I was the target of her insecurities. At that point in my life, I didn't understand why anyone would be jealous of me. My life wasn't easy. I didn't feel attractive, pretty, smart, or worthwhile. The only things I had going for me were my youth and my determination to overcome each obstacle.

I started dating a man, and he showed me moments of care. One Sunday morning, my mother called early and told me they had heard I had filed for bankruptcy from someone in my hometown. They were embarrassed and upset. My mother took it out on me and called to say they were seriously considering disowning me. I tried to explain that I had made the best decisions I could, but she didn't listen. She kept repeating that I needed to pay everyone back. She didn't understand how that would jeopardize the bankruptcy. She said I brought shame to the family, and they didn't need a daughter like me. She said my father doesn't want to speak to me anymore.

After we hung up the phone, I broke down crying. I felt my life was spinning out of control. How many more blows can a person endure?

My boyfriend was there during the phone call and was furious that they would treat me that way. He was shocked that money and family shame seemed more important than listening, understanding, and showing compassion to your daughter. He took me to breakfast that morning, hoping to offer me some support and kindness.

Gradually, I started rebuilding my life. I bought another car, kept working for the apartment community, stuck to a strict budget, and ended my relationship with the man I was dating. By then, my Assistant Property Manager had tried to manipulate my Property Manager into firing me, although I don't know why. Fortunately, my Property Manager saw through her schemes and realized I wasn't the problem. Then, one day, my Property Manager approached me and asked if I wanted to take a job as an operations manager for a company that furnished and rented apartments to large companies that needed their employees to stay in Phoenix for at least a month. It was an alternative to staying in a hotel for months. The General Manager of the Phoenix location was a client of ours, and since we knew each other well, I eagerly accepted the opportunity.

A New Door Opens

With this new job, my salary doubled! I had some breathing room in my budget and decided to move to Ahwatukee, an up-and-coming part of Phoenix. It was beautiful and located on the southeast side of South Mountain. The sunrises were spectacular from my apartment window. There was a lovely park next to the apartment community where I took my dog every day. The area offered great shopping, dining, and grocery options. I felt like I had hit the lottery!

For the first time in my life, I went on vacation. I got in my car and drove through Utah to Glacier National Park, then along the Lewis and Clark Trail. AMAZING! I have never seen anything as spectacular as the Rocky Mountains in Glacier Park. I felt at home. At peace. At ease. I never wanted to leave. I felt like I had been there before, and it welcomed me back.

From there, I drove to Yellowstone National Park and then to the Grand Tetons. I couldn't believe the beauty and peace of it all. I wanted to live here—the freedom of the outdoors, the smell of fresh air, and the tranquility. My soul felt recharged—at least for the moment.

I returned to Phoenix after my vacation feeling refreshed and ready to go. I really enjoyed this line of work; I was good at it. My Vice President would come into town every few months, and we shared a connection. She understood what I was going through. She had struggled in her twenties to make friends with women her age. She understood my pain and loneliness, and she would tell me over and over that those women my age were jealous of me. WHAT??? WHY???

Alahnah was an outstanding entrepreneur. She didn't form many friendships either, as the other women often felt she was competing with them. Now in her late thirties, she reassured me that things would change. She said women would start to appreciate each other in their forties. I felt encouraged. However, it was 12 years before I turned forty.

One fateful day, she showed up unexpectedly, and my world was about to crash again. My GM and I have not gotten along well the past few months. She was making business decisions that I felt were not aligned with our success. She was a great salesperson but needed to develop the skills to evaluate business decisions with clarity and objectivity. She did not understand the impact on our financial status or the legal risks we faced.

During my discussion with my GM, I didn't realize she had been talking with Alahnah about the situation. Little did I know, Alahnah sided with me on what she believed was the best course of action for the business. She thought my GM was making poor business decisions, so she demoted her and told me to take her place. When my GM was informed of her demotion, she flew back to California to meet with the owners. She manipulated the situation to protect herself and convinced them that I was clueless and responsible for those terrible business decisions.

Alahna spent the entire week trying to fix the damage my GM caused. She wanted to save me, but the owners refused to listen to her. They trusted my GM because she was a California girl, and they disliked my East Coast manner. Once again, I was let go. My VP was upset about the decision. She confided in me that she planned to leave the company soon and start her own. I stayed friends with her for a long time and never saw my GM again.

When I returned to my apartment after being fired, I felt utterly devastated. I was let go despite doing my job well. I was on track for a deserved promotion, but my career ended because of another woman's jealousy. She lacked the skills and knowledge to run a successful company, and I became a liability. This was becoming a broken record. I was fired again because of another woman's envy and my East Coast upbringing. Moving to Phoenix turned out to be a terrible decision, leaving me stuck in limbo and feeling devastated at every turn.

Where should I go now? I didn't have the answers, so I spent a week in bed feeling incredibly wounded. My life felt like a punching bag for others' whims. I accepted my mistakes, but I was young and naïve and let someone take advantage of that. Why shouldn't I trust my boss? Why would someone be so jealous of me? Enough to ruin my career. I didn't understand it.

At that moment, I felt entirely unprepared for life. I was making every mistake imaginable. My faith in humanity started to fall apart; women were jealous, men only wanted to sleep with me, and no one cared or offered a helping hand. I had no value to anyone. I was alone in the desert with nothing and no one I could trust. Despair was taking over my life. I turned to watching movies to escape the emptiness of my life.

Shortly after I was fired, I learned that the Phoenix office had closed down due to poor business decisions. I smiled that day; karma has a way of handling things you can't.

I found relief from my misery and despondency by driving around the state of Arizona. I saw beautiful sunsets and magnificent saguaro cacti in the Tucson area. The first elk I ever encountered was in Grand Canyon National Park. I was driving down the road, and it nonchalantly walked in front of me. I had to slam on my brakes so I wouldn't hit it. It looked at me and kept walking, and I thought, *"What a dumb animal."*

A Reprieve?

I visited every Catholic Church I could find on my road trips. However, none of them ever gave me the peace and acceptance I felt at the Catholic Church I attended in college. I sat in the pews, said the rosary, lit a candle. Nothing. It felt empty, just like the emptiness inside me every day. I didn't understand the change. Why did one place in my life give me so much, while similar places gave nothing? Was it me? Did I outgrow the need for the Church? Or was I too far gone to be helped?

As I sat in the pews searching for answers, my mind kept drifting to the Beatitudes. They resonated deeply in my soul:

1. *"Blessed are the poor in spirit, for theirs is the Kingdom of Heaven."*
2. *"Blessed are those who mourn, for they will be comforted."*

3. *"Blessed are the meek, for they will inherit the Earth."*
4. *"Blessed are those who hunger and thirst for righteousness, for they will be filled."*
5. *"Blessed are the merciful, for they will be shown mercy."*
6. *"Blessed are the pure in heart, for they will see God."*
7. *"Blessed are the peacemakers, for they will be called children of God."*
8. *"Blessed are those who are persecuted because of righteousness, for theirs is the kingdom of heaven."*

I felt like Jesus' Sermon on the Mount was a direct message to me. Yet, I couldn't relate because I didn't believe it applied to my life. I had hoped the world and my life would change for the better. But based on my experience so far, it seemed impossible. Still, I kept hoping. I contemplated my existence every day. I knew I had to survive, never realizing this was just the start of life's harsh lessons. The school of life has only just begun.

One of the first movies I watched was *The First Knight* featuring Sean Connery, Richard Gere, and Julia Ormond. I felt a connection with the characters and the story. I knew the story wasn't entirely true; however, I believed the depiction of the Knights of the Round Table's workings was accurate. I could feel myself immersing in the court politics and strategizing how I would handle it. Was this just escapism, or was it something more?

Then, I became intrigued by a movie called *Last of the Dogmen*, starring Tom Berenger and Barbara Hershey. I admired the Cheyenne and their dog soldiers for living peacefully and in harmony with nature. I was never deterred by The Dog Soldiers' fighting skills or their unwavering commitment to preserving their way of life. Their actions were justified. They were fighting to defend their lives and culture. I was rooting for the white men to leave them alone and never find them. Why? Where did this deep passion for the Native Americans come from? It has not diminished since I was a child.

During this period of unemployment, Princess Diana was killed in a car crash in Paris. I watched the coverage nonstop. I saw the love and widespread grief the world expressed for Princess Diana. In regular times, I would feel hopeful to see a hint of compassion; I didn't. Misery loves company, and I had plenty to give.

I continued to immerse myself in movies and watched *Contact* starring Jodie Foster. I was captivated throughout the entire film. Why was I mesmerized by the messages from space? Why did I feel drawn to the Vega Star System? Why did I feel compelled to understand the differences in time between Earth and other places? Why was I so happy to see Jodie change her mind from a focus on scientific evidence alone to opening her heart to something bigger? Those were questions that haunted me for a long time.

Luckily, my previous job helped me build business relationships with vendors that turned into friendships, and eventually, a job opening arose. US West was hiring salespeople for its Home Office Division, and my representative there encouraged me to apply. He told me he knew I could do it. So, I did, and they hired me within the month. Welcome to the world of telecommunications!

Finally, My Luck Changes

I never considered telecommunications; it was never on my radar. I didn't realize at the time, but my job at US West marked the start of a journey toward peace, prosperity, and unforgettable experiences. The merging of financial, mental, emotional, and spiritual paths led to a pivotal moment in my life. Even now, that job and the new friends and acquaintances I met remain the most significant part of my journey.

My new life began on October 6, 1997, when I started working at US West. I participated in a four-month training program along with many others. There was a lot to learn to succeed in this career. For this Gemini girl, who loves all things tech, it was an exciting and rewarding experience. It brought out my inner "geek." I loved working at the phone company. Every day, my job gave me more satisfaction, and I became completely hooked on it.

After four months of training and building some confidence along the way, I successfully passed the final test and became a full-time employee. It was a professional office. Business professional attire was required, and everyone appeared helpful and friendly.

My first manager, Harold, helped me succeed. I remember being frustrated with a process and asking him for help. He told me I needed to accept it and work within it. I replied, *"I can't accept it; it just doesn't make sense."* He patiently explained that I have a minimal window of acceptance. If circumstances fell within those boundaries, I could move forward, but if they didn't, I was fighting for change. He was the first person to gently tell me that it would be helpful for me to be less judgmental. I knew I had a long way to go, and that was a life lesson that would take decades to learn.

Working for US West in a sales role was a lucrative career. After a few months, I realized I could afford to buy a home. Wow! After struggling for two years, I finally bought my own house. I looked at many existing homes and decided to build a starter home with Shea Homes. Unbeknownst to me, I would feel another one of those sparks.

Greg was the person I collaborated with during the construction of my home. I was utterly infatuated with him, almost to the point of feeling lovesick and consumed by an obsession. I made excuses to see him. We had a good working relationship, and I hoped there might be more once I closed on the house.

In October 1998, I closed on my house. I had never felt prouder of my accomplishments than at that moment. I did it. I scraped and clawed my way to a place where I could own a home. Many people my age were still renting apartments with others, and they hadn't endured the adversity I had. With that change, I hoped a relationship with Greg would grow. He lived with his sister in a house on the same street as mine. Once again, it did not develop. He had eyes for someone else, and she was at his house quite a bit—another loss. By then, I was doing well in my career, and I tried to focus on that rather than another man with whom I felt a connection that wasn't reciprocated. It didn't work, but I tried.

My second manager, Faith, was well-loved in our department. She was promoted from within, and my entire team was excited to have her. I didn't know her before she became my manager; little did I realize we had some unresolved business to attend to.

Faith was a kind and generous woman, but there was an underlying tension between us. That was karma. We experienced moments of deep understanding, companionship, and support, alongside times of suspicion, misunderstanding, and contradiction. I felt a sisterly bond with her but couldn't fully trust her. Due to my past experiences with female bosses, I wanted to leave her team before she fired me. I applied for other jobs within the company, which was clearly a desperate move. I interviewed for a position, and the manager was ready to hire me, but he thought I had followed up too much and didn't see me as a good fit. Faith told me I had the job, but I believed I lost it because of my desperation. We talked at length and found common ground. She was an excellent manager, and we created a space where each of us could relax, accepting one another's strengths and weaknesses.

Faith discussed her spiritual beliefs with me, including crystals, meditation, and other metaphysical topics. She introduced me to a beautiful soul named Yvonne. Yvonne owned a metaphysical store at the local swap meet and began teaching me about healing, crystals, and aliens. I felt a wonderfully comfortable kinship with her. I spent many weekends at her shop, and during one of those visits, I met Angelique. Angelique was her autistic granddaughter, and Yvonne had full custody of her.

From our first meeting, I fell in love with that little girl. She was a willful, determined, and highly energetic child. Angelique was as attached to me as I was to her. She spent many weekends with me at my house, giving Yvonne a break. One time, Angelique had to have surgery, and I went to the hospital to see her. As I was walking to her room, I heard Yvonne scolding Angelique, telling her to lie still and calm down. The minute I walked in, Angelique was still and made no sound. Yvonne was stunned. Angelique never responded to anyone's presence that way. We didn't know why at the time, but we later discovered the reason.

After many months, Yvonne suggested that I learn about meditation. She had a friend, Hannelore, who held meditation classes at her home every week, and Yvonne thought I was ready to move on. In my first class, I wasn't sure what to expect. She began by playing her crystal singing bowls. She told us to relax and focus on our third eye. She guided us for a while and let us experience our visualizations. I remember seeing colors, and that was it. Hannelore told me it was a good start and that I should keep coming.

Hannelore would ask me questions about my life and try to understand my state of mind. I told her about my struggles with Faith, and she said that Faith and I were sisters in a past life. She mentioned there was a fight over a man, and I lost. Faith did not treat me very well in that lifetime, and it was time to clear that karma. That explains much of our connection, the give-and-take of companionship and warmth, as well as the anger and mistrust.

I was obsessed with learning about metaphysics during this period of new enlightenment in my life. In 1998, *City of Angels* was released, and I became fascinated by the idea of angels around us and the possibility of feeling their presence. It touched my soul deeply: imagining angels singing beautiful songs at a beach sunrise, offering comfort to someone about to cross over, and guiding someone away from danger. I felt in my core that it was true. It was like lightning struck me. I prayed I would see and experience those in my meditation.

After a few weeks of classes, I shared my experiences with Yvonne. She was happy for me and said, *"Soon, you will be ready to have your past lives read and meet Ashlem."*

"Who's Ashlem? And what is an Akashic reading?"

Yvonne responded to me in the kindest and most compassionate way, with the utmost patience. She explained that an Akashic reading is a record of your past lives throughout eternity, and Ashlem is an Ascended Master who speaks through Reverend Robert (Bob) Copeland. Ashlem chose to help the people of Earth by speaking through Bob while he was in a state of sleep, similar to Edgar Cayce, also known as *The Sleeping Prophet, who* did this from the 1920s to the 1940s. She continued to explain that Bob's profession was a truck driver and that he could not speak Tibetan. She pointed out that you could see the difference in Bob's face when Ashlem communicated through him.

Yvonne kept emphasizing how special Bob was. There are few in history who have allowed a Spirit to speak directly through them. This is direct contact with a Spirit, not channeled through someone else or their words interpreted. Ashlem does not judge you for making mistakes, as that is part of the experience here on Earth. He is a loving, caring soul who wants to do his part in the larger scheme of life.

I was intrigued. In the following meditation class, I shared that conversation with Hannelore, and she said, *"You are ready now. Here is Bob's card."* I didn't call him right away because I didn't feel it was the right moment. I placed his card on my refrigerator and waited a few weeks. One day, as I walked past the fridge, I was told, *"Call now. It's time."*

Upon meeting Ashlem and having my first Akashic reading, my entire world changed. My first reading took place on March 11, 1999, and it would have the most significant impact on me, even to this day.

Chapter Three: Ashlem

On the morning of March 11, 1999, I felt nervous and excited. I had experienced many tarot and intuitive card readings before, so I thought it would be similar. However, that wasn't the case, and I never expected what was about to happen.

I arrived at Jurkovich's beautiful home in Sun Lakes, AZ. They hosted Reverend Bob Copeland for his readings. When I entered the house, I was greeted by a stunning painting of Jesus.

It was one of the most accurate paintings I had ever seen. How did I know that? I was unaware at the time. I was taken to the front bedroom for the reading, which was decorated with crystals, angels, and statues of Quan Yin, Buddha, and Mother Mary. I could not move. I stared at the statue of Mary, and it seemed to have started smiling broadly. I felt at home.

Bob prepared me for the reading by explaining what would happen. He would start with a prayer, then see images forming. After he revealed those images and any messages, Ashlem, his guide, would ask to speak through him, and he would give his permission. From then on, Bob would be in a state of sleep, and when he woke, he would not remember anything that had been said.

Bob continued to explain that Ashlem would provide you with at least two or three past lives. The first one would be the lifetime you spent with Jesus, if you were with him during that time, and the second past life would be what your life and mission are in this lifetime. Afterward, Ashlem would ask you your questions, and he would answer them.

Akashic readings are sacred and can only be shared with the person whose records are being accessed. Bob made sure I had my questions, and we began the Akashic reading.

Ashlem March 11, 1999

"March 11, 1999. This is an Akashic reading for Tracey Renee Walker by Bob Copeland. This reading is being done in person. Tracey Renee Walker, you have asked to have your Akashic read. Do you give your permission?"

"Yes, I do."

"Then I ask God if He will place His Light around Tracey Renee Walker and myself, that only God's Truth and Love will exist between Tracey Renee Walker and myself. I ask the Lords of the Akashics if they will open the records on Tracey Renee Walker and allow me to remove from the Records that information that would be valuable and pertinent to her in her present incarnation. I call upon Ashlem, my Guide, to come forth and take me by the hand and lead me through these realms and keep me from harm. I ask this in peace and love.

"I see a beautiful soft pink light. The light is oval-shaped. The light radiates energy from the center out in beautiful waves of pink light that expands from the center outwardly, to fill the whole picture with beautiful soft pink light. The light of universal and impersonal love. Now, a pinpoint of golden light appears in the center of the pink light, and the golden light of wisdom and knowledge expands rapidly, shooting forth tongues of golden light and expand and blend with the pink light. Through this blending is produced a beautiful, soft violet light. The great light of spirituality. How beautiful this is. For this is the blending of the attitudes that are

necessary to produce the true being of Tracey. Magnificent. It fills the whole picture now. The magnificent violet light. A pinpoint of white light appears in the center of the violet light, and the white light expands rapidly without pulsating and consumes and blends with the violet light, leaving behind beautiful, soft White Light. For the White Light is the All-Consuming Christ, Light of Creation, as it now fills the whole picture with White Light. Now images are forming in the White Light. Once again, The Beautiful Blessed Virgin Mary has a magnificent smile on her face, her eyes twinkle. Around her, as all that is projected is the bust around her head. And around her head, small, tiny angels fly around in a circle. Now they begin to fade away.

"More images are appearing in the White Light. Once again, roses. Beautiful roses. There are eleven beautiful white roses in full bloom, and a white rose bud that is partially open. There are eleven beautiful pink roses in full bloom. There are eleven beautiful golden roses in full bloom. There is a single red rose in full bloom. These roses all grow from a single stem in a field of beautiful wildflowers. Poppies, bluebells, chrysanthemums, daisies, morning glories, tiger lilies, some jonquils, daffodils, snapdragons, lupines, larkspurs. Flowers of all the imagination growing here in this beautiful little clearing in the forest, a little valley. I can smell beautiful flowers. I see the magnificent trees on the hillside surrounding; trees of all kinds, sizes, and shapes. However, in the far distance, there are many, many trees that are barren of leaves, and scattered here and there throughout the forest are quite a few trees with brown leaves on them. But most all of the trees are in beautiful green foliage. Trees closest to the center of the forest have

44

beautiful pink blossoms on them, and I can count twelve trees with violet blossoms on them.

"In the center of the clearing, there is a White Rock that stands above the flowers. On the edge of the forest comes forth a little waterfall produced by a spring of water coming out of the side of the hill. The little waterfall flows over moss-covered rocks and falls into a pool of water. And from that pool of water, another stream is formed and continues to flow down through the clearing only to disappear down through the forest. The sky is magnificently blue. Upon the horizon, beautiful white clouds seem to be wind-swept across the horizon. And the sun peaking over the horizon cast beams of light across these clouds, turning them into hues of purple, and orange, and red, and yellow. For this is a dawning of a new day, and new era of time in the life of Tracey Renee. How beautiful.

"Birds of the forest flying from tree to tree as usual: orioles, and cardinals, robins, bluebirds, mockingbirds, all singing beautiful songs. And honeybees are collecting nectar. And the butterflies are flittering here and there. How magnificent this is!

"A little doe deer comes out of the forest. She stands looking into this beautiful valley, this little clearing in the forest, and she seems to shiver a little bit. Then the little doe deer seems to make her way down the hillside, being very careful not to step upon the beautiful flowers growing there. And the little doe deer comes down to where the stream is. She is frightened and turns around, all ways. Then she puts her head down and drinks a few drinks of the water and raises her head back up again. She is expecting something. Then she becomes calm and drinks more of the water. She walks downstream.

"After drinking the water, begins to eat the sweet grass surrounding the flowers. Then she stops, and she looks across the stream where the hillside goes up. And she looks up where the forest ends. And out of the forest comes a beautiful buck deer. It seems as though the little doe deer has grown in size considerably. Greatly matured now. She can't take her eyes off the great buck deer. The buck deer does not see her as she is standing very silent. The buck deer comes down the hillside, being careful not to step upon the flowers. And he comes down to the stream of water and drinks from the stream of water. He looks very calm and serene. Then, raising his head, he looks across the stream and sees the little doe deer. He wags his tail wildly. Then he comes down to where, adjacent to the doe deer, across the stream. Wags his tail again, and his ears perk up. The little doe deer wags her tail just a little bit. Then he merely steps across the narrow stream, comes over to the doe deer, and she is no longer frightened. She just looks at him. They nuzzle their noses together. He walks around her as though he was admiring her. Then they walk downstream together, shoulder-to-shoulder. Stopping here and there to eat the sweet grass. Then they come to where the stream turns, and they both step across the stream in unison together. Then up the hillside, on the other side, upon a new pathway, and entering a new place of the forest.

"On the White Rock appears a beautiful pink flame. A flame like a candle flame that flickers only at the top. The light is very bright and very fulfilling as it grows in size and intensity. Now it begins to soften and diminish. Ashlem is standing in that flame. Ashlem is wearing a beautiful pink robe that is trimmed in gold. Around his waist is a beautiful green sash. Ashlem has come forth in the flame of universal and impersonal love, wearing the beautiful robe of universal and impersonal love that must be governed by wisdom and knowledge, and all held together by the force of healing. These are things that Tracey Renee must do. Ashlem has that beautiful smile on his face, and his eyes twinkle, and the flame goes out. Ashlem stands looking and turning on the White Rock. Looking at all of the trees of the forest. For the trees in the forest represent all the lives lived by Tracey Renee. Trees without leaves indicate many negative lives lived by Tracey Renee. Trees in brown foliage indicate depressions of lives lived by Tracey Renee. Trees in green foliage indicate completed lives lived by Tracey Renee. Trees with pink blossoms indicate loves of those lives, and trees in violet blossoms, indicate lives of spiritual servitude lived and served by Tracey Renee.

"The White Rock is the rock of truth and purity upon which Ashlem always stands. Flowers in the field represent all the beautiful life experiences of those lives lived by Tracey Renee. The little stream of water is the destined course of the present-day life of Tracey Renee that flows over the rocks; the barriers of this life, and falls into the pool of water, the total sum of the present-day life experiences of Tracey Renee. And the little stream is the life stream of Tracey Renee that continues to flow down into the clearing only to disappear back into the forest of life.

"Ashlem stops turning on the White Rock, and he steps into the flowers; briskly, he walks through the flowers. He is

47

going where the roses are growing from a single stem. He stops and picks the stem containing all of the tiny roses. He turns and walks back to the White Rock with all the roses. Now, the roses have grown to full size. As he comes to the White Rock, he strips the red rose from the base of the stem. He takes that red rose, and holds it over the White Rock, and turns it upside down, and a red flow runs from that red rose. And the red flows down and strikes the White Rock and stains it red. But the White Rock of truth and purity is consuming the streak. The red rose is turning lighter in color. Ashlem is emptying the final vessel of heartache, and sorrows, and negative karma of Tracey Renee. Now, that rose is beautifully pale pink, and the fluid has ceased to run, and Ashlem turns that pink rose upright. He places it on the White Rock and there is a flash of white light.

"An image is forming on the White Rock. Once again, the Blessed Virgin Mary has appeared, and Mary shows herself in her youth. Mary is wearing a beautiful light blue gown. She has a white robe over her shoulders and head. Ashlem picks up the pale pink rose and hands it to the Blessed Virgin Mary. And Mary takes the rose and smells of it. Mary begins to speak, and golden words come forth, and the words say:

"Blessed art thee called Lina. For in that period of time, that thee did come out of Damascus, and ye came to the Temple of the Essenes at Carmel. And thee were a beautiful little girl. You were one year younger than I. And we became friends in the Temple of the Essenes of Carmel. Your skin was so beautifully olive-colored. I loved to touch thy skin. You were of the Bedouin tribe in that period of time, and your age was,

at that period of time, was 13 years. And we became close friends. Ye left your home out of Damascus because you were being molested by your father of that time; which was an accepted practice. But thee did not like it. And you ran away from home. Nomads found thee upon the pathways of roads alone. And it was truly not bright to be alone on the roads, especially for a young girl. Your body had developed to womanhood, yet you seemed to be ashamed of it.

"When you came into the Essenes Temple, you weeped an awful lot. And thee and I became close friends in that manner. And I explained to thee, and expressed to thee, the gratitude of the Essenes peoples who gave us refuge. For I entered the Temple when I was but three years of age. I had known thee into the Temple of that period of time for two and a half years. At that period of time, my womb was fulfilled by the Light. There were many, many in the Temple who thought I had slept with my betrothed, Joseph. And even Joseph thought I slept with another man because he knew I did not sleep with him. I was in great turmoil until the Angels came forth. I was with child, and they explained to I. I was the appointed one to give birth to the Son of Man, as it was called into those days.

"Ye did not ever forsake I. I weeped an awful lot in the Garden. You would come forth as others would, also, and hold my hands. Sometimes you would comb my hair, which seemed to soothe I. And I felt that I was not worthy of even your touch. And I went forth, after the Angels spoke to Joseph, with Joseph, and we were married. And we went into Bethlehem, where I was delivered.

"Of that period of time, you remained with the Essenes for two more years. Joseph, Jesus, and I fled into Egypt to escape the wrath of Herod. And thee went forth and into the land of Cana, ye did go forth too. And there in the marketplace of Cana, ye did begin to weave baskets. For all girls were taught to weave baskets. It was a good thing for thee. Of that period of time, you were a great artist into basketry, and you would paint with pigments you would make out of only the stones and rocks you could find. And bash them together to make your stains upon your baskets. You drew pictures of the Essenes, and no one knew who the pictures were; people you had known.

"After two and a half years, Herod had passed away, and we brought Jesus into again to Nazareth. And there, Joseph took upon him his carpentry, and we raised Jesus to the age of 12.5. But when Jesus was of the age of 10, you had heard of our being, and you made your way to Nazareth, which was not a good distance. And there we renewed our friendship, and I was filled with joy. For you brought with you your husband, and his name was Rene, and he was part Roman and part Hebrew. And you loved him dearly. And your womb was fulfilled, and you were in your eighth month when ye attended I, Mary. And you would sit and hold Jesus' hands, and looked into his eyes and say, 'I knew thee when thee were in your

50

mother's womb.' And he said unto thee 'Yea, it is so. For I felt your touch upon her stomach. Know that thee are blessed, and the child in thy womb shall come forth, and ye shall call of her Marian, and she will be known here and there for your blessedness.'

"You returned to Capernaum, where you and your husband had moved to a larger marketplace. I saw thee occasionally. I, also, after Jesus left at the age of 12.5, Joseph and I became consummating our marriage. And I became with child, and James was born through my womb. And you have heard of this, and you came to visit I again. And you gave aid unto I of that time. That, I come now to thee, and to these times, and say you are blessed. Let the Light of the Christ shine within thee always. Though thee have been oppressed in this life, it is over. Stand into the Light and form. For I will be with thee forever and forever. And at the ending of this Sixth Day, ye shall be with I, Mary in the Seventh Day, and we will walk through the gardens again. This I promise thee. Peace."

"Mary fades away and takes the beautiful pink rose with her. Ashlem smiles. Ashlem then turns, and he walks from the White Rock through the flowers to the pool of water of present-day life of experiences of Tracey Renee. Puts his feet on the surface of the water. He begins walking around the perimeter of the pool. He holds the roses in front of him, and the rose petals begin to fall off the roses and begin to multiply in the air before they strike the water. He is leaving a trail of rose petals behind him, the white of truth and purity, the pink of universal and impersonal love, and the gold of wisdom and knowledge. After making two revolutions around the pool, he stops and walks directly to the center of the pool where he stands, holding the roses high above his head. The petals still falling off and multiplying. It is now snowing rose petals. Then he begins stripping the roses from the stem and dropping them in the water one by one. He saves a white rose, a pink rose, and a golden rose in full bloom, and the white rose bud that is not yet fully opened. Then he walks from the surface of the water.

"Out of the forest come three white doves. They fly around Ashlem, and he smiles. And they land upon a little tree at the end of the pool of water, and the little tree is barren of leaves. And the doves land upon the tree, save for one. Ashlem whistles, and it comes to Ashlem. He puts into the beak of that dove, a beautiful White Rose in full bloom. It lands upon his finger he does of this. And the dove flies back to the tree and lands upon the topmost branch. And another dove comes forth, and he whistles, and he puts into the beak a pink rose. And it does the same. Lands upon the tree. And another comes forth. Lands upon the tree as he gives a golden rose to it.

"Now out of the forest a flock of white doves come forth. The tree begins to grow in size. Beautiful. The doves land upon the tree. Ashlem smiles and turns, and he walks from that pool of water. A new pathway opens up before him. He puts his feet on that pathway, and begins walking on it briskly as it wanders through the clearing here to there to the other side of the clearing, where the forest is most dark and ominous. He holds forth the white rosebud, as it bursts fully open, and the White Light comes out of that rose, and it surrounds Ashlem.

52

And he steps into the forest, and the darkness flees from his Light as he passes through the forest to a beautiful white mist. I can no longer see this beautiful place, but I can see movement that I'm being drawn through time and space.

"Then around the surface, the mist is dissipating. I hear humming. There are some ladies sitting around in a circle. Most of the ladies are older. They have bonnets on their heads. We are in Virginia. They are sewing. They are sewing on a flag that has red and white stripes. A field of blue. One is Betsy. The other Dolley Madison, I believe. I don't know all of the ladies' names. There is a younger lady. She is twelve years old. She has honey-colored hair and beautiful blue eyes. Her hair is worn in braids on each side of her head, and she is very carefully sewing on this flag. The girl's name is Charlotte Applebee. The girls seem to stand up and say, 'It's enough today, and we will do more tomorrow.' Each one tucks their needle into the flag, and they fold it together. Everyone is helping. They go out of the room. Charlotte remains behind and is picking up tiny pieces of thread and material that has been dropped upon the wooden floor. She stops for a moment and looks at the flag. It is folded up. Ashlem approaches her and places at her feet, the beautiful White Rose. Ashlem bows humbly wishes to speak through. I give my permission."

"I am Ashlem, known as Golden Image, I say to thee, 'Hail'. We brought thee of this period of time that thee incarnate as a beautiful, young female. You were of the Applebee clan of that period of time of peoples, during the great forming of the United States of America. At that period of time, it was said that the Council needed something to carry with them. A flag

was instituted and commissioned to do so. And the one who is called Betsy Ross is the one who came forward, and ye were a friend of Betsy Ross in that period of time; a young friend, and begged of her if thee could put a few stitches into the flag, and it was granted unto thee to do this. You were so proud that thee would do of these things. You loved America and wanted to be part of it. As ye grew forth into the colony that is called Virginia, ye knew of the one that is called Washington; George Washington, who later became President; First President of United States. And you know of Dolley Madison also. And, all of the works at that period of time.

"You met a gentleman whose name was Eric, and ye married with him at the age of eighteen years. The flag had been completed, though, it had been changed a few times. Everyone was proud of it, and you were proud to have put stitches upon it. It is so. Into the life force that thee did of that period of time, being married, ye moved to the region that was necessary for life to come forth. A wilderness area called Pennsylvania. Your husband was an adventurer of some sort. Provided a good living for thee. Through thy womb came forth three children: two sons and a daughter. And thy daughter, ye called of her Virginia, because thee missed Virginia so much. Knowing of the great first born into America also. As ye grew forth, you were taught by thy parents to read and to write. And ye passed this on to the students that ye formulated into a little place called Hickory.

54

And ye found of thyself of that period of time. Thee lived to be of the age of 47 years and perished from what is called tuberculosis.

"Now thee incarnate in this present time upon the Earth's Plane. Know that thee are blessed of this period of time. You are an old soul, my dear. You have lived into the Earth's Plane 7,384,216 years. You have incarnated in flesh in that period of time upon the Earth's Plane, 4,444 incarnations. You have completed thy masculine effect and thy feminine effect. You volunteered to come into Earth's Plane at this period of time that others may repay karma to thee, as it was a practice of that period of life thee were born into. Some have done this, others have not done this. Since the Harmonic Convergence has come upon the Earth's Plane, ye have been freed of the obligation of karma. We honor thee, my dear.

"Now there are many questions that I will answer for thee. Please begin."

"Who are my soul guides?"

"Your soul guides? Would thee accept Jesus? Would thee accept the Blessed Virgin Mary? There are instituted to thee. There is a Master Teacher, who is called, Rebezar Torres. He is thy Master of thy soul to help thee upon this way of Light. Ye have been with him many, many lifetimes. But he serves thee in spirit."

"What is my soul name?"

"Your soul name is Ahaleaiah. It means like the Aurora of Light."

"When people talk about Jesus, I back off from it, and I don't know why. When I'm alone, I think about him, and I'm fine."

"Could it be thee know more than they about Jesus?"

"It could."

"Aye. Were thee not with him?

"Yes"

"Did he not say to thee you are blessed?"

"Yes"

"Now back off, not away from people who speak about Jesus. Sometimes they know not what they say. But the blessedness is within thee. Let that blessedness shine in thy eyes, thy heart, and from thy smile. Do not worry about what other people say, for ye know the truth within."

"I would like to ask about Gregory."

"Did I not give thee the picture of the deer?"

"I thought so. When I was in meditation, Ramashamir came to me, and I just about fell on my knees when I felt his presence."

"Ramashamir. He is a wonderful wizard, is it not so? In that period of time, that thee did live into Mayan incarnations of the Bronze Race, you certainly knew of him into the early stages. Ye came from a beautiful planet that is called Myopia; third planet of the Vega sun system. Come to the Earth's Plane by the Brotherhood of Light into the land of Mu, that is called Garden of Eden, and into the city of Ra. Ye did come forth in thy first life was of the Bronze life. And thee

56

knew of he, in that period of time also. For other lifetimes, after many times, that thee did incarnate with him. And ye found the grace. Though his wisdom is great, even thy wisdom is greater. It is time to bring it forth. Now ye knew of him also into India, when he was a Sadu. You would come upon him as a young lady at the headwaters of the Ganges River, and into Gangotri. There ye would kneel before him, and he would get agitated that thee would kneel before him, like a god. And he would say unto thee, 'I am here to serve, not to be served.' Though you would always bring him a bowl of food."

"There is also a young girl named, Angelique, and the first time I met her, I felt she was my daughter in another lifetime."

"She is what would be termed adopted daughter. In a lifetime that is into Egypt in that period of time, what is called Cleopatra and Anthony rein.   Thee were there also, at that period of time. Your womb was barren. Your husband was angry with thee. Your name was Dahalia, of that period of time. Ye found upon the roadway, a child abandoned. And thee took of her into thy home. Any thy husband weeped because he had no child of his own. And ye said unto him, 'If I cannot give to thee a child, let us take this one and make her our child. She may give honor to us.' And she did. Spirit recognizes Spirit."

"I've been having this dream ever since I was young of me being shipwrecked or washing up on shore somewhere."

"In masculine incarnation, it is so in the period of time of 1487, you were masculine, at that period of time into what is called pirateers. Into England and there upon a ship, ye sunk into the ocean. Washing upon the shore, ye did, on an island that was between Spain and England. And there ye remained. Ye used to get excited about story of Robinson Crusoe. Is it not so? Thee were like Robinson Crusoe of that period of time. Ye had no companion. Ye wrote chronicles of thy life there, talking about the people that ye knew, and you fashioned a stone knife. There was plenty of food to eat and fresh water to drink. You were very lonely in that lifetime, but your chronicles were found later. And way, peoples wondered who this person was: Reginald Wingate."

"I went to the Renaissance Festival, and I was attracted to this talisman by Marie Laveau."

"Spirit recognizes a lot of things, does it not? In the period at the time of Camelot, thee were into England also and ye lived into Camelot. And the Knights of the Realm were prevalent at that period of time. It is not fable. That period of time your name was Maria. Many ladies were called Maria, but you were called Maria of Ascot of that period of time. And thee were treated like royalty. You were related to the Ascots at that period of time. Greatness within thee rose forth. Ye married with a gentleman who was called Roland. He was a good man who always desired to be knighted. He spent his life being good, so that he would have opportunity. But upon the

58

roadway of one day, he was returning with deer that he had killed to help feed the family. He was slain for his prey. This broke thy heart, but thee never did stop loving of him."

"I am very attracted to Atlantis and I feel like I've been there."

"Into the second breaking up of the continent of Atlantis into the city of Alta, thee did reign at that period of time. And thy profession of that period of time was working with plants and flowers. The Brotherhood of Light was prevalent upon that period of time, upon the country of Atlantis and especially into Alta, where there were great greenhouses of that sort. When the Brothers of Light would bring plants from other planets throughout the cosmos, and bring into the density of lower light of third dimension of Light, which caused them great difficulties. The Brothers of Light determined the vibrations of Light into these buildings like greenhouses, where they placed the plants. Ye were a caretaker of these plants and loved flowers of that time. Raised the vibration of these plants."

"How about Greece? I am very attracted to Greece?"

"Aye. After the incarnation of Atlantis, ye went to incarnate into Athens, Greece. Athens, Greece, the true Athens Greece, of that period of time, was close by Atlantis. But not so that thee could see it. The pillars of Gibraltar separated it. But thee were born into Athens, Greece of the ancient city. There was great grace and understanding at that period of time. Ye were feminine of that lifetime also. Guyana were thy name. Marriage of that time was also that thee did do, and had six children: four boys, two girls. Good life for thee. But thee recall many things in thy greater Consciousness."

"How many more incarnates do I have?"

"This is the last incarnation upon the Earth's Plane. Mary has said to thee that you will walk with her in the Seventh Day. Hold thy head high and be proud of the Force of Light with thee. Take ye this hand. Press it upon thy heart. Upon the force of life, with thee and through thee, that thee must understand. I am going to bring into thy being at this period of time, and through thy heart, I shall put forth the force of healing. And ye will know of thy force of healing. Ye will begin to know the greater value of healing, and ye will heal with thy great, beautiful heart. In thy touch of thy hands, ye will heal many. I have summoned thee forth of this day that thee may understand of these things. I want thee to imagine in thy mind the beautiful White Rose I have given to thee. Now repeat after I, Ashlem.

"I and the Father are One.

"I stand forth into the Light of the Christ.

"For I am Light. I am LIGHT.

"I AM THAT LIGHT.

"Breathe deeply, receiving the Christ Light into thy body. This energy passing through thy heart, the muscle that pumps the blood through thy body, permeates the vascular system of thy body, enters into

60

every atom and every cell of thy body. There it stores itself into thy body. By through thy proclamation, ye bring the Christ unto thee, and through thee. Therefore, each morning when thee awake, you must imagine in thy mind, the beautiful White Rose I have given to thee. By placing thy hand above thy heart, breathing in the White Light, you will breathe in the Christ. Making the proclamation that thee and the Father are One, as we have just done, exactly. Then the Christ will shine around thee, and protect thee daily. It is very important for thee to understand and do these things.

"Now, thee will sit up with feet on the floor. I balance thy chakras.

"Into thy throat chakra, breathe in beautiful sky-blue light. Breathe it into thy throat chakra. Feel this energy welling up into thy thyroid. Feel the energy entering into thee. Breathe the light deeply, slowly, and ye relax thy body as you breathe this light. It is important that thee do this each day, three times per day. Put thy hand upon thy throat chakra and breathe in the blue light twelve times, each session. Do this for two months. It is important. It will help calm thy nervous condition, and make thee feel much better, and cause thee to think better.

"Into thy heart chakra breathe in golden light for this is the energy of the cosmos, the oedic life force of Creation. The oedic life force of thy own spirit. As ye go forth and do thy healing work, you will dissipate much of thy own oedic life force of thy spirit. To

replenish it, ye must put thy hand upon thy heart chakra, and breathe in that golden light until thee feel comfortable again. Lest you become very weary.

"Into thy solar plexus breathe into beautiful kelly green. Kelly green is the healing light of the cosmos to all things of nature. Breathe kelly green light into thy solar plexus. Breathe it deeply. Feel it entering into thy body expanding into all directions. Here the center of the cosmic body, and the center of the astral body, and thy center of the flesh body, as this energy goes forth from the tip of thy toes to tip of head to thy fingertips. There it is stored into thy body. It begins to heal thy body and redirect thy body. And with mind power thinking, thought will create thee to the Oneness and Goodness. And never say that thee are not worthy of this, because ye are worthy of this. You have been a healer in many times of thy lifetimes. It is now time to heal upon the Earth's Plane with thy goodness of thy heart and thy being.

"Into thy heart breathe deep pink light of love. Love is the creative force. Without love, there is no creation. Breathe love into thy heart. Breathe it deeply. Let it come forth. Feel it expanding and radiating through thee. Expanding into all directions. Let it pass into thy aura so they who come into thy aura, they see the light of divinity and be fulfilled by thy grace.

"Place this hand upon thy forehead." (Ashlem says a Tibetan prayer.) "As I place upon thee, the sign of peace of he, who cometh. I open thy inner eye that thee *may see a greater wisdom that knowledge is. And I open thy crown chakra to let the Christ Light flood unto thee. That thee become one with the creative force to know of thee.*

"Hold thy head high beautiful one. You are blessed.

"Peace be unto thee. I take my leave."

After the reading was over, I felt a peaceful numbness. As I drove home, the enormity of the experience began to settle in. It felt like I had spent the last 90 minutes in another world. Spending time with an Ascended Master can be confusing and overwhelming. Their energy is more attuned than ours on Earth. I was exhausted.

I arrived home, lied down, and then revisited my first Akashic reading. There were many affirmations of my experiences in my youth.

1. The dream memories of running across the desert at night, hearing Bedouin, Bedouin, and knowing a father in my past abused me.

2. My reactions to Betsy Ross's flag and my love for Elton John's 'Philadelphia Freedom.'

3. Hearing the song 'Ah! Leah' and turning around as if someone were calling me, because my soul's name is Ahaleaiah.

4. The TV show where the main character washed up on the shore and didn't drown in the sea.

5. My love for gardening.

6. Why I already knew the history in the Mediterranean and the Tigris/Euphrates River basin; I was there in another lifetime.

7. Why Angelique and I had a connection, and she listened to me when she wouldn't listen to anyone else.

8. Why I was drawn to the Vega solar system because it's my true home.

I pondered my past life as Charlotte Applebee and what it meant to me in this lifetime for quite a while. Ashlem said that is the one that is most like my path now. What does that mean? I knew the political leaders who were creating a new world at that time. Does that suggest I should go into politics? I didn't feel that was the correct answer.

Ashlem told me I got married, left my family in Virginia, and went off with an adventurer to the new frontier, where I taught in a small community schoolhouse. Am I supposed to prepare and introduce this "new world" to those who cannot see it? That seemed to make the most sense and felt more correct. But how does the power of healing fit into teaching? I didn't know for sure, but I did know that answer would take me a long time to understand.

It took me a long time to come down from the high of this reading. I needed to share it with someone who would understand, so I went to see Yvonne to tell her about my Akashic reading, especially the parts that pertained to her granddaughter. She told me she now understands why Angelique behaves so well with me: I saved her.

Now that I have this knowledge, my next question is: where do I go from here? Ashlem gave me the power of healing, but what does that mean? Do I go to medical school? Do I learn massage and Reiki? What about acupressure? What about my new career at US West, which I loved? Am I supposed to change gears already?

I didn't have all the answers, but I knew one thing: I was hooked. I wanted to learn more about my past lives. I never shared any of my youth experiences because I didn't trust anyone with them, and now a spirit knew the truth about me. It was the first time in my life that I felt understood and accepted. I wanted more, so I scheduled my second reading for July 8, 1999.

Ashlem July 8, 1999

"I see a beautiful pinpoint of purple light. The purple light expands. As it expands, it becomes more etheric, and a violet light comes out of it, expanding. The purple dot is consumed by the violet light, leaving violet light. And now, a pinpoint of golden light appears in the center of the violet and expands in four different directions, causing a four-pointed star. Now, the star expands, and a golden star invades, and blends with violet light. This leaves behind White Light. The All-Consuming Christ. There is nothing but White Light in the picture. Images are forming in the White Light. It is the Beautiful Virgin Mary appearing once again. I cannot see enough of Mary appearing. How beautiful She is. Beside her, a magnificent Angel. The Angel is tall and slender, and has beautiful black, wavy hair with white highlights in it. Her name is Delaitha, the Builder of Dreams. Mary is holding in her hand a beautiful pink rose. Now, appearing in front of Mary is a golden flame. A flame like a candle flame that flickers only at the top. Grows in size and intensity and begins to soften and diminish. Ashlem is standing in that flame. Ashlem is wearing his white robe of simplicity. The flame goes

out. *Ashlem bows humbly to the Blessed Virgin Mary and the Beautiful Angel, Delaitha.*

"*Mary reaches forward to Ashlem and gives Ashlem the pink rose. Ashlem accepts it, and it turns into a beautiful White Rose. Mary begins to speak, and golden words come forth, and the words say,* **"I have returned, and the Light of All Creation is upon thee, and I have come unto thee of this time, that thee may remember the significance of life. I have gone through the cosmos, upon that period of mission that I had to perform, and I have accomplished it long before I should have. Yet with love, I come forth unto all peoples of Earth again. Look thee to the Light to find my image. Look thee into thy heart to find my words. I shall be in thy mind always, as it is before, it is now. I bring to thee this beautiful Angel, Delaitha, and her mission is to aid with thee through the dream of dreams of life. And for thee, thy shall find the greatest of great within. For when thee think, and speak her name, then the dream will begin, and a dream may come to reality. Reality is that which lives. And I am with thee. Peace."**

"*She fades away. The Angel remains, and Ashlem sits on his White Rock in a lotus position. The Angel seems to hover above Ashlem. Ashlem bows his head and wishes to speak through. I give my permission.*"

"**I am Ashlem, known as Golden Image, I say to thee, 'Hail.' Here come forth, the beautiful Angel, Delaitha, that she may understand thy purpose of life of this period of time. She will be with thee to work miracles upon miracles of love through thee of this**

66

period of life. There are no prophesies into life, and I do not prophesize for thee of this time. But Delaitha has come forth to help thee create dreams. Remember, dreams are things that peoples' existences or needs or projections. Then project thy life into the force of love around thee and let love become a part of thee. She will lead thee down thy pathway of grace and understanding. Mary have brought forth your Rose of Love that she has accepted from thee. She has returned it as a Christ Rose unto I, thy Christ Rose. Now let it begin within. There are many questions that I may answer for thee, please begin."

"During my last time here, you gave me a parable about two deer, and I thought it was about myself and Gregory, which you said you had spoken to. But I didn't quite understand it and was wondering if you could explain it to me?"

"But I have given it to thee into symbols for thee to explain, not for I, Ashlem."

"The two deer walking down the stream together are lifemates. So does that mean Gregory is my lifemate?'

"Are thee still with Gregory?

"No."

"Has he gone away?"

"Yes"

"Then was it Gregory or someone else? Do you see, I bring forth a picture of time for thee. For this picture of time, I use a symbol. It is for thee to interpret who it is and who it is not. And at the moment of time, you were with Gregory."

67

"So, you are saying I will not be with Gregory?"

"I do not say yea or nay to that question, my dear. It is for thee to understand. Will thee walk down a pathway of life with a gentleman? The answer is yes. Will it be with Gregory? I do not know. It is according to thy course of destiny. It lies within thy greater being in thy heart. Then, if it is not with Gregory, then, it must be someone who is in thy heart. Is it not so? If one carries love in their heart always, with truth and expectations, would it not be so that the thought creates? Has Mary given to thee an Angel of Dreams? Then ask her to dream with thee. And create through the thought Consciousness. If you wish Gregory to return unto thee, then put forth the thought of love. Do you understand?"

"Yes, I do. Can you tell me about a past life with him?"

"To the period of time in Rome, you were with thee into Roman lifetime that is of 273 BC. In the building and creating of Rome of that time, you were luxurious, Roman woman of that period of time. Marcana, thy name, of that period of experience. Very beautiful. Haughty type of person; head high. And loved music; played string instrument thee call harp, which was popular in that period of time. Strings were made out of what they call cat gut. But stretched and dried properly, they would give off beautiful tones.

"Ye learned to thee play music which ye loved the most, which was gentle flowing music. People from all around found thee to be of love and peace at

68

that time. He was the creator of the instrument for thee. And ye came to love of him of that period of time. His name was Decarnes; he was a good man. He was a craftsman working with his hands and carved the beautiful arch that was necessary to make the instrument. He cured the cat gut and so forth.

"Ye fell in love with him and then thee, and he became grace in that period of time of love. Ye married with him. His services were required by the Emperor, at that period of time, when he became well-known. And ye went, was it called, seventy-two leagues into Rome, where thee he was employed by Emperor to create an instrument such as thine. And he did of this.

"The Emperor was pleased, but Emperor was very poor in what ye say, tone deaf. But he had others who could play the instrument beautifully. He gave honor to both of thee at that time. Marrying he and thee together produced through his seed and thy womb six children; three females and three males. Into this lifetime coming forth, you have met for a reason. Is it not so? Have ye discovered of this reason?

"No."

"But thee did not like each other in the beginning. But did not care for love at that time. Spirit recognizes spirit. Where has he gone?"

"He is living down the street with his sister and working at a different property. I do not see him much anymore."

"Do ye not contact of him?"

"I have not."

"And why have ye not done of this?"

"My fear."

"What is fear?"

"Fear is something that I create."

"Aye. Is there a basis for this fear? Do thee and he have argument?

"No. My heart has been broken before, and I think he could do it again."

"He has broken your heart before?"

"No, not this lifetime."

"Then I say to thee my dear, 'Fear not, but stand forth into the Light.' If ye are in a garden of flowers, do all the flowers, all look as beautiful? Or is there one special flower always, that one may find to be a personal thing? They are afraid to pick that flower, they would lose that moment of love. Would it not be so? And is it not so also with thy friend? Then thee must learn to pick the flower.'"

"And not be afraid? I guess my fear at this point is that I lost that moment."

"You lost it?"

"I feel like I have."

"You have not lost that moment. Why do thee not contact him and say, 'I have not heard from you in a period of time. I kinda miss thee.' Would it not be pleasant to do that? Can ye say unto him, 'Can we get together for dinner or something to that effect?'"

"I can say that"

"But of course thee can. It would be saying to him, 'I am interested into thee.' And let him come forth. Man always like to be the aggressor. But he likes woman to be a little aggressive too."

"And let my fear go away."

"The only thing he could say is, 'Nay, I am busy.' Or say to thee, 'Nay, I am busy with other woman.' Would that hurt thy feelings?"

"Yes."

"It should not, because you are a better woman, and you would stand forth and say, 'Ah, it is alright; we are still friends. Then let us be friends.' You are a better woman, do thee understand?"

'Tell me about my connection with Montana. About two years ago, I was up there, and I didn't want to leave. I felt more peace than I have ever felt."

"Into the wilderness, is it not so? Ye loved it there. Ye were native there. It was in the period of time, thee would call 58 BC. That period of time, ye were feminine. You must understand the Red Race came across the Bering Straits from the land of Mu. They crossed over from the place called Siberia. It was at that period of time, not very cold; it was tropical. The Bering Straits were walkable of that period of time; a land bridge, as it is called by scientists. And it is so, the Red Race crossed it and made their way down with their tribal customs into what is presently called North America.

"In that region of time, ye lived into a village called Wakicheta. And of that life experience,

northern wooden natives, ye loved to make dresses.
They were called wichutas. And there ye put little
beads where thee found bushes of some sort, with red
beads, ye loved red beads and green beads. Ye make
dried of these little gourds, and stringing them
together. Ye would sew them upon, the cloth or what
thee call deerskin. Many of the tribe was envious of
thee of that period of time for the life force within thee.
When thee return again into the wilderness, ye feel
comfort there, because there was love."

"Tell me about my connection with the ocean."

"Thee loved the ocean in Atlantis, off of the
island or coastal city that is called Murdoch. Thee
lived upon Atlantis of the second incarnation of
Atlantean incarnation. Ye were there, a fisherman,
and thee love the sea, and provided food for many
peoples of Atlantis. Ye were one, who could sing well.
Always they could hear thee going off the shoreline
with thy fishing craft. Singing; waiting for the tide to
go out. There were many women would sit and watch
thee go. For ye had many lovers at that period of time,
also. Loved the sea and loved the animals of the sea,
ye call of them dolphins."

"Who are my Guardian Angels?"

"Guardian Angels? Ye have guardian Angel who
is other half of thy soul, called soul mate. Name of
Edwina. He is masculine."

"Ever since I was very young, I felt the physical deaths
of many people. I would feel it physically in my body, and it

was overwhelming, so much so that I asked the Universe to take it away from me. And my question is why did I feel that?"

"Ye have been masculine into many incarnations, have ye not? Ye have been a warrior into other lifetimes and different aspects of life. And ye did slay many peoples as a warrior, for that was a part of the experience of the Ancients is to come forth and have war with each other. You blame thyself for all of these souls that thee set asunder. But I say to thee that the karma is finished and ended. And there is no need to reflect upon this. Sometimes subconscious mind pops into wrong time, and ye feel the remorse of these things."

"Even at the exact times of their death?"

"Aye."

"Tell me about the South Pacific. I want to go there. Tahiti."

"Tahiti? Polynesian Islands? You want to go there again? Island Samoa? May find great love. As a native there, you were there into the ancient time also. Feminine. Hawaiian Islands, or what is called Polynesian Islands, also, refer to Love Islands, eons of time ago. For sailors were brought forth and sometimes it said unto Ancient, that the Sirens or the Singers, would bring ships too close to shore, and they would become beached there, so that the women of the islands would have husbands. You were one of the women. There was a time upon an island that is called Katcha'chulea, not now, but it was then, and thee were sitting and seeing a sailing vessel far away. And ye sat

there and said, 'I wonder if there are any men, gentlemen like.' And ye kept thinking and thinking and wondering like about this, and closed thy eyes, and dreamed, and soon thee opened thy eyes, and there was a ship close. And it hit upon the rock, and men were jumping into ocean. Then thee began to run inland, because ye were afraid they would think that thee brought them to the shore, where they were shipwrecked. It was not so.

"Out of that shipwreck, ye did meet a gentleman. He was of good attitude of life. He was injured badly into the battering of the rocks from the sea. And ye found him upon the shore. Ye helped him into thy place, which was a grass hut. There were very few men born upon the island into thy reign of time. Mostly were women. It is part of the stories of the Amazons. Tribes of women; they had to be strong and govern themselves into that period of time. You fell into love with this man, and to the rituals of the tribe, ye did marry with him. You were very happy. It is why you look into that region and find love, but do not know where it is."

"How about Chile and the Incas? Was I there?"

"Of masculine incarnation, you were Mayan incarnation, but of course. Chilean temples, ye called pyramids – topless pyramids. You were what is called, the Rajah or Holy One, to bring truth to all, and especially you loved most of all, the children, to bring them together. Male-to-Female and Female-to-Male– to bring them together with dignity and love. And you

74

would call, marry of them together. It was a ceremony that thee created at that period of time. To bring the inner love force."

"Last time when we had talked, you gave me some directions for healing, and I started to take classes. And I am just wondering if I am on the right track with those?"

"On the right track? Do thee feel good with this information?"

"Of my classes? Yes, I feel good with it, and I seem to pick up and understand the information very quickly."

"Why do thee question this?"

"My question is, should I be going a more formal route with classes or learning with a teacher?"

"It is based on the route that thee are going with now. You do not need a certificate. You are learning about herbs?"

"Not yet. Right now, I am learning about qi or ki energy. Qi Gong and Tai Chi."

"The qi is first important to learn about, to bring it within thee, upwardly and outwardly. It is most important to control the qi, and it's rising up. If it rises too strong, too quickly, it causes mental breakdown. But rising gently, brings a great flowing energy within a person. Then, continue to learn how to do this. For it is qi that is needed to do all things with. Into thy gardening, also, that will come forth, you will put upon the plants the thought of the qi. The energy."

"So, I should go into herbology then?"

"I would say not so much formal herbology. We try to bring teachers of growing for the peoples in this vicinity. If the people show up, and they wish it to be so, they will learn many new things. So, that people can find theirself. It is not all there into the reality of growing, but it will be a beginning for many."

"I had a dream about my friend, and it was very frightening. There were a couple of us, and it was like an evil force had taken her. She said it was ok and that she would sacrifice herself and go with it and not to worry. I didn't know if it was a message for me or for her. But if it were for me, I didn't get it. Would you be able to help me understand that dream?"

"It was not a message for either. It was a projection. You will find at this period of time, there are many negative thought projections, as well as positive thought projections, that come into thy mind. Treat them just as projections. The guidance within each is to promote love. Then, your friend, you dream of her doing what?

"Sacrificing herself for the love of others."

"So, she was taken by a cannibal?"

"No, it was like she was possessed by something."

"A negative entity possessed her? Were thee champion to her?"

"Yes."

"And did thee feel comfortable with this?"

"Yes."

"Then it is not your friend that you are speaking of. But thy own greater Consciousness. To bring these negative thoughts into action, of the positive direction for thee. Then see it as it is truly. You want to find inner peace. Find peace within thee. Seek of it. Change thy thought to peacefulness. Ye will find it reign upon you soon."

"I met my neighbor, Nancy, and from the moment we met, we had a strong connection between us. I was wondering if you could tell me what my past was with her."

"You knew her into Atlantis, thy feminine incarnation there. Ye had peace and understanding with her. Women had to bind together because men were oppressive to women all time. So, women had many lady friends. Close friends and speak intimately for confirmation of learning. She was one of thy friends into that period of time in Atlantis. Gave to thee wisdom and knowledge that ye used properly."

"And she's here to give me knowledge again? To help?"

"Aye."

"I made copies of my first reading with you and shared with a few people. A few of the copies are missing, and I did not know if there was a reason?"

"There is no reason purposely why they have been misplaced. But thee will again make other copies, then thee will be able to understand all the words within it. One must listen carefully to the words spoken. For one day they mean one thing, and the next day they mean something different to thee. Because the interim of time, comes forth with greater wisdom and knowledge. That is why I put them into parables."

"Last night I was meditating a little bit, and there seemed to be an older Oriental man who came to me. I saw a vision of him, and I would like to know who he is."

"Does he have beard?"

"Yes."

"He is large entity?"

"He did not look large."

"Did thee call him Rebazar Torres? Is he not your teacher guide? A beginning of a long journey."

"A long journey?"

"Aye. Are there more questions?"

"I don't have any more questions."

"Into this force of life upon thee, it is time to begin thy directive. It is time to begin growing of herbs and learning about them. I make this especially to peoples. You will find older people will need medications. You are not to prescribe any medications to anyone. Remember this sternly. Government will be upon thee quickly. But unto learning of the herbs, you would say to the person, 'If I had that condition, this is what I would take.' If they say, 'Should I take it?' Then you say unto them, 'Do thee have this condition?' And leave it at that."

"Have I ever been a medicine woman with the Indians?"

"You have not been woman, but ye have been what is called Shadu or Holy One or Medicine Man. Do thee find interest in the Runes Stones?"

"Yes, I do."

"At one time, into the ancient time, you used to use rune stones and bones to tell fortunes to the

78

tribesman. Most of time, they came to pass.
Tribesman gave to thee great wisdom and
knowledge."

"And that is why I am attracted to them. What about
Celtic? There was a Shamanic piece that I saw, and it brought
me so much interest. The owners said it was from the Aleutian
Indians."

"It is so. It is part of that experience. Ye find
greater interest. Are there any more questions?"

"No."

"At this time, I ask thee to go forth and begin thy
growing of the herbs. It is not too late. Learn to dry
herbs. It does take a little art. Learn to use what they
call brown paper bags. Put the herbs in a bag, and
punch holes into the bag, and hang them in dry place
where it gets very warm. And the herbs will dry
quickly. And learn to store them properly. Ye will
learn the combinations that is necessary to heal with."

"Will I be doing healing with my hands?"

"Is not creating herbs, healing with thy hands?"

"Would I be doing things along the lines of Reiki or
massage?"

"Reiki is very good therapy. But one, the
patient must believe into Reiki to be cured. Or believe
into their doctor or the one who is putting forth the
Reiki. But to make Reiki Masters, as they call unto
ourselves, the thought coming forth into the healing
force must be strong. And two people working on a
body can heal quicker than one person."

"So, what I am hearing is that I should spend much more time working on herbs?"

"I would do it."

"Tell me one of my past lives with my sister, Kimberly."

"I would say go to thy home this evening. I want thee to picture the two white doves who sit upon the tree. I want thee to picture in thy mind the Force of Light into what is called Ireland. I want thee to envision thee and thy sister as you look of this day, both together there. Let thy Akashic come forth and see thy own life."

"So, we can see our own Akashics?"

"Aye."

"I have been seeing a lot of visions of past lives. Is it my own creation or a message?"

"It is a message to thee of life so that thee can find thy inner self. That which thee are striving very hard to find. But thee are filled with doubt of thy abilities. Take the doubt away. Throw it away. It has nothing to do with thee. You say, 'I am that I am and all that I am, I am that." To that positive thought, you begin to create a circumstance of life, so that will be happier and a greater achiever. It is as simple as that."

"It is harder in human form."

"It is because the conscious mind cannot function to the degree of the subconscious. When you put everything to the subconscious mind, it comes forth abundantly. You begin to understand."

"There is an Angel that I see many times in meditation, and I cannot tell if it is masculine or feminine. It is a younger person with blonde or fair hair. I saw him for first time with Mary."

"Romero. His name is Romero. A special angel for thee."

"He is young?"

"When he is in spirit, does he have to be old? I, Ashlem, are ancient, but then I showed my image unto thee, and it is not so that I am ancient?"

"No, you are not ancient in the image. You said he was a special Angel for me. In what respect?

"An Angel of Creativity."

"Creating what I am here to do?"

"Aye. You will have to close the door so that he can work alone."

"I don't understand that."

"Ye will. Take this hand and place upon thee heart. Through the force of Light, I want thee to picture the Blessed Virgin Mary. Now the beautiful pink rose. Now the White Rose of the Christ. Breathe in the White Light through the White Rose deeply. Receive it. Feel it go through thy entire body, and it begins to reverberate back and forth. Entering every cell group that thee have. Feel that love force upon thee and through thee. Let it begin with the Light. The Light is the creative force. In this period of time, one with thee, the Christ, one with thee, the God. Place it upon thy forehead." (Ashlem sings in Tibetan.)

"Into thy Greater Mind comes forth the wisdoms of time. Here into thy inner eye as it begins to open upon thee and through thee. Let it begin. Lift the Veil and open the crown chakra, and the Christ Light enter into thee of all time. The Light is strong, and the Light is pure within thee. It is time to hold thy head up, not doubt. And go forward and begin to create. You will find a greater peace within thee. Here is my covenant to thee:" (Ashlem creates a circle with this thumb and his forefinger.)

"Of the Father and the Son, and of thee and thy Holy Spirit, that the circle of God is eternal. Never beginning, never-ending, and never to be separated from the whole, and that is thee. And the force of Being be upon thee at this time.

"You are doing well, my dear. Stop doubting thyself. Walk with thy head high. Thy love in thy heart and thy stead. Go forth to the gentleman and speak to him, and to be friends with him without fear. And then he will return to thee with greater love and peace. And you will find the inner self is a greater person than you have ever felt before.

"The Angel come forth to help thee. Use her. Walk into the Light. Peace be unto thee. I take my leave."

"Thank you, Ashlem. Thank you for helping me."

Chapter Four: I Have Much Learning

I had many questions and doubts after my last reading with Ashlem. What does he mean? Why do I feel more lost than before? It's not so much about the knowledge of past lives I can see, feel, or dream of—that makes sense to me. But should I hold my head high and not doubt who I am? Really? Are you kidding me? Doesn't he see what my life has been like? The mistakes I've made, the anger I had and still have, the ridicule, sabotage, and rudeness from people I barely said hello to. He wants ME to reach out to Gregory even though it feels like he wants nothing to do with me. Why would I want to put myself out there like that? Why would I want to feel rejected again? Haven't I had enough experience with that? Life often feels full of rejection and pain. I pushed those questions out of my mind. I wasn't in the right place to think I was worthy, and I didn't want to relive all the pain and heartache of the past. I preferred to work on other subjects that are much less painful and emotional.

I started with the easiest subjects. I wondered how our minds jump to the wrong time period. How can that happen, and why does it happen? I concluded that since we carry all the knowledge, experience, and wisdom of the past, our subconscious mind reverts to that time frame when triggered by a smell, sound, feeling, or experience.

I could do without the feeling of someone crossing into the Spirit World. It's hard on both body and mind. I wanted to abandon that penitence; however, I felt it was right to honor those I had lost in previous lives. I didn't feel remorse for their deaths caused by my hands back then, and it's only proper to do so now, even if Ashlem said I didn't need to think about it anymore because it is over.

I started thinking about the Hawaiian Islands and the past life he mentioned there. I do remember learning in middle school about the sirens from Greek legend, who seduced sailors and lured them to their islands. I recall feeling a strange sense of awareness at the time. Now I understand why.

Ashlem said I should look in the Hawaii region for love, but I can't find it. Strange. I don't want to go to Hawaii. Fiji and Tahiti, yes, definitely! But not Hawaii. My mind drifted back to childhood when I had pictures of places around the world. Waikiki Bay was one of my favorites, and I couldn't quite put my finger on why. Could this be the reason? Was my lifemate from Hawaii? Or was there more? I didn't know, and I'm not sure I could solve that mystery right now.

As I continued my classes at school, including massage, reflexology, anatomy, and Reiki, I wondered how qi and the Christ Light could be the same. I came to believe that it was an outlandish statement. How could they be the same? Christ meant light, and qi meant the energy of the body. Why would Ashlem tell me something so wrong? I had a sneaking suspicion that I was the one who was wrong or didn't understand the concept. I decided that lesson was for another day. I may someday understand all these lessons I have been given.

I moved on to the herbal conversation. My school didn't offer herbal classes, and I wasn't comfortable learning about it on my own. They offered aromatherapy, but it didn't resonate with me. I purchased several books on herbology, including one specifically titled *"Back to Eden"* by Jethro Kloss. It contained many traditional herbal remedies from the 1700s and 1800s, and it was very informative and comprehensive; however, it didn't entirely resonate with me. I bought a few herbal remedy books that focus on herbs used by Southwest Native American tribes. Still, once again, it felt like I wasn't on the right path. I also bought a book about Traditional Chinese Medicine (TCM). As I started reading it, I felt intrigued. Maybe this is it!

In one of the first chapters, the book begins to explain the diagnosis process in TCM, covering wind, heat, cold, damp, dry, phlegm, yin, yang, jin, ye, blood, and qi. What are they talking about?

I re-read the chapter several times. I decided to put it aside and try again another day. When I did, it still didn't make sense to me. I thought they were crazy, or maybe I wasn't smart enough to understand. I pushed it out of my mind and kept searching to learn about herbal medicines. The idea of the government coming down on me for healing with herbs without a license scared me to death. I wasn't ready to step into that world of healing without at least a formal certificate. And would that protect me from government persecution? I wasn't sure.

The world was changing rapidly, and what had once been accepted as American rights was being challenged and altered daily. Pharmaceutical companies began influencing the FDA's decisions on herbal medicine, making it increasingly difficult for self-taught herbalists to practice their craft under the new guidelines.

I decided to wait a while before starting any herbal certification program. Instead, I met Yvonne at her shop and discussed the rune stones. She encouraged me to learn as much as I could, and I bought my first set of clay rune stones. I practiced with them every day, reading all the meanings of each symbol. I found wisdom in the process, so I decided to "up the ante" and buy a set made of lapis lazuli. During this same period, I also started studying crystal healing. I purchased the book, *"Love is in the Earth"* by Melody. I was very drawn to smoky quartz, amber, moonstone, labradorite, and ametrine (amethyst and citrine). Each had qualities I needed at the time. However, my favorites seemed to be smoky quartz and labradorite. Is it a coincidence that the legend of labradorite says it fell from the Aurora Borealis, and my soul's name means 'like the aurora'? Maybe. But are coincidences really just that? No, I was learning that wasn't true.

Comfort Comes to Town

Life was going smoothly until I received a phone call from my younger sister. She still lived at home with our parents and wanted a change. I offered her the chance to come live with me. It would be a new experience for her and provide me with some company. We were very close when we were young but drifted apart during college and after I moved to Arizona. I ran away from that situation because I needed to find myself, and I thought it would be a good step for her.

She moved in with me, and life felt good. I missed her company. She gave me a unique sense of peace that only she could provide because we grew up together. She understood my background. She quickly found a job, and we spent all our time together, going out to eat and hanging out with friends. She was also searching for love and hoped to find it. Phoenix could be a good fit for both of us.

While home life was good, my work began to suffer—not because of my own actions, but because of the changes that occur in everyday corporate life. My manager, Faith, accepted a new position, as she deserved, and the department promoted a man within it. He was young, bold, and brash, and he didn't understand — or didn't want to understand — how to treat employees, especially the female ones.

My new manager wasted no time in creating a counterproductive environment for our sales team. He was rude and condescending to the men, and he made sexual comments to almost all the women, especially to me. One time, he rubbed his back on the pillar while looking at my breasts and saying, *"I'm like a bear, I need to rub myself up against something."* I was immediately uncomfortable and felt like I was going to vomit.

We were a very close-knit team, and we communicated effectively with each other about what was being said and what was happening. We supported one another in every way. No one was better or worse. It was a gift that Faith instilled in us. Everyone on the team had a story about our new manager, and we felt like we needed to do something about it.

One night, I talked to my friend Nancy, who suggested I document everything. She pulled out a notebook and started writing down everything that happened. It turned out to be a blessing.

The team decided to bring the complaints to our Union leaders. One by one, we met with them, and they knew they had enough documentation to present to the Director, especially with the accurate details of time and dates I had provided.

The day arrived when it was arranged that each team member would have thirty minutes with the Director. I, however, was allotted sixty minutes. I remember feeling sick to my stomach as I sat in her office, reading page after page of documentation about the sexual harassment I endured. After twenty minutes, you could sense the tension in the room. She was jotting down everything I read to her, and once I finished, she asked if I had anything else to add. I distinctly remember her saying, "*Not that there needs to be anything else. There's a lot here.*" She then rolled her eyes in disgust and condemnation of the repeated acts of abuse. She hired this manager, and she understood her role in this situation.

She asked me what I wanted from this. I told her I wanted him punished for what he did. I also said that I never want anyone else to experience what I went through. She sighed in relief, and at that moment, I didn't understand why.

After the meeting, I rarely interacted with any of the managers. I came in, did my job, and kept to myself, except for conversations with my team members. I felt more vulnerable than I did before the meeting. What were they going to do? How would I be treated afterward? Did I do the right thing? Would they do the right thing?

I became very apprehensive and anxious that nothing would happen to my manager, and I would be forced to keep reporting to him. During this time, a few managers tried to speak with me, and I withdrew even further. The two most difficult parts of the situation were that he was still my manager and his wife worked in the same department. Luckily, she was on a different floor of the building. Always looming was the possibility of running into her and being confronted about the situation. I didn't want to be called a liar or worse, and I didn't want to have to justify my actions. I did what was right for me and the other women in the department.

As the days and weeks went by, my anxiety overshadowed my ability to do my job well. My manager maintained a professional distance from me, and when we needed to speak, he was always polite and concise. Another manager I felt comfortable with, because he had always been sincere and professional, casually told me some stories about workplace sexual harassment, where women received a substantial settlement instead of continued employment. He said the women were genuinely harassed, but they wanted a large payout for their suffering. I told him I wasn't after a settlement. I just wanted to keep my job and do it well. If anyone needed to leave, it should be my manager, not me. He nodded, and we ended our conversation.

At that moment, I realized why my Director, Darla, asked me what I wanted from this. She was expecting me to demand a payout from the company. I didn't want blood money for this. To me, that was like taking money for performing a sexual act. I'm not a prostitute, and I wouldn't act like one. The company had no control over his behavior. They would have become victims of his misconduct just as I was.

As time passed at work, I received a voicemail one day from a competing company looking for sales representatives. I decided to return the call and apply for the position. I was immediately hired and gave my two-week notice to US West. I felt relieved; I needed a break from that environment.

My Director, Darla, asked me to meet with her after I gave notice, and she informed me that my manager had been punished for his actions. They didn't specify what the punishment was, but it had happened and significantly impacted him. She wished me luck and said she hoped I wouldn't leave, but she fully understood my decision.

A New Path Opens

In January 2000, I started my new role at Cox Communications, and I decided it was time for another reading with Ashlem. Many things had happened, and I needed reassurance from Spirit that I had made the right choice. I left a job I loved because of a situation that didn't have to occur, and I was on my way to another.

Ashlem January 13, 2000

"I see a beautiful pink light emanating from an oval shape of light. As it expands slowly in the center of the picture, turns to violet light. Continuing to expand, begins to turn to white light. The larger it gets, the whiter it gets. The light is magnificent as it fills the whole picture now with soft White Light. An image forming in the center of the White Light.

"It is the Beautiful Blessed Virgin Mary once again. Mary is standing; she has on a white robe trimmed in gold over her shoulders and head. A light blue gown. She holds in her hand a beautiful White Rose; an aura around her is magnificently pink as it seems to fluctuate. Now, Angels appear around her: three beautiful Angels. One to the right, she has silver hair; her name is Delaitha. There is one above Mary; she has very light blonde hair. Her name is Regina. One with dark brown hair on her left. Her name is Jimaith. She is beautiful. Mary smells the White Rose, and before Mary

appears a golden flame—a flame like a candle flame that flickers only at the top. The Light is very bright and very fulfilling as it grows in size and intensity. It begins to soften and diminish. As usual, Ashlem is standing in that flame. Ashlem is wearing his white robe of simplicity, expressing everything in life to become more simplified. He has that beautiful smile on his face, and his eyes twinkle; the flame goes out.

"Surrounding now are more angels; male angels also, and Cherubs appear. And now a host of music appears, beautiful sounds. Ashlem bows to the Blessed Virgin Mary, and she hands Ashlem the White Rose of the Christ. He takes the White Rose, and he smells of that White Rose.

"Mary begins to speak, and golden words come forth. **"In the life of the Christ, of one stands forth in that Light, one may find the truth within for the greater being of wonderment of life. And the lives beyond the lives have been forgiven. And all things are of grace at this time. We stand before thee, beautiful one, that thee may know of our truth unto thee, and the Light shall form within thee, and shed forth that others may see. I am one with thee, and all of the Angels are with thee also. Into the peace of this new year to come forth of this time, we stand in your name."**

"Mary fades, and Ashlem smiles. A beautiful light blue light shines upon Ashlem. What a magnificent contrast. Then he sits on that White Rock that always accompanies Ashlem in a lotus position. The blue light fades to white. Now images are appearing around Ashlem. The flowers, and the birds, and little animals of the forest. The forest appears. The gentle

92

flowing little babbling brook, bubbling over the moss-covered rocks, making its way down to the gentle sloping hillside, to the horizon before. Ashlem smells the White Rose again and bows his head and wishes to speak through. I give my permission."

"I am Ashlem, known as Golden Image, I say to thee once again, 'Hail'. The force of Life comes forth of this period of time. The force of Life is with thee always, as the Blessed Virgin Mary brings the host of Angels unto thee. That thee may know and appreciate those things that are happening into life of this day. For there is not a day that has gone by that thee have not learned a wisdom of life. So, sometimes it is painful, yet ye know many good things coming forth. God is with thee, and God is the Force within thee of all times of this period. Here now, surrounding the Grace of God, a heart. A heart that beats with joy and happiness, most of the time. That is good. I stand before thee, to ask thee now, what is thy questions."

"I had this pull to Siddhartha and this connection to him ever since I read the book by Herman Hesse. And my question is, what connection do I have with him?"

"But ye are not connected to him, only by the means that he stands forth into the Light of Creation. Then by that, it is what thee look with favor of the masculine image or the thought creation. It is that purity of life for thee, that thee did not know the entity before. But now in your heart, you know greatly of that entity and its creation. It is good to hold fast of that knowledge within."

"So, I'm a bit confused because I feel a strong connection to the woman in his life, Kamala."

"Aye. Kamala. But do thee not associate Kamala with thy own feelings? That is where the connection comes forth because of thy own about life and things of life. It is how the association begins. Ye have had friendships in other lifetimes with entities similar to those you have spoken of. It brings to thee a happiness within thee to find there is someone else who has a greater knowledge or a feeling such as thee have. That is comforting, is it not so?"

"A while back, I saw a Master who appeared in front of me. He was very dark-skinned in a turban, and he was wearing an orange robe. He was a beautiful person. Do you know who this person is?"

"Rebazar Torres. You did not recognize him?"

"I was not quite sure who it was. I recognized the Spirit, but I did not know the name. He was very comforting."

"You will see him often again. In different settings of different phases of the Consciousness. He will teach to thee many new things to come forth. When thee envision him again, envision sitting down before him and feel his power and thoughts upon thee. You will learn much wisdom and knowledge from this.

"I know at nighttime when I go to sleep, I spend time with him and Mary, but I don't remember."

"But the subconscious does remember, and when thee need knowledge, it is there. So, do thee not function upon this Earth's Plane with things you do and wonder, 'How did she and he know of this?' It is

where it comes from, the higher sense of Being. It is
called Superconsciousness."

"So, if they were to tell me something, I would
remember it when I woke up?"

"It would have to be so if ye needed at that
moment of time."

"Which brings me to a dream I had where I was in a
workplace. There was an older gentleman, and he and I were
becoming close, but another man came in."

"The older man that comes forth that thee were
seeking wisdom of life. And a younger man who came
forth and disrupted that wisdom moment. Is there not
a time in your life, where you were learning your
higher sense, and was disrupted by another being?
Who came forth, and then he turned that knowledge to
another being, and soon dissipated into Life?"

"My ex-husband?"

"Aye."

"Was there some type of karma that I needed to finish
with him?"

"It is finished."

"Good. One thing I feel all the time is that I don't feel
connected to many people of this Earth."

"It is understandable because of thy age and the
wisdom within thee. But ye must connect yourself
with peoples of the material plane of Earth that they
may know of your station upon Earth. Of these times,
you are to find yourself to be a beautiful woman, as
you are a beautiful woman, but, there are times where
you say, 'Why am I so ugly or disoriented to life?'

These things you are not to think of. But only of the beauty. Picture yourself as a beautiful rose. Even in the later stage of life, the rose does fade. But it still holds an inner beauty, does it not? Then the beauty lies in the eyes of the beholder. Thee do not have the right to judge yourself about beauty and grace. For ye are truly beautiful into the eyes of All Creation and your Angels who surround ye at all times. It is the world to be friendship and loving and caring to the best of your ability. There are no peoples upon the Earth's Plane are perfect. Therefore, you are not perfect. But you are a beautiful being here with great wisdom to share with other peoples of this time. Wisdom and Love. And you must allow yourself to be loved also."

"Is that why I feel there are very, very few people who understand me?"

"Aye. It is the reason."

"Because I don't allow people into my life?"

"You are afraid they will intrude into your thought patterns and way of life. But your way of life is protected by the Grace. When one opens up to see their inner beauty force, they do not worry about the person entering into their life scope to change their direction of life. But ye must flow with love. Understanding Universal Love to peoples. It is not an easy thing to do in times of Earth. But to open yourself to a person that does not know thee, is important. You are able to speak to strangers and yet *not be able to talk to the people who are close to thee. Out of this fear."*

"Because I fear they will hurt me and my emotions."

"Aye."

"That leads me to my next question. I always feel that I am searching for freedom of something."

"Freedom of Self. You are being afraid of Self. And afraid you will make more mistakes into life. But if ye have not made any mistakes into this lifetime, then how much wisdom would thee have?"

"Nothing."

"Aye."

"But I have made a lot of mistakes."

"So has everyone else. You know your mistakes because ye have lived them. They know their mistakes because they have lived them. They do not know your mistakes, and you do not know their mistakes because they have not lived those mistakes with thee. So, therefore, each wisdom is separate and individual. So, of this period of time, live your mistakes. Bring wisdom into your heart and the wise person who comes forth and say, 'I have learned well because I have made many mistakes.'"

"I had a vision of being on a spaceship. It was just a flash."

"It was not a vision, it was a recall."

"And what ship was I on?"

"Inashio. It is a beautiful spacecraft. There are many female Brothers of Light or Sisters of Light upon that ship and ye know many of them. Cerana, Teracis,

Wuhannah, Lynacha, Sotoyenah, Enaham, Wunsutti,
and Personas. They are the Beautiful Ones."

"Have I spent time with the Pleiades?"

"In the Pleiades? Ye have spent a lot of time in
Pleiades with the Brotherhood of Light aboard your
spacecraft. You have found wisdom of knowledge and
loved to go to the planet called Agola into the Pleiades;
it is a place of the yellow race. For there, ye have the
yellow race much different than it is upon the Earth's
Plane, but they are very loving, and deep-loving
peoples. And that is what ye loved of the Brotherhood
of Light and helping of them. Especially their children.
Into their growing up of that period of time, children
of Agola have a very short life. In other words, their
child life is very short. According to Earth children,
they grow up quickly there, but they know love
instantly. They were made to thee a good friend. They
used to call thee Masaleaiah, which means "a Flower
of Light."

"I was channeling a while ago and I heard the name,
Ranish, come to me."

"Ranish? It is one of your names, into the
ancient time, into Mayan incarnation. You were
feminine of that time. It was near the place that is
called Machu Picchu of the present time. But long
before Machu Picchu was into existence, a little village
called Tamiquia. Your living there, was small. The
village there, was only of 24 peoples. But it was a
loving family type of existence."

"Was I a person of wisdom at that time that they would come..."

"But of course, you were a person of wisdom. They would come and sit before thee, and ye would stroke the ladies' hairs on their heads, and ye would tell them beautiful stories of the ancestral beings who taught. Ye call them today, Brothers of Light. They were the Masters and Teachers. And most of the peoples into that ancient time, were afraid of the Gods that came forth. But ye told them and explained they are not Gods, but beings of another dimension, which was difficult for thee to explain to the peoples. They did not understand what is dimension or time period. It was a good life for thee."

"Since a person has had so many incarnations, are there different vibrations from each incarnation that is part of you?"

"It is part of thee, and thy experience of that lifetime brought wisdom and knowledge, the same as the experience of this lifetime is for thee brought wisdom and knowledge. But the wisdom and knowledge now is more intricate because of the density of Light that thy flesh is in. Therefore, it is harder for thee to realize wisdom. Where into other times of higher vibrations of Light, it is easier to understand wisdom into certain subjects. When thee have known all of the subjects that are into the Universes and the wisdoms of time and space, ye need not to come into flesh anymore."

"Is that going to be soon?

"I do not know."

"Am I close?"

"But of course, ye are an old soul."

"I had such a connection to Commander Hatonn when he came through the other night at meditation."

"Aye."

"Can you explain that?"

"But of course, you were with him in the Brotherhood of Light. You went to the planet called, Serancis, that is far away into the Alpha Centuri Galaxy. Of that period of time, ye and he looked upon each other with a great favor. It is not what thee would call carnal love, but a deep respect for each other. Ye do not forget good peoples. Good beings."

"I also saw a place during a meditation. Do we, as spirits, have a place we call home, or on a spaceship? Because I saw this place, that was silver and white, and it had like a sunken living room. And I remember a silver mirror. And I said, 'This is mine. This is my home.'"

"Ye dreamed of this when ye was a child. And it is a reflection of that dream. And that dream was caused by another life experience into another vibration of flesh."

"Ok. So, I was bringing that forth?"

"Aye."

"A lot of wisdom and recollections are coming to me now. Is that because I am working with Rebezar Torres?"

"It is so. Enlightening of the Greater Being of that density of flesh upon Earth's Plane, is not easy. There are too many negative vibrations surrounding all peoples of Earth, and one must wade through this,

what is called, this cosmic trash to receive the greater awareness. People say, 'Why, if I am such an old soul, why do I not have all the wisdoms of time?' But thee do have all of the wisdoms of time, it is the Veil of Consciousness that holds them back from thee. So, therefore, when you have done good in your life and bring forth the greater wisdom, the Veil becomes lighter, and more wisdom comes forth."

"It is lighter now?"

"Of course, it is lighter now than before because ye have been speaking to I, Ashlem."

"And in the last few months, it feels like it has really been aggressively growing."

"It is because of the New Age of Time that has descended into this region."

"When I was young, I knew what month and year my great-grandfather would pass away; May 1987. And it came to me that my passing may also come in May when I was 29."

"In this lifetime?

"Yes."

"Do thee think you are going to pass away?"

"I always felt that I would. Even though, I don't want to."

"But ye are not ready to go yet. The passing of that time ye speak of into May is a greater awareness yet to come."

"Why would I pick when I am 29? And we speak of May 5th, and I would be 29 then."

"There will be an enlightenment into that year of May 5TH, 2000. Ye will find a revelation into

interbeing. *You will be able to see the Light within thee and feel lighter into your sense of vibration. It is difficult for I, to explain to thee what I mean into that revelation. But for thee to become closer to God within, you find a greater beauty."*

"When I was a teenager, I feel my Veil was lighter than in early 20s."

"But in your early 20's, you were a different person. And doing things, ye considered wild? But ye learned great lessons of that period of time. The Veil of Consciousness will descend heavier, when there is negative thinking or negative actions. But it brings greater wisdom to yourself and knowledge, and the Veil is lifted again."

"I realized that life was not good for me, and I stopped my 'wildness', and I went to the Church. I was so connected to Jesus at that time. Was he saying to me, 'It is time to come back?'"

"Ye were at the breaking point of alignment of being. To be with Jesus means to open thy heart to the good things of life and put away those things that are not good."

"Are you saying I had broken that point of alignment?"

"It is so. Ye have opened up from that point of alignment."

"Last week in class, you talked about abortion. And some friends have had abortions."

"It does not matter. There is no karma connected with it. They would not allow a child to come through their womb. The child would be a

detriment to their whole being. They understood it before, and they understand it now. Then they should not worry about the karma connected with it."

"I wanted to understand when it is a karmic condition and when it is not."

"Karmic, my dear, is when thee hast gone forth and deliberately let yourself go, and become with child. And out of anger and frustration from the father of the child, you would abort the child. That would be negative karma. But, when you have decided in your life that would be disruptive to your condition of life, and your flesh body, it would be better to have the child aborted or to let it go. The spirit already knew that beforehand. So, there is no reason to worry about any personal things that come into your life experience. You are not to have a child at this time, unless that child is wanted greatly by thee."

"So, in this lifetime, I have not chosen to have children or not at this time in my life?"

"At this point in your life, my dear."

"When I was making my life plan, did I choose to have children?"

"But of course. But it is up to thee, what thee do, when you are into incarnate, then when you are into Spirit, designing your course of destiny. Would say that I need to entertain a child coming through my womb for this purpose or that purpose of life. Then it is up to the Spirit that wishes to come through your womb."

"It is not my free will that will stop that; a Spirit wanting to come in."

"It is not your free will; it is the Spirits. But it is your free will to decide if having a child is the best decision for your course of destiny at the time in thy life."

"My family, my immediate family. I always feel like I am the black sheep of the family."

"Ye are not black sheep of family. Merely have not incarnated with them often. Therefore, ye find yourself to be foreign in their ways of life. And it is nothing purposeful. But thee had incarnated with them several times before. Same family incarnate group. Your family incarnate group is not upon the Earth's Plane at this time."

"What do you mean by family incarnate group? I don't understand that."

"Your personal close friends of the family incarnate group is into another space or planet into the cosmos. Your nuclei. Ye incarnated into this family incarnate group whenever the occasion ye needed to be here on the Earth's Plane at certain times."

"So that is why I don't feel close to my family?"

"They sometimes fear thee because of your knowledge. Your peer group; your mother and father. They look upon thee and think thee are weird. But their word is wisdom and not weird."

"Helps a lot of past pains. What about my maternal grandfather? I feel very close and loving of him."

"He is like a guardian angel to thee. Into this life force of flesh and into the spirit. And will be a guardian angel to thee."

"I feel like I am at a crossroads right now."

"But ye are at a crossroads. Millions of peoples around thee are at a crossroads. It is to do with the millennium that has come. People have been so caught up into what is going to happen in the new year 2000. They forget to live in the present."

"I don't feel that I have been that caught up in it."

"Ye have not been. But all of ye friends have. Now, nothing has occurred. So, ye feel there is a void."

"Mary took me to a blue star in one of my meditations and said, 'This is where I will be.'"

"It is Star of love and grace. It is not blue representing a sadness, but the blue of enlightenment."

"Is that a planet I will incarnate on?"

"You are incarnate on the blue planet now. The blue planet is Earth."

"So, the Earth was the star?"

"Aye. The Consciousness of Earth."

"It seemed like it was brand new."

"Earth is brand new considering other planets."

"Ok. Let me rephrase this. It seems like it was a new birth or rebirth of Earth."

"Could it be now? With the millennium?"

"Is that why I see a baby in this crystal many times?"

"But of course. Your crystal: it is a very large crystal. Have I charged this crystal before?"

"I do not believe so."

Ashlem charges the crystal by singing in Tibetan. When he finishes, he says, **"The wisdom of wisdom come forth into this beautiful crystal, and the stories that it tells is of greatness. For it collects all the stories of Creation and holds them. And if ye want to know a thought, put thy hands such as this, and feel the energy of the crystal through your palm chakra of your hand. It does not matter what hand it is. And in your mind, you will find greater wisdom to come forth. Let that all be of love and peace."**

"Can you read this? This image right here?"

"Can I read it? It is for thee to read, for it lies into the eyes of the beholder. Then, put your crystal in one hand in the palm chakra, put your other hand on the top over the apex of the crystal, and you will feel the energy pouring through. Now meditate upon the Light, the Light of love and peace. Do thee see angels? Do thee feel the cherub singing? If you want to visit different planets, visit in this mannerism, and believe what you feel and see. That is all positive. Then end each session with, 'I am the Light and the Truth and Being, One with God.'"

"What else should I do to help other people at this time?"

"There will be a new direction upon your path to soon come forth. Ye will not have to look for it. It will merely appear, and you will walk down that pathway, and along that pathway, you will find others. Some will have an emotional hand they reach toward thee. Take of their hand and calm their being. Others will

106

look forward to be taught. Teach them of the knowledge that you have learned from I, Ashlem, and let them breathe into it. And the other beings you have worked with upon this flesh of this Earth's Plane. Take from each of they, the knowledge of wisdom of life. And give it to others also. Do not judge others. Merely say, 'This is the Light and the Way. And if thee see the Light, and feel the Way, then thee will be better off in your whole flesh existence.' People will begin to understand thee, and you will heal and you will teach."

"There are some people right now that I am helping. Is there a time that I will need to pull away?"

"Each one will find their own time. And they pass away suddenly or move away in another direction from thee. Then thee say, 'Let them go in peace and love.' And they will become teachers also."

"Is there anything else I can do to bring my lifemate into my life?"

"A lifemate?"

"The one that I have chosen to spend this life with."

"Continue on your course of destiny. That has been outlaid for thee at this period of time. Bringing love and teaching. I can only say when your life mate or love mate is upon the course of destiny designed to intersect with yours, then thee will recognize that spirit. People always say to I, Ashlem, 'Where is my lovemate?' I cannot control other entities' ways of life. They must control their own. If they choose not to be on the proper pathway, what may I do? Nothing.

107

There is nothing that thee can do for that. But bring love and be that shining star that they may see a beacon in the darkness of night, that brings Light to their heart."

"I know you cannot prophesize, but how long do I need to wait?"

"Ye have many years yet to go."

"Many years?"

"Are thee saddened of that?"

"Yes."

"Why are thee saddened? I say many years of your life to continue between now and then, ye will meet your lovemate."

"I get lonely."

"Does not everyone upon Earth get lonely? It is the nature of mankind and womankind to be lonely peoples. They are creatures of loneliness. They must associate. The greater association coming forth. As ye do your work teaching and healing, and then one will come forth and the first eyelight upon he, you will know that this is your lovemate. Do not turn over rocks looking."

"I wanted to ask about a situation at work. My boss was sexually harassing me and others on my team."

"Was it the truth?"

"Yes."

"Then why are you worried about it?"

"Well, I know it was the right thing to do, but in my heart..."

"You did not want to get the person in trouble. He was being a man. That is what thee feel bad about. He did not need to have that harassment."

"So, I did the right thing?"

"You absolutely did the right thing."

"I don't have any more questions."

"Mary stands into the Light with the Rose of the Christ. It is your Rose of the Christ.   Expressing to thee that thee are one with she also.   Speak to her often. Carry her into your dreams and your heart. And all of the cherubs of life. And Rebazar Torres, stand forth and say, 'My guide, my teacher, my love, let it come forth.' He may help thee guide thee into the direction of your love mate to find that truer greater being in all of yourself. You are the captain of your ship, guide it through the night by the guidance of the stars within. That thee may know of the truer being of that Light. That is the message and the word unto thee.

"Take thee hand and press it upon thy heart. Of this force of the Light for thee and through thee, see the Christ Rose. Repeat after I, Ashlem:

"I and the Father are One.

"I stand forth into the Light of the Christ.

"For I am Light. I am LIGHT.

"I AM THAT LIGHT.

"Breathe deeply and receive the Christ Light of the Cosmos. Feel it penetrate in every cell of your body, reverberating through your body. It is now changing your body. This is changing everything.

Bringing a greater awareness unto your being of this time. For this, Light will alter many things. Bring a greater peace into your heart of this time. One with God is the Way and the Word.

"I give to thee this sign of peace, My covenant to thee. (Ashlem creates a circle with his thumb and his forefinger.) *"That is of the Father, and the Son, and thee, thy holy spirit, that the circle of God is eternal within. Never beginning, never ending, and never separated from the whole. And that is thee.*

"As ye walk forth here, take the hand of the person who is troubled, and say to them, 'Look to the sky of Light. Look at the many stars. They shine for you. They shine for they. They shine for every creature upon the Earth's Plane. And when the sun is warm into the day, and you feel its warmth upon thee, be happy because there are places where it is not as warm. Let the Light of Happiness always shine within thee. Do not forget the Covenant: 'Of the Father and of the Son and thee, thy Holy Spirit, that the circle of God is eternal within, never beginning and never ending and never to be separated from the whole. And that whole is thee.'

"Walk forth with the Angels. Peace be unto thee. I take my leave."

After this reading, Ashlem answered the question about my life path that was unclear to me before: *"Teach them of the knowledge that you have learned from I, Ashlem, and let them breathe into it. And the other beings you*

110

have worked with upon this flesh of this Earth's Plane. Take from each of they, the knowledge of wisdom of life. And give it to others also. Do not judge others. Merely say, 'This is the Light and the Way. And if thee see the Light, and feel the Way, then thee will be better off in your whole flesh existence.' People will begin to understand thee, and you will heal and you will teach."

Chapter Five: The Lessons Continue

My life slowed down from the chaos and turmoil, and I began to enjoy the break. My new job was exciting, and I learned a lot. It was a different part of the telecommunications world. While US West/QWEST was built on the old AT&T network and corporate culture, Cox Communications was more innovative and forward-thinking. They were expanding into the telecommunications market using their cable company network. It was wired into almost every home in Phoenix, providing competition to the old dinosaur. I thought, *This should be easy. Everyone wants a choice.'* However, I quickly learned a harsh lesson.

Construction into commercial buildings might involve digging alongside a road, tearing up and crossing the road, or working in a parking lot, which often requires city and environmental permits. Even if the customer agreed to all these conditions, we still had to retrofit the buildings to connect to the network. This process would take at least three to six months, and companies could not wait that long for service.

Deal after deal fell through because of construction logistics. Fortunately, my company was dedicated to this expansion phase and kept paying us well for our efforts. I received a lot of support from my manager, who taught me a great deal about outside sales and the skills needed for success. It was unlike US West. They had a network everywhere, and it was integrated into the business parks during their development.

In my personal life, I focused on my spirituality and practiced regular meditation. Ashlem held lessons every Wednesday night, and a group of twelve students would always attend. Ashlem allowed the attendees to ask any questions they had. These sessions were not personal Akashics. Questions ranged from Jesus and Mary Magdalene to abortion, crystals, herb growing, Atlantis, and Mu. It was wonderful to learn from others, discover what was weighing on their minds, and gain knowledge I hadn't considered before.

One of the lessons Ashlem shared involved May 5th, 2000. On that day, most of the planets would be on the other side of the Sun, exerting a strong gravitational pull on the Earth. This could cause Earth's axis to shift. If that were to happen, irreversible changes would occur. The Earth's axis might flip; north would become east, and south would become west. The class was stunned. In those moments, we wondered how life on Earth could survive. We were silent and scared. If that happened, the profound childhood certainty that I would leave this Earth at age 29 would come true. Was I prepared? Was it the end? Did I live my life to the fullest? Did I do everything I was meant to do?

Ashlem assured us the Council was doing everything it could to protect Earth from this disaster. They were giving Earth more time to learn from the negative consequences it had caused. They hoped mankind would start reconnecting with the divine light inside us. I had hoped we were saved, but I wouldn't know for sure until May 5th came and went. I did my best to forget about it and live the best life I could.

On April 6th, Rene and Milo hosted another gathering with Ashlem for everyone. I vividly remember walking into their home that night, and feeling that something was about to happen, although I didn't know what. Then I looked at Milo and knew he was leaving that night. He had been in and out of the hospital for months, and it seemed he had recovered from his illness. But that night, he looked like he was close to death, even though he was cheerful and loving toward everyone who arrived. I saw it and felt it. Rene didn't seem to notice, and Bob appeared very distant.

Milo decided to sit in the other living room during the class, which he had never done before. As the class ended and Ashlem left, Bob had the saddest face I have ever seen. He seemed to want to keep the class going as long as he could. I remember feeling a wave of agony as the class finished. Most of the people left, and I was about to leave when Milo came into the room and told Rene he had to go to the hospital again. I had a foreboding feeling.

Rene was afraid to drive at night, and the hospital was about forty-five minutes away. At that moment, Milo's organs started to fail. Rene asked me to drive her car to the hospital. A friend of mine agreed to take me home while she followed us. Milo's family was called, and they planned to meet us at the hospital. I drove recklessly. I knew I had to get him to the hospital before midnight. I didn't understand why. The little voice in my head urged me to get there quickly, and I did.

Once we arrived, we said goodbye, and Milo pulled me into the biggest, strongest hug he could give. He said, *"I will always love you."* It felt like a goodbye.

As we were heading home, Rene called and shared the news with us. Milo had died, thirty minutes after we arrived at the hospital and just before midnight. He wanted to return to spirit on April 6th, and he did so just minutes before midnight.

I was sad. Not because he left this Earth, but because I could feel it and knew it, and I couldn't say anything to Rene. It was a shock for her and their family. That's the downside of my abilities; sometimes I am unable to speak. I need to let the situation unfold as it's meant to. I can't stop it, nor can I interfere with the circumstances. It's a lesson I keep learning every day.

I had three dogs: two Pomeranians and one Akita puppy. Reno and Buster were my Poms, and Tasha was my one-year-old Akita puppy. She grew up with the Poms, and Reno, who was the love of my life, tried to keep her in her place. He owned me as much as I owned him. He would snap at her if she came too close to me. He was jealous and didn't want another animal near me or to receive attention from me. One evening, I had errands to run and would be gone for a few hours. I left my dogs alone at home, as I always did. When I came back, I knew immediately something was wrong. I stepped onto the back porch and saw that Tasha had her head down, looking at Reno, who was lying on his back, not moving. He was dead. Tasha had had enough of his antics and fought back. She grabbed him and shook him until he was gone.

I cried more than I ever cried in my life. Reno was the other half of my soul, and I felt like I was ripped open and flayed. His death almost destroyed me. Tasha walked over to me with her head down, trying to console me. She knew what she had done was wrong, and she felt the pain her actions had caused me. I couldn't console her. I couldn't be near her.

I wanted to die with him. I felt I had no reason to live on Earth anymore. Everything I loved was taken away or never truly belonged to me in the first place. The only true love I felt was gone. Tasha was a good girl, she was an alpha, and she was establishing her place in the pack. Unfortunately, it was 70# vs 5#. I visited my friend, Chris, who loved Tasha from the moment I brought her home. I asked him if he could take care of her for a bit while I mourned. He agreed to it.

I would go to the lake to mourn. So many times, I thought about throwing myself into the water to drown. I was drowning in my sorrow, and nothing could comfort me. Over and over, I asked myself, what purpose do I have? Why can't I just leave right now? The pain of life almost suffocated me, and I couldn't breathe anymore. I honestly didn't want to.

I would visit Tasha almost every weekend for a few hours. I didn't blame her for this; I blamed myself. She did what animals do. However, I was not ready to bring her home. After a few months, Chris called me and said it was time to take Tasha back. Every time I visited her, she became despondent because I left without her. She paced and paced and paced. It took her hours to settle down. He said those visits were too hard for her, and she obviously belonged to me.

I agreed and took her home. It took time for my pain to lessen, but it did, and it brought me closer to her. I was grateful for the protection she offered. She was never far from me. She loved me, and I was her person.

Movies and music continued to serve as a balm against life's harsh realities. One evening, I watched a movie called "*Stigmata*" with Patricia Arquette, Gabriel Byrne, Jonathon Pryce, and Nia Long. Being Catholic, I understood what the stigmata were—manifestations of the wounds Jesus suffered during his crucifixion: wounds, scars, or bleeding from hands, feet, the side of the body, and the head. I recall that St. Francis of Assisi was the first documented case of receiving the stigmata in September 1224, followed by Padre Pio in 1918. Many parts of the movie affected me: the stigmata, the bullying by the Catholic Church, and, most of all, the moment I first heard the words from The Gospel of Thomas— *"The Kingdom of God is inside you and all around you, not in buildings of wood and stone. Split a piece of wood, and I am there. Lift a stone and you will find me."* Those words resonated deeply within my soul. The truth. It explained why my visits to the churches no longer brought me joy or peace. Maybe I found the Kingdom of God within me—perhaps only a small part of it.

Later that year, I watched the movie *"Castaway"* with Tom Hanks. The despair, isolation, and loneliness conveyed in the film brought me to tears. I cried for hours and was depressed for weeks. I didn't know why until the little voice in my head said, *"Do you remember your first reading with Ashlem? Do you remember your past life as Reginald Wingate? You went down with the ship and managed to swim ashore on a deserted island, where you lived the remaining years of your life."* Ahhh, now it makes sense. My past life memories were validated once again.

My life remained quite ordinary. I went to work, exercised with my sister, spent time with my dog, and attended meditation and spiritual classes. Unfortunately, everything changed one day. Time never stops for anyone, and I was about to start a new level of learning.

My Sister's World Changed

My sister met a man who worked at her workplace. They hit it off, and he asked her out on a date. Before leaving for the date, she asked me, *"How do I act? It's been forever since I was on a date?"* I told her what Ashlem taught me: act like you want to be treated.

I had hoped this man would be a good match for her. She faced challenges in life and was looking for kindness and a good man to share it with. From what she told me, Dean seemed to bring her happiness, and he appeared to be a friendly and likable man. When I finally met him in person, I had the exact opposite reaction. My body tensed up and moved away from him. My gut turned, and I felt sick to my stomach. I pushed those feelings aside and wished the best for my sister.

She seemed happy, and it wasn't my place to judge her choices. She needed to live her life and make her own decisions. I wasn't as good at hiding my dislike for him as I had hoped. My words were appropriate, but my actions and expressions didn't match them. A rift started to grow between my sister and me. Circumstances and incidents began to affect us in different ways.

It was my house, and I didn't want him to stay overnight. I didn't trust him, and I didn't want him to be there. My sister thought I was unreasonable. I understood her feelings, but it was still my house and my rules.

At the beginning of June, my parents were traveling from Pennsylvania to Washington and asked my sister and me to join them. We planned to fly into Seattle, and they would meet us at the airport. We intended to visit Mt. Rainier, stay at the lodge, then drive down the coast to Crescent City, California, and on to Big Sur, before finally heading to San Francisco.

My parents visited Seattle a few times, and the clouds always covered the top. My father was frustrated that another trip would be wasted, and he would never see it on a clear day. We had dinner at the lodge and settled into our routines. I first sat in the lodge and watched all the families spending time together, playing card or board games, talking in front of the fire, reading books, or attending talks given by the National Park Service. It was heartwarming to see everyone enjoying each other's company. A sense of peace washed over me; I took a deep breath and relished the love being shared among families. I had never felt such peace and joy within my own family, and I was grateful and honored to witness it. A spark of hope ignited in my heart.

Suddenly, I felt an urge to go outside and look at the mountain. WOW. Beautiful. Amazing. It was clear, and even better, a full moon was shining its beams on the snowy peak. It was magical and breathtaking. This evening revealed a side of life that was previously missing from my experience: Peace. Contentment. Love. Grace. Kindness. Charity.

To this day, I still see the full moon over Mt. Rainier in my mind, and I can feel the moments I spent watching the loving interactions between people. I am forever grateful for that trip and the experiences it provided. A glimpse of such a world could make it a better place for everyone.

The next day, our trip continued, and the tensions between my sister and me grew worse. We were all stuck in a vehicle together for hours. My parents stayed out of the conflict, although I felt they blamed me. Growing up, I was often punished for things my sister did. They would tell me, *"You are the oldest, and you should have known better."* Things didn't change. They still took her side, even when she was wrong. I guess my 'weirdness' will always be a reason for them not to treat me like a daughter should be treated. I didn't do what they wanted, and I didn't live my life according to their plans. My thoughts and opinions were different from theirs. At this point in my life, I didn't need to follow their requests. I was 29, and in a few weeks, I would turn 30. It was time to stand by my principles, not theirs. The trip ended, and we returned to Phoenix, but not for the better. I decided it was time for another reading from Ashlem. I reflected on the following lessons in my life.

Ashlem June 1, 2000

"I see a pinpoint of golden light in the center of a violet background, the pinpoint of light goes up and down in a thin spire, and now sideways from one side to the other. A four-pointed star being formed. Spires are very thin. And now, the golden light fades to white light. And the white light expands now outward, upward, invading the violet light, leaving behind beautiful, soft White Light; the All-Consuming Christ. Images appearing in White Light. There are white roses. There is an array of these roses in half-moon circle. There are three rows of white roses, three deep. There are 33 roses in all. These roses are arched to top of picture.

"Now, below a beautiful violet shape light that expands from an oval shape outward. An image forming as it expands. It is the Blessed Virgin Mary. Such a beautiful place. Mary stands with her white gown trimmed in gold and a blue robe

120

over her shoulders and head in her traditional garb. The roses above are white and now pink roses trail down from underneath. It is like a grotto. But Mary is not a statute. Now, Angels appear in the background. The Angels are faint; all kinds of cherubs and angels.

"Mary turns, and she reaches above her and picks a White Rose. She smells the White Rose and turns back around again. She bows her head and begins to speak. Golden words appear, and the words say, **"Blessed art they who believeth in the Christ Consciousness. Blessed are they who understand the movement of the roses. Blessed art they who believe into in I, Mary. Blessed art thee upon this Earth's Plane of this time. For each white rose represents a lifetime of my son, Jesus who served mankind into his fulfillment of his destiny. I stand now before thee and always will, into the force of Light. Here is your Christ Rose."**

"Mary fades away, and that Rose remains. The Angels are singing. The arc of roses disappears, still the White Rose stands alone. Behind it, a golden flame appears. As always, Ashlem is standing in that flame. As it diminishes, Ashlem is now holding that White Rose. The flame goes out. Ashlem is wearing that white robe of simplicity. Ashlem has that beautiful smile on his face as always.

'The Angels just seem to fade away and taking their place, is the beautiful forest. Roses are everywhere, growing. Ashlem is standing on his traditional White Rock. He looks up into the sky. The sky is beautifully blue. Here and there, is a little twist of clouds floating by. Ashlem sits in a lotus position holding that White Rose. He looks from left to right, from the right back to the center. Ashlem bows and wishes to speak through, and I give my permission."

"I am Ashlem, known as Golden Image, I say to thee, 'Hail.' To the blessedness of life, one comes forth. Such a beautiful place and such a beautiful day. It may align into the mind of mankind here upon Earth's Plane. But yet, it is heavenly, to speak of. The Blessed Virgin Mary has come forth again and will always appear in her image for thee. For thee to understand the truth and purity of your life of this time. There are trials, and troubles of all things that come to Earth's Plane concerning new things.

"I come before thee with the Christ Rose that Mary has chosen for thee of this time. Walk your pathway with your head high. Do not look constantly on the pathway, ye may not see where thee are going. But walk with dignity, look everywhere upon the pathway. When ye sit upon the pedestal of life, look around ye at the beauty and enhance the beauty with your beauty. That is the thought of creation. Now there are many questions I will answer for thee, please begin."

"I feel like I am on the wrong path for my life right now. There are lots of things happening now, troubles and turmoils, and I think I need to change, and I don't where to go or what to do."

"Ye feel like ye are walking down a long corridor, looking for a window or door to escape. There are no windows or doors, is there?"

"No."

"Have thee looked up to see if there is a ceiling?"

"No."

"It is like walking through a maze of life of this time. But all is for a purpose, is it not so? Have you learned wisdom and knowledge through this life experience of this present time?"

"Yes."

"It is what ye are doing. You are walking down this corridor of life, and you look here and there, and different accesses happen upon your pathway. You meet different peoples, and some peoples are filled with hatred and discontent, and that annoys thee. And other peoples are filled with universal love that thee cannot grasp yourself, at this time, do you understand fully?

"But yet, there is love in your heart that reaches forth for companionship and understanding. This is part of the human experience upon the Earth's Plane. Indulging into the material plane to love creative forces. The love is an important thing that thee may not be able to purchase yet. If ye purchase love, it is a false love, is it not so? Therefore, love must be earned. Then what is the problem walking down your corridor of life? If ye wish to tear away the walls, see them dissipate. Begin a pathway that is filled with roses, but yet keep your eye upon the pathway. But not stare at it, as we have demonstrated to thee. Your life is going to change, my dear. Do thee want it to change?"

"Yes."

"Then ye have learned a wisdom of life that is needed. Ye work hard for your money, is it not so? Do not waste of it of this time. Ye have made your way without the aid of a man, is it not so? Yet your heart is waiting for love to enter. I say unto thee it shall come to pass, but do not turn over stones looking for love. It does not lie there. But love is upon your pathway unto this experience. It is not a prophecy, I say, it is your course of destiny. You have learned the business world, working in this world. Now you are bored with it?"

"Yes."

"It is time now to venture forth remaining steadfast to your business. In other words, you are good employee of this time. You work hard and have good faith to your employers. They think you are good in your business. Maintain this attitude that thee have learned to appreciate yourself. Then if you wish to change into another venue of work, then seek out that which is in your heart to do. If it requires schooling to do that work, then by all means, take the schooling. But it is thee who must decide which course of destiny ye shall follow now.

"You are at a crossroads into your life. And one crossroad, one pathway, you will find again repetition of the past experience of this present life. On the other crossroad that thee take or decide to take, ye may find new horizons. Then look towards the new horizons to come forth. It is simple a feeling within.

"When thee decide to do this in life, then go forward to it. Work as best as you can toward it. Always placing into mind the destination. In other words, a runner who runs upon an oval-shaped field, a pathway, is first goal in prime purpose is to reach the goal. In order to reach it first, must run harder than the others. Into this lifetime, also, is that same experience for thee. Look at your goals into life, the finish line. It shall always move away from thee. Therefore, will thee ever reach it? You do not want to reach your finish line because, when thee have reached, as ye have now reached a finish line in your life, boredom sets in. Then you are looking for another finish line. Then if you are going to finish, ye must be steady into your flesh life here.

"New horizons will open for thee. But not only if ye knock upon the door, that the door be opened, look in. See if it is what thee desire. Then go for it. But if you stay at present place of work and your same thing, then thee must find new and exciting ways to rebuild or continue to grow into that field. There is never an end to anything, if one puts their mind to continue to create a different wisdom.

"Ye have reached a plateau unto this business world of yours, there is another plateau if ye wish, continue on or another direction that thee wish to take. Always roadways have bumps in the road, is it not so? You must learn to flow with those bumps in the road. You have learned a great wisdom into these few years of life, young life. There is still much more

125

to do. It is best that thee do this without the aid of a man and his ability to create work or monies.

"It is alright to be independent, but your heart still needs love and understanding and fulfillment. As ye walk down this pathway of strength within, allow others to join with thee to walk a short distance with thee. When ye have found the right person, ye will know this and flow together. Then each of thee working together will build a greater castle."

"May I ask more about the new horizons and the plateau? There is a position at my current job that would be a promotion. And right now, at this point, it sounds like something I would love to do. But, there is also a part of me that wants to get out of the business world and do my own thing. I just don't know what that is."

"Be like the runner that runs the circle. Do you understand? They must prepare for the race. You are at the start line, now, of a new race. What thee are to do now, ye must choose. I cannot make thy choices for thee; it would be wrong for thy Ashlem to do this for ye. Your heart is filled with that which ye want to do. Ye have saved some monies?"

"Yes."

"Hold fast unto them, do not be foolish with your funds. Very important for thee. For ye have learned many sacred wisdoms about money. You have just overcome a portion of that problem of life concerning money. Now, when ye start upon a new pathway, ye must work again. But into working, look forward to the excitement of something new. Then ye

126

will fulfill yourself with this new excitement. New direction. Think about the wisdom you will learn along the way going up. But ye must make the choices, not I, Ashlem."

"Ok. What about my home and my personal life with my sister? I'm running into some..."

"There are going to be changes, my dear. Do not become angry with your sister. If she is doing something that is against your household, then ye say, 'My darling sister, do understand this, I cannot stand this or what you are doing here. Would it not be wise to find your own place?' And she would say to thee, 'I cannot afford to go to another place.' Ye say to her, 'As long as ye are here, you will never be able to afford another place. It is first to go out and find other place and then seek the work with continuance of it, then thee may be able to support your ownself. Then thee can have your boyfriends in anytime thee want.'"

"That's a big problem."

"She is a young girl yet. It is good to be young, but it is better to be responsible for your life. Do not become angry with her, she might become angry with you. Then thee would say to her, 'Kimberly, I want you to look at yourself. Listen to what I am saying, 'Build your life for your life the way you want it to be. But you must do this upon your own. Then, ye will reap the harvest of whatever ye sow into life. If you continue your way now, I am afraid the harvest will be a poor harvest.'"

"Just like I had to do."

"It is something thee have been putting off for a long time."

"Yes, I have. Why do I feel so responsible for her? Ever since I was young, I felt so responsible for her."

"Because you are the older sister."

"And that's it?"

"What else could it be?"

"I don't know."

"Past experience. She has been your mother before, it is so. And ye took care of her when she was very ill into China. When she were your mother at this time and you were her son. And ye cared for her as it was your responsibility to do in those ancient times in China; to care of elderly parents. And ye, which was he in those days, took care of she until she perished. But the spirit does not forget. So ye feel responsible that ye should take care of her. But if ye do this, she learns no lessons. You are doing her a greater favor by saying to her, 'My darling, sister, go forth and do your thing.'"

"That is very hard to say."

"But ye say to her, 'This is my house.' Not angrily. But say, 'You are disrupting it. I do not want to control your life. Do not try to control mine. Go forth, my sister. Get your apartment that thee need and stay there. If you want a house, you have to work for it, like I did.' Be polite and loving, but yet firm."

"I have a question about the night Milo passed. Was I supposed to be there, or did that just fall into place?"

"Have thee not made a bonding with Rene? Then that bonding is for a purpose and reason. You are a strength for her at this moment of time. Be that strength with her. She will begin to stand upon her own way for your inner strength that thee show. Yes, you are to be there for a reason and a purpose. It was important for thee to see and feel the pain and the suffering. Yet he wanted to go home. And that was the most important thing, and ye helped him see to that. He will remember thee unto the next lifetimes."

"How did I help him?"

"You helped by helping his mate and are still helping his mate. And that made him feel closer. It is important. Robert and Milo had a talk before he passed on. He told Robert that he was going to leave that evening. It was a harsh thing for Robert to sit and watch him. Robert wanted to say to him, 'Do not go, you are my friend.' Could not say this to him, only to make him feel bad. He wanted to go home. He was being called. Through your efforts at that time, ye gave peace to many peoples. You will see this in time yet to come."

"I heard that I was supposed to be here that night – was that the reason?"

"It is so."

"And I heard, and I saw Angels in the house. And I knew immediately when I saw him that he was leaving."

"All for a purpose. You were there to serve those moments of time. You are not obligated to remain or to hold her hands. You are there for that purpose of

time. Ye have been a good support for her. It is very much appreciated, no matter what they say or others may think. It has been greatly appreciated by her, by I, Ashlem, by Milo, and they who are involved. Your strength will help. Then do not place yourself here upon the presence constantly. But ask if ye are needed, then go if you are needed. That is the reason for this. You will find a period of closeness between she and ye for a period of time. It is good. She will help thee eventually. You will see this in time. Good friends must honor each other, must they not?"

"She has been in a lot of pain, especially in her head. I put my hand on it, but I don't know if it helped."

"Of course, it helps. The healing force, my dear. If one touches upon the emotions of enlightenment and love, is it not a healing factor? I say a doctor cannot heal your wounds, only thee can heal your wounds, and others, also theirs. But when thee put forth a love action of caring, it begins a healing force ten times stronger."

"But going into the healing, is that what my path is? To heal my friend's emotions?"

"Of course. But are there not many ways of healing?"

"Yes."

"You allow yourself to be caught up into their trash of life. Do not do this. So, if you are counseling someone, use wisdom into counseling them. Do not put your heart upon your sleeve with emotion. You can stand back and see the picture entirely. If you stand too close to the picture, you cannot see the whole forest. So, therefore, counseling a person, do not become involved into their emotional dip of life. That is important to remember."

"I feel like I'm being pulled into a thousand different directions."

"Do not let this happen to thee. Ye must be a pillar to stand forth. But because of your emotions, you are pulled here and there, because you want to help. And your help comes forth strong that thee want to do this and that, and people want to lean upon thee. Ye would have them lean upon thee, but it becomes weary after a while. So, you help this person a little bit here, that person a little bit there, and another person a little bit there. They must learn to stand upon their own two feet, like your sister. The greater service to her is for thee to say, 'Go forth.' Always keep yourself open to counsel your sister. If she becomes angry with thee, forgive her. Say unto your sister, 'I will be here to help thee, emotionally, with wisdom and knowledge if you want my help.' Then, give her good wisdom. Do not do it for her."

"I am becoming more aware of different things. Could you help me by describing the difference of projecting things and receiving information?"

"There is a fine line between projection and receiving through your imagination, as ye are talking about. But the thin line is wiped away by the action of the thought of creation. Ye must remember that all thoughts create. Therefore, your imagination, as ye *put it, ye are not imagining, ye are creating that circumstance. Then accept it as a creation, not as an imagination. Ye may see and envision future things for thyself in this mannerism. Become greater clairvoyant into life. And then, be able to help others in time, through your clairvoyance. To look upon their love and their place of life. It is part of a counselor's way of life. It is how it must go. But if ye think, 'That is my imagination working overtime.'*

"You see these beautiful colors and things such as that, 'I am not worthy,' then thee will never be worthy of it. Because you already limited it through the being by thought. But what you say when you see things, 'Is that not beautiful?' Enhance the beauty of it. Let your imagination grow upon it, because it is a creating force. Let it expand and continue. You do not have to tell other peoples about it. But to yourself, you will see different images appearing, and for that purpose of those images. But first, colors and lights, then the images, and then the purpose of those images. It will come forth. All in time. It is a learning experience for thee."

"What about the feelings I get. Like the other night when I was going to bed, I felt presences."

"There are always presences around thee, my dear. The Blessed Virgin Mary is one of them. And your Angels also."

"Why do I feel them sometimes and not others?"

"If your thoughts are negative, then ye attract around you negative spirits. Not bad spirits, but

negative thinking spirits. Let us put it more harshly. If there is an alcoholic and the alcoholic has a negative attitude, it breeds spirits that were before alcoholics in the flesh. And they tend to group around the alcoholic, causing it to drink more alcohol. So, they can see and feel the effects of the drink. A person who says, 'I cannot stop smoking,' is being influenced by spirits who at one time smoked. Maybe even has perished due to smoking. So, they will enhance people to smoke more. The urging.

"But if a person who dismisses the attitude of this alcoholism, and they feel free of their being, then there is not a problem with the spirit. So, when you are there thinking thoughts of goodness and love, who is it that thee attract around thee? Spirits who have goodness and love. And that brings what? A greater way of life. Then bring forth peoples who have passed on with greater wisdom and knowledge. And let them come into thy life like Plato or the wise ones. Confucius and so forth. Think about their sayings. They will guide thee without pointing the way for thee."

"Are they around me?"

"It depends on what thee are thinking about. If thee are creating, they are around thee. If you are not creating, then they are not with thee. Ye cannot walk a straight line down the pathway of life, my dear. Ye must go off the pathway here and there to learn the experience. That is the wisdom of time. Work upon it. Do not wander too far off of pathway."

"A couple weeks ago, I walked into a store, and I always looked at that Buddha, but that day, I could not walk away from it. I kept hearing, 'You must take me home,' and I could not walk down the aisle away from it."

"Buddha is always with thee, also with the wisdom of time. A Master Teacher for thee. You brought the Buddha home because you heard the inner voice saying, 'I am yours.' Then you wished to bring him to I, Ashlem, is it not so?"

"I forgot it."

"Ye did not forget it. He is with thee now. When thee go home, I want ye to say these words, (In Tibetan), **'Buddha, my friend, the blessedness of Ashlem upon thee of this time. Stand with I and guide I.'"**

"Is he now another one of my Master Teachers?"

"He has been a Master Teacher of thine for a long time, because ye adored him."

"Was I with him?"

"In the period of time he walked upon the Earth's Plane, ye had known of him. Ye did not walk with him, but ye had known of him."

"And I had loved his teachings. Was one of my incarnations...?"

"One of your male incarnations, you were a Buddhist priest into the Tibetan plateau."

"Why did Nathan come into my life at this time? What lesson did I need to learn?"

"Ye have to figure that out. When ye have a purpose that is recent, what did you receive from the friendships of Nathan?

"I learned to open up a little bit more."

"It is a wise lesson. Have thee put a greater hold upon thee emotions from it also?"

"Lately, yes."

"Then what is the purpose of Nathan to be in your life?"

"To help with my emotions."

"Aye. Do thee want more?"

"I thought I did."

"Then cherish the thoughts and the wisdom ye have gained. Upon the pathway of life that continues to flow on. The pathways may intersect."

"Is he my lifemate?"

"I cannot say that to thee. I cannot make your decision. Ye must make the decision. When he and thee are in the same place, thee will know. And you will answer your own question."

"I saw the light in his eyes – the golden light."

"Knowing a person, being with a person, does not know the person. After ye have spent a lot of time with the person, then thee will know. Absence makes the love fonder. Sometimes it puts forth a cloud, and one needs, and wants love so much, the mind blocks out the bad things. But in reality, when one opens eyes and sees the entire picture, then there is a different story. If ye want to see the entire picture, ye must be with him to do that. Do not thee move."

"I almost did. If he would have asked, I would have moved."

"But it did not work out. Then what is on the other end? Great aspirations? Expectations? Would they have been true or false?"

"It would have been false."

"There is time. Continue your pathway. If he cares about thee, the way you care about him, then he will be by your side."

"Why did I hear to give him my moonstone?"

"We have discussed this already. Ye will see in time, that is all I can say to thee, about this moonstone. It will carry a new vibration."

"I want to ask about the amber ring that was given to me by a friend. It was green with some red, and now it is golden."

"It has been purified."

Ashlem asks for the ring and prays in Tibetan. *"Now come forth the energy of this ring. If the rings turns back to the way it was before, then ye are walking down the wrong pathway."*

"So, it is telling me that I am walking down the right pathway because it turned golden, which is the wisdom and knowledge. Was it my vibration that..."

"Thought is the creative force. Thought impenetrates everything."

"On May 5th, 2000, was my spirit lifted?"

"There are avenues of that period of time. It was not the reason for May 5th, 2000. The reason for May 5th, some peoples say the spirit shall be lifted and your karma shall vanish. Good thought. But in reality, it is thee who has wished away your karma,

136

because you purified yourself with the thought. Have thee been lifted emotionally? There is some residual still hanging there. Then your answer to your question is nay. But I say to thee, there is still time remaining, the vibration of the Earth is continuing. This year is not finished yet."

"Why was I feeling so ill and dizzy and sick on my stomach that night?"

"Thought. You were afraid innerly, thinking about all the things people have said about May 5th. The World to come to an end? But ye did not want to come to an end. Nor did anyone. But ye felt the movement of the Earth's Plane. All of the planets that were aligned were pulling the surface of the Earth greater. Many sensitive people such as yourself felt this pulling. Made nausea and or fainting spells. But as far as changing your physical makeup, nay. But your emotional makeup has risen, one would say, lighter vibration."

"I didn't know if I was being positive right now. I'm trying to be. I don't know if the emotion is bringing down my positive thoughts."

"Be positive and knowing. You are now questioning yourself. Do not question yourself anymore. 'I am love. I am peace. I am happiness.' That is your thought that ye must maintain. By the thought maintaining, things are not going smoothly for thee, you will find it will again regain that senses for thee to be smooth. because of the thought pattern of creation.

I have said the bumps in the road, have I not? You must let all anger go away best you can.

"Jealousy is a perversion of anger. Promotes it. There is no need to be jealous of anyone. If a person does greater than thee, say, 'I am happy that person can do greater than I.' That eliminates all jealousies. Does not promote anger. If ye say, 'She does not do as good work as I do, yet, she has been promoted.' That is negative. Then you have put yourself down another notch. Do you understand?"

I paused to think about what he said.

"There is more?"

"One more. I was at dinner with friends, and we were talking about the movie, Gladiator. And I said that I would not go to see it because of what happened with the people and the animals in the Colosseum. I was probably killed there, which is why I have aversion to it."

"Your good friend was killed there during the persecution of the Christians."

"I was not killed there?"

"Ye did not suffer the pains there. But all people who are elevated, their Christ Consciousness to a greater degree, feel pain and suffering in the Colosseum. Accept it as those days being the way of life for those people. Often, people who are called Christians of this period say, 'You cannot be born again, or you cannot enter the Kingdom of God, unless ye believe in Jesus.' And I say to they people, 'Before Jesus was born, all those souls who lived and perished

138

were refused from the Kingdom of God? Because they did not know about Jesus?'

"Usually, the excuse is that they have a dispensation. People do not know what they are talking about. It is a matter of understanding this time. Those people who died in the Colosseum, it was their destiny. Unless, they would have not died there. Into those ancient Roman times, the Colosseum, before the Christ Consciousness and before Jesus was born, thee being a Roman woman, lost your loved one as a gladiator. But if ye go see this movie, I guarantee thee, ye will weep tears. Not tears of great hatred and discontent, but understanding what love is. For thee have felt the same pain in another lifetime. It is good movie, not entirely true. But it is a good movie. There is not much killing of animals in. It has its battle moments, but the ones who created the movie, had good thoughts about peoples turning their stomach."

"One of the aversions I have is all the animals killed in that arena."

"The people are being slain in the arena, not the animals. A battlefield. That is how the movie starts out. The Roman Conquerors. It is what they were known for throughout the world. Conquering most of the world. The inhabited world. The cultures that thee have today, some of them are from Rome during that period of time.

"They left their mark everywhere. But they did not be able to hold it because of arbitration. They

fought battles with sword, and the spears, and fireballs. A terrible battle.

"If ye go to see this movie, you will see man at his greatest negativity against his own kind of peoples. You will see and learn more of the Roman nobility. Some parts of the nobility are true. But they show more slaughter in the arenas than there really was. But not animals. There are tigers in the arena, but you will not see them devour the gladiators or be slain totally. You will find also tiger, cat or lion life was worth more than a gladiators. And valued more. So why would they slay them?"

"I also saw a movie, What Dreams May Come with Robin Williams. I think it helped me understand love a whole lot better. I cried and cried."

"Tears cleanse the soul. Do they not? Is there more questions?"

"No. Thank you Ashlem."

"Take this hand and place it upon thy heart. Of the force of life through thee of this time, the Blessed Mary pays honor unto thee once again, and with each time, ye come forth. The Rainbow Roses, Christ Roses, she has explained on what they are. I want thee to picture the beautiful White Rose. Once again, repeat after I, Ashlem.

"I and the Father are One.

"I stand forth into the Light of the Christ.

"For I am Light. I am LIGHT.

"I AM THAT LIGHT.

"Breathe into the Light force of this time. For the energy pour into thy body strengthening every tissue of your body, every structure of your body from the atom, the molecule to the cell, to the bone and muscle tissue of your whole body. You are one with the Christ, and the Christ is the Light and the Christ is Truth, and Christ is with thee at this time.

"Let the force always be with thee, never let it hide."

Ashlem speaks and prays in Tibetan. *"I have lifted thee Veil making it very thin so that greater wisdoms flood into thee. Only anger will set it afire. Then walk with your head high, love in your heart, and smile upon your lips. I give to thee the sign of peace* (Ashlem creates a circle with his thumb and forefinger) *that is of the Father, and the Son and thee, thy Holy Spirit, that the circle of God is eternal within. Never beginning, never ending, and never separated from the whole. And that is thee.*

"I say to thee, 'Forgive they who have trespassed upon thee. Forgive I, who for my trespasses also.' Let love abound with thee from a pure heart.

"Peace be unto thee, I take my leave."

"Thank you, Ashlem."

After reading, I knew it was time for my sister to leave my house and start her own life. Our relationship had worsened to the point that I didn't think she would take the request very well. I didn't trust myself to have the conversation without getting emotional. I felt guilty. But I needed a break. I wanted her to be happy with her new boyfriend, even though I doubted she would find true happiness.

A few weeks later, she moved out of my house and moved in with Dean. We didn't talk for months afterward. I regretted the rift, but I finally had peace in my home. I found the quiet to be fulfilling and refreshing.

Maybe Not the Peace I had Hoped For

My parents were upset about the situation. They disapproved of my sister living with Dean out of wedlock and were clearly displeased with our relationship. My mother told me that Dean has a drug problem. She was worried sick about my sister's safety and the baby's health. She didn't know if the baby would have birth defects. She also said my sister was concerned about the baby's health, but didn't think he was using drugs when she became pregnant. I didn't know Dean had an addiction problem, but his behavior now made sense.

Because of all the drama, emotions, and worry my parents experienced, I became their outlet and punching bag. I often heard that I should have handled things differently and accepted Dean. There was no discussion of my feelings—only what they believed should have happened. And once again, I was the one to blame.

At 30 years old, I once again failed to meet my parents' expectations. Nothing I did ever pleased them. I stopped calling them, and they stopped calling me. The pain from this situation and their disapproval felt as strong as when my mother previously told me they were close to disowning me because of the bankruptcy.

I was alone once again, deserted by my family. At this point in my life, I shouldn't be surprised, nor should I let it hurt as much as it did. I cared deeply for my family and was taught to show them respect. However, no one should have to endure this kind of love from their family or anyone else. It wasn't love; it was manipulation and control.

I was learning that you cannot rely on anyone; only yourself. You, alone, are the captain of your ship, and you must leave the harbor when it becomes too overwhelming to handle the expectations of others. Go out and find your way, and only your own way.

As summer faded, I took more road trips around Arizona. I felt alive. Maybe it was the freedom of the open road. Maybe it was an escape for the day. Or maybe that is just my life. It reflects the past life I shared with Mary and Jesus. I ran away from that Bedouin home to escape the cruelty I faced and to find happiness. I am doing the same in this lifetime as well.

I didn't hear from my family, and I wasn't upset about it. My sister was living her own life with her boyfriend, and my parents kept out of my way. As September ended, I made plans for a holiday trip: Christmas to New Year's. I submitted the request at work, and it was approved; I was excited to have that time off.

I started to feel "normal" again. I felt like I was in control of my life and destiny. As you can imagine, that changed. On December 23rd, I got a phone call from my parents. They were flying to Phoenix to spend the week here, and they wanted me to host Christmas and New Year's with my sister and her boyfriend. They felt it was time to mend the rift. They also said that my sister had something important to tell me, and that was the reason for their request. They never asked about my holiday plans, and I never mentioned them. I responded to their email very angrily. They expected me to go along with their requests, and I did, reluctantly. I planned the holiday dinner at my house with the family.

I was angry with myself for not standing up to them and telling them I had plans, and that they would have to figure it out themselves. I put their needs and wants before mine. My plans for a peaceful vacation of rest and relaxation were ruined. I was now fully immersed in planning this farce to please my parents and sister.

A few hours later, my sister emailed me to say she was six months pregnant and hoped I would be happy for her. She wanted me to try to find common ground with her boyfriend since a baby was on the way.

I was shocked because she had never talked about wanting to be a mother. I told her I was happy for her if this made her happy and if it was what she wanted. It wasn't my place to judge how she lived her life. Her choices were hers alone.

I wasn't sure it was the best choice for her, but I couldn't be hypocritical. I don't like it when I am told what is best for me, and I definitely didn't want to do that to her. I focused on controlling my anger and suppressing it for the good of the family.

Christmas Day arrived, and they came to my house. Within the first ten minutes of their arrival, my sister's boyfriend broke a plant pot I had on the counter. Accidents happen; nonetheless, I thought to myself, "Is this a bad sign for the day? And if so, how am I going to make it through dinner?"

144

The Christmas dinner, also known as the farce, ended, and everyone headed to my sister's apartment. I made it through the meal and the company. I felt miserable. Why didn't I stand up for myself and say, *"No"*? I had plans, and I wasn't canceling them because they called last minute. Why couldn't I prioritize myself and my needs? It's a lesson that will repeat throughout my life.

I scheduled another session with Ashlem to discuss recent events, my feelings, and my options. Luckily, Bob had an opening on January 4th, 2001. It's just one week away.

Ashlem January 4, 2001

"I see a blue light emanating from a pinpoint of light as it expands slowly outward in all directions. Now, that light seems to be about ½ way across the picture. Now, it suddenly turns to a green light. And now, a golden light. And then changes again to a red light, or as you would say, magenta. The colors of the rainbow coming forth. Pulsating from that circle of Light. And now the circle seems to explode sideways, and it forms a rainbow.

"And now behind that rainbow, there are clouds; soft, gentle clouds. It seems to be going downward below the rainbow. There is Earth and a forest, and it is now raining. But the rainbow remains in the sky. I see the flowers, magnificent flowers. There are very large petaled flowers. Some of their plants have small leaves that seem to be light green.

"Now, the clouds are dispersing, dissipating. The rain ceases, but the rainbow remains. I seem to turn to a side where there is a beautiful crystal cluster, a large crystal cluster. I

would imagine spires on the crystal clusters about 6-7' in length, maybe reaching 1-2' in diameter. It is where the rainbow is emanating from. Turning 180 degrees around, in the distance, I can see another crystal cluster of the same magnitude. Below them is a White Rock that has small crystals around it. Growing out from it.

"Now, on top of that White Rock appears a beautiful image. It is a female image. She has beautiful, long black hair that seems to shimmer in the light that is surrounding it. She has a perfect figure. She is dressed into a white jumpsuit type of garb. I do not see any seams. She is pretty. Her name is Chaleaiah.

"She begins to speak; words seem to form and disappear in golden letters. She says, '**I am Chaleaiah. I am your sister in the Brotherhood of Light. I have been upon the planet that is called Shekalia, far away into the Alpha Centauri galaxy. But I have come here to Ancora, the crystal planet, that I may meet with thee through the advisement of Ashlem, a Speaker of the Spirit. That of this time I say to thee, 'My Sister, I am with thee. I will leave here and return to the planet, you call, Venus, in your system. There will be an intern time. But I will call upon thee and your name, and you will then come out of your body, and you will join with I, for a brief period of time, as you call Earth time, and we will get to know each other once again. Please understand this is difficult for I. I have never done this before. But I am here. You may call I, your Angel, if it pleases you. But I am your sister. We have roamed the cosmos for many centuries. We have been**

146

separated for a long period of time. Our assignments were apart from each other. I have asked for this opportunity that you may know I. I will converse through your mind in time yet to come; have patience. Namaste.'"

"The image fades away. In her place appears a beautiful golden flame. Ashlem is standing in that flame. Ashlem is wearing his simplicity robe, the white robe of simple material. The flame goes out, and Ashlem stands. His hands are folded down in front of him. He is looking down upon the White Rock, where the little crystals are growing out of them.

"Now, he looks up at the rainbow. It is still there. Now, he turns and sits on the White Rock in a lotus position. The light from somewhere seems to reflect from those crystals, creating a flickering state upon his face as it was a candle flame. Ashlem smiles, bows his head in meditation. Puts his hands together.

"Now, he ends his meditation, opens his hands, and puts forward, and there is a small White Rose in his hand. And now, the Rose begins to grow and fulfills his hands together. Then, it stops growing. Ashlem smells of it. Ashlem bows humbly and wishes to speak through, and I give my permission."

"I am Ashlem, known as Golden Image, I say to thee, 'Hail.' We have come forth at this period of time by your request and the request of your Sister of the Brotherhood of Light. You will be together in time yet to come. This introduction to thee seems to be strange, but you will understand in time yet to come. There are many things you must still learn on the Earth's Plane. We have heard your prayers and also your negative

thoughts about some issues in your life. But it is alright. Remember, always you are humankind, and subjected to these thought patterns. But understand, my dear, you are truly blessed. Accept it. Now there are many questions, please begin."

"What is the importance of the rainbow above us?"

"The rainbow is the significance of symbol of your life. The colors of the rainbow are significant to life itself. And each one has its own vibration. Then the rainbow is designed, and through it comes forth the force of All Creation. It was your sister's gift to thee."

"What about the rain and clouds?"

"Must there not be rain if there is to be beauty? Then beauty falls into your life as rain. Then what is life without rain or rain without life?"

"There is none."

"There is life abundant."

"So, the rain doesn't signify something I've gone through?

"Why do you think negative? A rain is a blessing. Look upon it as a positive manner, not as a rain that would ruin your best day upon a picnic. But the rain must come forth for growth to grow. It is part of the Earth's Plane. It is different in other planets. Some planets do not have rain. The water is needed for its plants through the process of osmosis through the roots of the plant from the center of the planet."

"I feel lost in my dreams and meditations. Feelings have come to me that I lag behind in my spiritual development. But

148

then, I am told I am not doing the things I came here for, and I need to take it slowly."

"Ye have a habit of rushing everything. Speed is not a thing. The quality of the experience is what ye have come for. It might behoove thee a little to slow down your life experience by relaxing a little bit. You do great work into your job, and you are very efficient. There is time for a person to work quickly and a time for a person to sit quietly and meditate. And when you begin to combine both of them together, you begin to reach a higher plateau.

"So therefore, at this point of your life, it is time to slow down a little. Begin with your speech. That will be the greater problem for thee. Sometime, you speak too fastly and the person receiving the words you are speaking, do not hear them all. That causes confusion to them. They do not wish to embarrass thee or embarrass themselves. So, they say they understand when they don't. So, as they, between you and I, slow down a little bit, but not your thoughts. Your thoughts are great, and you will begin to create.

"But when thee have learned to relax a little bit, then your destiny will begin to flow much clearer for thee. Do not run down thy pathway, but walk down your pathway. Take a little bit of time to smell the flowers along the way.

"Your sister has chosen the planet Ancora to meet with thee through the spirit. That thee may know of this time. You have spent much time with her upon that planet before ye were separated by the

Brotherhood of Light, and she was assigned to a faraway place. And thee, then was assigned to Venus, and then you again returned into flesh at this period of time. It is all fitting and proper. Your confusion now will begin to erase itself.

"As you slow down a little, your Consciousness of Meditation will increase its value upon thee. And thee will be able to see things more gently and completely. It is an exercise for thee to begin with your life. Slow down your thoughts, not your way of life. Your mind is constantly racing and even thee cannot keep up with it.

"We feel your patterns of Consciousness. It is what we are speaking through. For ye to increase the value of this year to the next year upon Earth, you will have to be able to slow down and listen to other people's experiences and needs. And if ye think too quickly, ye will miss much of what they say to thee.

"For your course of destiny is increasing upon thee. Your value. And you will learn some more experiences. We understand that you are disappointed with love. But, my dear, there is love to come forth. You have spoken to I, Ashlem, often about your disappointments. You must understand when it is, that proper, whenever it is to be, it will occur with thee. This ye must understand.

"Now you have resigned yourself with the thoughts, 'It's alright, I don't need anybody.' But it is wrong because everyone needs somebody. Love is part of the vibration of Earth. Love is part of your vibration. You will find a realization soon to come if ye learn to slow your thoughts down a little bit.

"Not the wisdom of your thoughts, but merely, you will begin to enjoy more of the beauty. An exercise to do this would be to sit in a garden of flowers and slowly look at each flower. And if a honeybee comes by, pay attention to the honeybee as it is upon its daily task of extracting the nectar from each flower. It is the way man is truly.

"Each day mankind must select and extract their nectar of life. Then, through these moments of life, you may find your greater self. We do not say for thee to become lazy; we are saying to thee to slow down your thought patterns, so ye can see clearly everything about thee. You will recognize a love mate when it comes your way. Do not become discouraged. I say soon, but to I, soon can be 50 years from now. But to thee, soon means next two minutes.

"But I say to thee of this life, many have come before I, Ashlem, and said, 'You have said I have a lovemate. Where is my lovemate?' And I say unto thee, 'Walk down your pathway. Do not run. Do not turn over rocks looking, or ye may find another scorpion.'

"But only a few have heeded my words. Do not become flustered of things I say to thee. All is done for a purpose and a reason. I want thee to think hard for yourself. Try to figure problems out, and the meaning of many things. Ye had a vison recently, is it not so? Speak of them."

"I was watching TV, and I saw this rainbow appear like a picture sitting in the corner next to my TV. A couple of days later, I also saw a line of bright lights. They were about four or five wide and four deep. And one day, when I was driving home, I looked up, and I saw two pink ships that were in the sky."

"What does the pink ships represent to thee?"

"That ship is here for love for the Earth; universal and impersonal love."

"And today your Sister, Chaleaiah, came to thee under a rainbow. And you saw a rainbow next to your television. Then could it be your Sister was in communication to your higher self? Then stop and think about these things; everything has a reason. It was your Sister trying to communicate to thee, and the message was that you had to come and find out what was happening unto your visions, so she could speak to thee. Do you see how it works?

"Now of this period of time of life for thee, your inner visions will increase, and you will see many, strange things. The two pink ships are you and your Sister in the Brotherhood of Light. That was a representation. Your Sister will communicate with thee into various ways. You now know her name, and you will then be able to speak by using her name with her, and she will reply in your mind, not in your ears.

"Then, thee must learn to trust your own mind, which most humans do not do. And happiness will come upon thee. You will find your lovemate, do not

be discouraged. Continue with your life. The less you ever think about a lovemate, then he will appear."

"So, what you are saying is that I already put that creative thought out there, and now it is time to surrender and release it and move on."

"Aye."

"So, when you say that I need to slow it down and not think..."

"No, do not do that. Do not misunderstood, I, Ashlem. You have a great Consciousness. You have a great ability since thee were a little girl. Your mind races forth, and great wisdom comes out of it. And you have amazed many peoples, but your speech have turned peoples away, who were important in your life, because they could not understand thee. They are embarrassed to say so.

"So now, slow down your speech by thinking about slowing down your speech, your mind will automatically slow down. Then, you will be able to see all the details of life. Then, as you begin to slow your Consciousness, then you are able to envision more of the beauty of life surrounding thee. When was the last time thee walked through a garden of flowers?"

"I don't remember."

"Aye. But if ye decide to walk down or by a garden of flowers, look upon the flower and notice that each flower is different. Different properties, different reasons for being there. But the most important reason of all, is for thee to enjoy the love

that they bring forth by their color. Then, ye must concentrate upon the artist who puts those flowers together in an arrangement. Growing. Because it is an artist's ability. Then, what was in the artist mind when he put these flowers together?"

"Love and beauty."

"Ahhhhh. Then, understand the creation of someone else, brings a grater creation to thee. You are doing alright. Do not misunderstand, I, Ashlem. We only wish thee to continue to the higher force of your greater Consciousness. But we want thee to walk to it, not run to it."

"Just like the dream I had when I jumped down the ladder, instead of walking the rungs?"

"Aye."

"When I was in meditation, I feel like I persuaded the Council to let me come back to Earth, but they didn't want me to. Was that truth, or...?"

"It was decisive the other way around, though."

"They wanted me to, and I did not?"

"Aye. But it was granted. Ye wished to come after ye were shown to this flesh vibration. You have a mission to fulfill. Although, ye may think it is a simple mission, but it is a very complicated mission. You are working into a field of communication. Then, it is a reason to learn to communicate with others now, so that thee will be prepared for the changing of your destiny later. You are to communicate, which is why we speak to thee about your speech. You are a

beautiful woman; only your inner anxieties are causing difficulties for thee."

"How do I calm those inner anxieties?"

"**Stop hating yourself. That seems strange to thee.**"

"I don't know if I hate myself."

"**My dear, you blame yourself for every little mistake you make, and then you lash out at others for it. Humans cannot be upon the Earth's Plane without making mistakes because one learns from them. And the one that makes the most mistakes has the most wisdom and learns best. It is why ye have been summoned forth here now, because your life is going to change if ye allow it.**

"**In consideration to your family coming forth. Your earthly family; your sister, your mother and father. Each have their own rights of life. Even though they do not coincide with your destiny, but, they must learn their lessons, and you must learn your lessons of this time. You come together as a family unit for a purpose and a reason. And that reason is not to hate, but to love.**

"**You cannot control your sister's life; she cannot control yours. Mother and Father cannot control either of these lives. But, they are still flesh and blood units together. Now, ye must make amends with your family. Be kind and loving. But ye do not have to be with them constantly.**

"**Say to your sister lovingly, 'If ye need my help, I will help thee. I do not have monies, but I can help**

you emotionally. You will always be my Earth sister.'
Ye must know of these things to come forth. There is
an inner peace that comes upon thee. And then when
something happens, ye do not fly off the handle with
anger."

"Especially with my parents and trying to control."

"It is so, but parents are parents. They
controlled most of your life, did they not? Do thee
expect them to stop now?

"I would hope they would stop now."

"But they haven't reached that point yet. Say to
momma and to daddy with respect, 'Mother and
Father, I love thee, dearly above all things in life, but
we do not see eye-to-eye upon life and its missions of
life. I will do things in my life that I see and deem
necessary. I allow thee to do what thee wish to do. But
most of all, my request to Mother and Father, love me
for what I am, your daughter.'"

"That is very hard for them. To let me go and live my
life."

"But of course. They love thee. But that is not the
way to show love. And ye say to them, 'To love me, is
to let me do what I want to do in life. If it is wrong,
then I pay the consequences, not thee.' But they will
continue unless you say to them those words, I have
spoken of."

"I did send an email back, and I know that I was pretty
rough, but I felt that I needed to draw a line in the sand. Did
that make any effect on them?"

"They were very heartbroken. Was that your objectivity?"

"No. It wasn't to break their heart."

"Then a letter of apology would be appropriate. Heartfelt apology. Words were taken out of context. Say to them, 'I did not want to hurt they emotionally. I wanted you to know how I felt.'"

"And they don't see it that way?"

"Of course, they don't see it that way, my dear. How can they see it that way, when they want thee to live their way?"

"That is why I thought I had to be pretty strong."

"It is alright."

"When I was talking to Renee about my past life with Jesus, she thought I should ask a question about it. I was married to a man named Rene, and have I met him in this lifetime? And is he going to be with me in this lifetime?"

"The person is incarnated at this time. He is in Rome, Italy. He has a beautiful wife and three children: two girls and one son. The youngest being a son. His name is Ramono. Your course of destiny does not show crossing."

"What about Marion, my child at the time, blessed by Jesus when she was in my womb? And that she would be known by my blessedness."

"She is your guardian angel."

"Chaleaiah?"

"Aye"

I broke down crying with emotion. It took me a minute to ask the next question.

"The crystal I am wearing. I have worn it in different lifetimes, and I would like to know what purpose or importance it does have."

"It is to enhance your being. Place it into this hand."

Ashlem begins to pray in Tibetan.

"I have placed the chant of tranquility into the crystal. To help slow your vibration down."

"Renee said this crystal reminded her of Pocahontas. Was I with Pocahontas, and did she have this crystal?

"No, you were not with Pocahontas. But she say, it remind her of it."

"Was this crystal with Pocahantas?"

"No. Pocahantas had one similar to it. It was of a different value. The crystal is your vibration. If it were billions of years ago, at its inset and start, no one else owned it except thee unto your own life vibrations."

"I have had this crystal since the beginning, and no one else has had it?"

"It is so."

"It keeps coming back to me?"

"Aye."

"I had a vision that I used to wear it on a headband, and it would be over my third eye. Was that in Egypt?"

"It is so."

"Atlantis?"

"In Atlantis, they did not wear crystals upon their third eye. The crystal vibrations by the pyramids in Atlantis were called a great headache."

"Because the vibration was very light."

"Aye."

"All of the crystals that I have in my house, I've had before?"

"Not all of them. Some are new to thee. But when ye see a crystal and ye say, 'This is the one I want.' It has a vibration that coincides with your own psychic space; your oedic life force. Therefore, it is likable to thee. The ones that thee have turned away, they were not likeable to thee."

"I am confused about the selling of my house. I am building a new one, and I have not had anyone look at it. It's been on the market for over 90 days."

"Continue to put good thoughts in your mind. What have they said that works for real estate sales. I believe it is to take an image of St Joseph and plant it into the ground in the front yard of the house, facing the house. He should not be upside down. He should be facing the house upright. Say these words when you do this, 'My beautiful friend. This is a house of love, and house of family. You are a family man. I place this house in your care. Find a family to occupy it that has love.'"

"In a previous reading, you said that I wanted Freedom of Self, and I do not understand that completely. Freedom of my human self?"

"Freedom of your own convictions of yourself. You have formulated in your mind who ye are, and yet you do not even know yourself. Ye have desires and needs. Some of the desires and needs are from the

Spirit, and some are from the flesh. The flesh must work with the spirit. When ye separate the spirit and the flesh, you separate your life. You bring God into your heart to find the fulfillment of experience with thee. Bring love together with happiness and thought. Then you will have the complete self.

"I said before, 'Stop hating yourself.' You say I do not hate myself. But in turn, you do. Because you are not satisfied, ye say, 'I am too fat,' and you try to work upon losing weight only to gain more weight. Or to become ill, because you have starved yourself. Did I not say to thee before on how to reduce the same way you have gained your size?"

"I don't remember."

"When thee have your meal, no matter what it is, do not consume all of it. Leave a little bit upon your plate. And next time you help yourself to the meal, take a little bit less and leave a little bit. It is easy thing to do. And before ye take the last bit upon the plate, ye merely say to yourself, 'I am full.' And then little by little, you begin to lose the weight ounce-by-ounce, not pound by pound.

"The thought is the creative force. When ye badger yourself to lose the weight, ye only cause an insensitive thought to gain more. And your body is saying, 'No, I don't want to be starved. I want more food.' It is a negative circle. So ye accept; I am growing thinner. I will be back to a good normal size. 'I love me.'

"Then ye will reduce your size gently and forever unto its size. As long as ye remember the following: ye get overanxious, ye get angry, ye overeat. Now, when thee get overly angry, pour yourself a good glass of clear water and drink it. Not a hot chocolate."

"Yesterday, I was reading a book by Nick Bunick, and he said that Jesus was receiving training in Temple of the Essenes when he was a youngster. And that did not ring true to me, so I don't understand why."

"Jesus was not teaching at the Temple of the Essenes when he was a youngster. Jesus was teaching at the Temple of the Essenes when he was 12 years old, not receiving it. When he was 8 or 9 years old, he was a tyrant. But a good boy, in a manner of speaking. He did become angry with the Rabbis of the churches. But Mary would take him sometimes on a sojourn to Karnak, where he was accepted into her womb. He would say to her, 'Mother, remember I was there.' And that would upset her, because it was not the normal for normal peoples to do.

"But sometimes, he would go to Qumran and speak there. But Jesus learned to control his own greater I AM with the Masters and Teachers of the Far East, which is into the Himalayas. They came to receive of him as the Brothers of Light instructed them to do. They brought him forth and took him through India and then into the temples. Some have not even been discovered yet. But upon the scrolls and the

161

tablets there, cuneiforms, there is a mention of St Issa. There he had to control his I AM."

"Because he was so aware of it."

"It is so."

"I had a dream the other night, well, it wasn't so much of a dream. I was falling asleep and felt like I was being taken. I saw feet and looked up and, I believe it was Rebazar Torres. Then I don't remember anything else. I was gone."

"But of course, it was Rebazar Torres taking ye out of your body. He is very fleeting. He does not like everyone to see his image. But it was important for him to speak to thee. He took thee to his home and there conversed with thee to bring knowledge to thee. Ye do not remember all of it in your conscious mind. It is all there in our subconscious. In time, you will use of it."

"I see him quite a bit."

"It is good."

"I know you said Jesus was one of my guides, but I do not see him often or speak with him."

"Jesus is your spiritual guide. In other words, your incentive to the Christdom of Life. He does not tell ye, go here, go there, hither and that, and do thee that. But he is an incentive to maintain the flow of the Christ energy."

"I ask and see Mary much more."

"Mary is there to serve thee, and she serves millions of others who ask her. Who asks of her, she gives to."

"When we were doing some meditations, and I channeled a couple of different Masters so far. Is that what I will be doing? Channeling many or just one?"

"And what is the purpose of this?"

"For teachings?"

"Aye. Then thee have answered your own questions. Continue with your meditation. Listen to the word of wisdom that comes into your conscious and unconscious mind and from the Masters. And ye have a problem with names upon them, do thee not?"

"Yes."

"It is alright. Name them any name you want."

"Thoth was with me at the meditation. What is his purpose?"

"Wisdom. He is to bring wisdom. If ye listen. Everything is in order. Continue your life force. Stop belittling yourself. Love yourself in order to change your flesh body. Do as I have said to thee. Especially about the anger part that causes ye to overeat. When you become upset and angry, do not reach for something to eat. But drink a nice cold glass of water."

"I heard Mary and Chaleaiah say, 'Namaste.' What is that?"

"Namaste is the salutation like amen. It is what it means, to have a good day. Have a beautiful life. In Hawaii, they say, 'Aloha.' It also means love."

"I don't have any more questions."

"We are pleased with your progress. We do not monitor your life. But it is your thoughts that when

we come into view with thee become disturbing to us over the row of your sister and your mother and father; very disturbing to us, the Brothers of Light, as teachers. Because you upset your entire balance by your anger. You are so frustrated causing vibrations like almost sparks running from your aura. It is not good. It is why we speak to you today. If you listen to what we have said, it will discontinue, those flares of anger. Remember when she becomes mamma, send a card."

"I am very worried about her. But it is her life."

"It is so. You cannot control her life.

"Take this hand and place it upon thy heart. Through the force of life and being, and your Sister bring a Rose to thee. I want thee to picture The White Rose of the Christ, and passes it to thee. See her passing it to thyself. Image the Rose and repeat after I, Ashlem.

"I and the Father are One.

"I stand forth into the Light of the Christ.

"For I am Light. I am LIGHT.

"I AM THAT LIGHT.

"Breathe. Receiving the Christ into thy body. Breathe it in. Let it flow completely up. As it reverberates through your body, it expands into your aura, and your aura expands to the Christ of All Creation. One with the Father. Let us take all the anger from thee, and we throw it away.

"I give to thee this sign of peace of Covenant (Ashlem creates a circle with his thumb and forefinger) **that is**

164

of the Father, and the Son and thee, thy holy spirit,
that the circle of God is eternal within. Never
beginning, never ending, and never separated from
the whole. And that is thee.

"Walk into the Light. Peace be unto thee, I take
my leave."

"Thank you Ashlem."

After finishing my reading, my thoughts drifted to the crystal I wore around my neck. Ashlem said that this crystal has only been with me and that it represents my life's vibrations, psychic space, and life force. I was stunned. This crystal came to me in the most bizarre way, and now I understand why it had to be mine.

One day, I was at Yvonne's store when the vendor across the aisle, who sold high-end crystal jewelry, mentioned he knew how much I loved smoky quartz. He told me that a customer had purchased the stone and put a deposit down on it. They had been making payments, but it had been a couple of months since the last one. He said he had reached out to them many times, but there was still no payment. He warned me that if they didn't pay within a week, he would sell it. Then he asked if I wanted it. The moment I saw it, I knew I had to have it. I told him I would buy the stone if the other customer backed out. It wasn't the best time financially to buy such a luxury, but I had to have it.

All week, I prayed and hoped they wouldn't come back. It was a double-edged sword: I dreamed of owning this amazing crystal, but I also worried it might set me back financially for the month. I tried to quiet my mind; if it wasn't meant for me, then it wouldn't happen, and if it was meant to be mine, I would find a way to cover the cost. The weekend arrived, and I drove to Yvonne's store, eagerly awaiting the answer. As I walked in, she greeted me with a big smile and said they had been waiting for me. The other buyers never made a payment, and the crystal was mine if I wanted it. Of course, I wanted it! After paying for it, I gazed at it intently. It touched my soul, bringing a sense of familiarity that's hard to describe. I was elated; my heart soared. It was mine once again.

The Work Is Never Over

I continued working through my lessons on overcoming self-hatred. It's hard to believe in yourself and your worth when you have little support and life pushes you down at every turn. The truth was, I did hate myself. I couldn't find love. I didn't meet anyone who made me feel wanted. My family judged me for every mistake I made. They wanted me to do what they wanted, and I was berating them for not listening to me. The truth is, I was tired of being a punching bag for them. They made me feel responsible for my sister's life. They did this when we were kids, and it continued into adulthood. I numbed these feelings by eating them away. Some people use alcohol to numb the pain; I used food.

I wondered how to free myself from these negative thoughts. Then, I realized I needed to believe I was worthy, and that those thoughts shouldn't come from someone else. They had to originate within me, and my mind had to accept it. Otherwise, it would be like building a castle on the sand. My mind could not accept that I was beautiful and worthy. Ashlem and Mother

Mary would say it a hundred times, and a hundred times I would reject the idea.

As each day passed, my determination to shield myself from more emotional pain grew stronger. I built what I believed was a wall around my heart. Every emotional wound left a scar and gave me another reason to toughen up and brace for more hurt. I felt alone. I needed to find a way to heal, but I didn't know where to begin. I needed to believe in myself, but at the moment, that didn't seem possible. One thing I knew I could do well was channeling. Ashlem said it would help me teach others, and I focused on refining that gift.

Chapter Six: 2001 and Many Changes

During the first few months of 2001, I had little contact with my family. I knew the baby was due on March 20th, my paternal grandfather's birthday. The family was excited about the birth of the first grandchild; I was nervous. I felt it would be a difficult birth for my sister, and I was anxious about how to handle the changes in the family dynamics. I had a tenuous relationship with them, and I felt I would be pulled into a space I was not comfortable in.

I was not ready to be an aunt. I had hoped I would not be called to babysit. I knew nothing about babies, and I never changed a diaper in my life. I had hoped that streak would continue.

On March 6th, my mother called to tell me my sister's water had broken, and she was at the hospital. I went there that afternoon, but she hadn't made much progress. The baby was stuck, and they hoped he could push through. She was told that if she didn't progress, they would need to do a C-section. I didn't stay long because I felt uncomfortable. I didn't know how to act or what to expect. I felt like an outsider, and my relationship with my sister was fragile. I'm not sure how she felt about me staying or leaving. My leaving might have seemed like I didn't care, but that wasn't true. I didn't want to add any extra stress to her, since she had enough going on. Looking back, maybe I should have stayed—perhaps that was the right thing to do.

A day later, my parents arrived in town to meet their grandchild. They stayed at my house, but I never saw them. They spent all their time at my sister's apartment with the baby. I felt their disdain for me because I was not more involved with my sister and the baby. I scheduled a reading with Ashlem before the birth, and it was time for me to pour my heart out to him. I was in emotional pain, and I hoped he could guide me.

Ashlem March 8, 2001

"I see a beautiful pink light emanating from a pinpoint of light. Slowly expanding. Fills the whole picture. Soft pink light. Now, in the center of the pink light, a darker pink heart is formed. Now, the heart fades away. Beautiful little cherubs come forth floating here and there. Now, a pinpoint of violet light in the center appears and expands slowly, blending with the pink expanding. The cherubs remain, but now there is violet light. In the center of the violet, appears white light expands rapidly, and it consumes everything, including the cherubs. There is nothing but White Light.

"An image forming in the White Light, oval shaped. It is this Blessed Virgin Mary once again. Mary shows herself with a white gown and a white robe over her shoulders and head. So beautiful. The cherubs appear behind her again. Mary is holding in her hand the White Rose of the Christ. Mary has that beautiful smile on her face. She smells the White Rose, then bends and lays it at her feet. She disappears, but in her place, appears a White Rock, and the forest is appearing around.

"The cherubs are gone. Doves singing; turtle doves, white doves, morning doves, cooing. I can hear in the background a mockingbird singing songs. What a magnificent forest. The stream of water that seems to be pure water flowing over the rocks into the pool, and the flowers look especially bright.

"On the White Rock appears a pink flame. Ashlem is standing in that flame. And Ashlem is wearing his white robe of simplicity. The flame goes out. Ashlem has that beautiful smile on his face, and his eyes always twinkle. Then he bends down and picks up the White Rose that Mary left. He sits in a lotus position on the White Rock.

"He smells the White Rose. He bows his head and wishes to speak through. I give my permission."

"I am Ashlem, known as Golden Image, I say to thee 'Hail'. The force of Life come upon all who stand into audience of it. And, of this period of time, always I come forth into the forest. For the forest does give forth life and purity and trust and truth, and that which lies into all creation upon mankind of this time. Through the endeavors of life, come forth The Blessed Virgin Mary, that she shows herself in this period of time, when she was into the garden of the Essenes of Carmel before she became with child. Her innocence and her purity and her beauty raised within thee also of this time. As one comes forth into life, they see and do many things upon the Earth's Plane. All for the experience of being. The glory of the God Creation upon Earth is peace and love. It is cherished and given forth. And they who refuse love, refuse life.

"Now, there are many questions I will answer for thee please begin,"

"The first one, Ashlem, is I heard the name Solaris about a month ago. I believe it's spelled S-o-l-a-r-i-s. Why did he appear? Or the spirit appear to me?"

"This is Brother of Light. Also, very close to the spirit world who works with the Spirit World often of that period of life force. The name of the Brotherhood, Solaris means one who stands with the Son of Creation. The Giver of Light. That is what his name was positioned for of that time. He comes forth to guide thee upon the Earth's Plane. And to rid thee of false thoughts."

"So that's why I heard him was because of the thoughts and he was clearing them?"

"Aye"

"Will I be hearing him more or seeing him more?"

"It is up to thee, my dear, if ye had accepted his wisdom, then he may return to thee again."

"OK. I've been reading the book, Keys of Enoch, and there is a name B'nai Or."

"And what did it say to thee?"

"Well, I guess I don't really understand. It's a group that works with the Creation in the different worlds and bringing the Brotherhood of Light to different worlds, but I don't understand that."

"B'nai is also the word of giver and of the aura, which is the Light again and they who give of the Light. For B'nai is a word that is of Jewish descent or Hebrew descent, do you understand? Meaning Bringer of Truth. So Light within thee is the truth. That is why within thee, ye feel a different vibration and the word stuck with thee."

"Was I part of that group?"

"Are thee part of their group? Nay."

"OK. Have I worked with that group?"

"Ye have known some entities who have involved themselves with that group. But it is all right. Do not worry about it."

"OK, I keep seeing flashes of light; flashes of pink light, white light, purple light all the time, and I don't know why. Is someone trying to get my attention?"

"Could it be your greater Self trying to get your attention?"

"Of course it could be."

"But of course it could be. Everything has its purpose does it not? What purpose could it be upon thee?"

"Well, it could be that they're trying to give me information and my Higher Self is trying to come through, and through my human form so that I can see it and recognize it."

"It would come through as thought, would it not? Then, has it altered your thought patterns?

"I think I've been better lately."

"Well, that is good. Have thee given love, spirituality and wisdom and knowledge to others?"

"I always try to do that."

"Then could it be the realization of those factors of life for thee to be upon this period of time for thee. These are things you need not to ask I, Ashlem, but ask of yourself and listen carefully to the greater One within thee."

"I've been hearing a lot of different things lately, and I know last time when we were here, you said Chaleaiah had been trying to get in touch with me, and I didn't know if this was another way of her trying to get in touch with me as well."

"Have thee spoken to she? What has she said to thee?"

"Well, when I don't know if I've heard it consciously. I mean, I've asked her for help and to guide me through it and if there's any advice that I need. Going into a situation, that's when I ask."

"What situation?"

"Day-to-day things of, you know, my job and my financial situation and with my sister."

"Your sister? Has she given birth?"

"Yes, she has. I kept hearing Spirit saying that a baby is coming through. Is it this one?"

"But of course."

"So, it's not a baby or spirit that wants to come through me?"

"But you are true to see a spirit desires to come through your womb."

"Am I hearing that spirit or both of them; the one that came through my sister's womb?"

"You are hearing the spirit that wish to come through your womb.

"Well, doesn't that spirit have to bring someone into my life to make that come true. The father that it has chosen, I should say."

"It is possible. Thee still have childbearing years. Do they wish to have a child?"

"I don't know. Some days yes, some days no. I'm more open to the idea than I was a couple of years ago."

"Then if you have a child, it will disrupt all things you are doing now. Are they ready for the change?"

"Not right now. I've been hearing lately from my Higher Self or someone that we can't hold Mother Earth in its place without causing a lot of karma and a lot of disruptions. Is that true?"

"Cannot hold Earth in its place?"

"Into its cradle?"

"In other words, what the Brotherhood of Light have done. Holding Earth from the pole shift. It will not cause more havoc. Except for the people who are already involved into their own havoc. Do thee understand? OK, then they will be increased, will it not? But they who sit on their hands, they have been shaken violently, because the power shift did not occur. Their faith have been shaken. Do not worry, the pole shift will come forth. It is only a matter of time when things are completely right. Next step to worry about this Armageddon."

"Explain that to me. What does the spirit say that it is?"

"It is coming together of the Arabic communities uniting with secret treaties with each other. Then they will unite and gather against Israel. And America will have to defend Israel. And then will come into the picture, Russia against with Israel along with China. Also possibly North Korea, North Vietnam. They also come forth. Then that would be the coming of Armageddon; Nuclear War. Worry more about nuclear war coming forth in the next three years.

"So, I will see that then?"

"It may come to pass. I do not know. At this moment of the time, treaties are being made."

"What about the earthquake that happened in Seattle?

"There shall be more. You will see it will work its way down coastline."

"Are we going to lose California completely?"

"You will never lose California completely. But lose many lives into California."

"Because of the earthquake? The land just won't break off and fall into the ocean."

"Portions will."

"Is that coming forth soon?"

"I have been saying for over a decade. It'll come soon. I do not know when."

"Because Bob mentioned 30 days and I don't know where that came from."

"If there is a northern earthquake or an earthquake into Mount Pelee or Vesuvius, a large quake and great eruptions of either one of them, then California has 30 days."

"So, when we see the Vesuvius and Pelee? We know that it's 30 days."

"It is so."

"Because, you know, we have a lot of friends in California, who are up there, and they feel that they are safe in California. Should we be warning them?"

"You should not have to warn them of anything. They already know."

"And I have chosen to be there at that time?"

"They have chosen to cling to their material plane. If their material plane is destroyed; if they cling too tight to it, they may be destroyed also. They who stand one with God in favor, they will be saved."

"Even during the earthquakes?"

Ashlem smiles and nods.

"Is there anything else that I can be doing? During this time, or am I doing all that I should be doing at this point?"

"It's time to reflect upon your life with wisdom. Not with anxiety of negativity. You think of all the things you have done that were wrong. And you blame yourself for it."

"I'm trying to do that less and less."

"Stop doing it, period. You are a beautiful woman. We have given to the instructions on how to be more of a beautiful woman. But they get into fits of depression. And you blame yourself and ye weep tears, is it not so? You say you want to have a man. The man that ye wish to marry is a man who would not tolerate weeping all the time. But he is looking for a woman who can stand upon her feet with wisdom and aid the family. Do thee understand?

"When he and ye mate with each other to bring offspring, that is to be upon the offspring that wishes to come through your womb. And your desires of that time. You're a good woman. Enjoy your lifetime now. But you must try to help other peoples willingly. To help them, you will find your movement of the position of work that they are in. You will meet many different peoples. Especially ye will meet some men. When thee

176

meet a man new, you will look into his eyes. And if you feel that vibration, then let it pass. Then be a woman. Let the man step forward and say, 'I would like to be with you.' Then the man that he treats you like a lady. Be a lady. He will respect thee. And you will know this is your mate."

"Are you saying that I will probably meet him during my work?"

"It is how it has been arranged so. He will not come to your house."

"I don't expect him to. I guess though, now that we're talking about men. Why is Steve not with me anymore? Was it my fear that drove Steve away?"

"Your fear was part of it. It was not his direction. Why do they use word drove away?"

"I guess that's a common English word."

"Did thee force him away from thee?"

"No, I didn't."

"Did thee desire him to return, yes. And why is this?"

"I had a good time with him."

"That is good. But if he were your love mate, he would be here, would he not? And you were saddened because ye felt he rejected again."

"Yes."

"My dear. It is a stepping-stone down the roadway of life. That period of time, there were a few roses that they may smell along the way. But the pathway continues on to the greater garden of roses. Whenever there is a stumbling block, as ye call of it, there is a reason and purpose for it. One should seek out the reason and purpose, not always is it negative."

"That's all the questions I can think of."

"On this roadway of life that thee have placed your feet, ye lose much ground when thee become depressed, disgusted with your material life. If it was to be that they would have this or have that, it would be placed in front of thee, would it not? Then thee know the truth within thee and have faith of it. Continue your works. Each time they become despondent, ye step three steps back. Stop being that way. Do not look at everyone who you think is trying to take advantage of thee in business or in friendship. It is up to thee. You must make your decisions. It is important to finish the book to the best of your ability. It will be good enough.

"Take thee this hand placed upon thy heart. The White Rose. Mary come forth. What did Mary say to thee?"

"She did not you didn't say anything."

"But she said many words without speaking. She smiled. She smelled of the Rose. To thee there were many words. Remember they."

"She was happy, and she's there with me."

"Picture the White Rose I have in my hand. breathe in the White Light. Repeat after I Ashlem:

"I and the Father are One.

"I stand forth into the Light of the Christ.

"For I am Light. I am LIGHT.

"I AM THAT LIGHT.

Ashlem begins to pray in Tibetan. *"I have said unto thee, into thy heart, into thy body, bring forth the force of the energy of the creative force with thee. Let God lie here, into thee of goodness, and create your goodness from here. Your body. Your mind and your soul. As you walk hither to there, upon this Earth's Plane, stop doubting yourself. And be loving. But be this with humility. Not vanity. There is a fine line between. Seek it out and stay away from vanity.*

"Am I being vain?"

"At times thee have been, though, thee say ye were humble over it. But there is a fine line. We are pleased with your progress. Ye should be pleased with it also.

"I give to thee this sign of peace of Covenant (Ashlem creates a circle with his thumb and forefinger) *that is of the Father, and the Son and thee, thy holy spirit, that the circle of God is eternal within. Never beginning, never ending, and never separated from the whole. And that is thee.*

"As you walk on the Earth's Plane, be a woman. Enjoy being a woman, but protect yourself, woman. Then thee will not have the pains that you have had recently.

"Walk into the Light. Peace be unto thee. I take my leave."

After the reading, I drove home, reflecting on the information Ashlem had shared. I decided to let things unfold naturally with my family. There had been enough drama before, and now everyone's primary focus would be on this new baby.

No Peace with the Family

My parents flew out last week to see the grandbaby and stayed at my house. They would leave first thing in the morning and wouldn't return until after 11 pm. I was already in bed. This happened every day. It was disheartening that they didn't spend any time with me, but I tried to understand; they were here to see the baby.

As April approached, my parents made plans to spend another week here, staying with me. Once again, I didn't see them. When May arrived, they planned to visit again, and I asked if they would spend time with me. My father replied, *"We are not coming out to see you; we are coming to see the baby."* This time, I told them, my house was only a hotel for them, so it would be best if they stayed at a hotel close to my sister's apartment.

I felt used, and I knew it was time to stand up for myself. Many disagreed with my decision; however, they never walked a mile in my shoes nor experienced the life I lived and the heartbreaks I endured. I was 30 years old, and it was time for my parents to respect that. I didn't want to be a punching bag for them anymore.

On the first day of their trip, Dean called me. I recognized his number and chose to ignore the call. He left a message criticizing me for not caring about family, calling me rude and disgraceful, and saying I wasn't a good daughter for making my parents stay at a hotel when I live alone in a three-bedroom house and had the space for them to stay.

I exploded with anger. What right *does* he have to call me, and what right does he have to judge the situation when he only sees things on the surface? He never asked how I felt or where I was coming from. I was blinded by rage and called my mother's phone. She answered, and I unleashed my fury on her. She was flabbergasted. She said she did not know that Dean called me, and she had no defense for the words that were said. I quickly ended the conversation after I said what I needed to say.

I left for about 45 minutes to run an errand, and when I returned, my father was sitting in my driveway. When I pulled up, I knew I finally had the chance to say the things I had bottled up inside me for 30 years.

We went inside and sat at the dinner table because that's where all Italian families have their serious talks. He seemed calm on the outside and told me I didn't need to talk to my mother that way. I responded that I didn't need a call like that. If they felt that way, then they should have said it to me directly rather than relaying it through Dean. I made it clear that they made me feel unwanted, and I was as good as a hotel for them. I continued my rant and reminded him that I own this house, I pay the bills, I don't rely on anyone for help, and I am 30 years old. I don't need anyone to tell me how to live my life.

At that moment, recognition lit up in his eyes, and he understood. He slowly nodded and said, *"You are right."* We reached an understanding about life and my need to live as I pleased. They had done their job as parents, and now it was time to let me go. After that, we continued with small talk, and my father seemed to have a new appreciation for me. I was elated. Finally!

He returned to my sister's apartment, and the debate about how I should behave toward her choices, her life, or the need to take responsibility for her ended. I felt peace. Sanity. The exhausting merry-go-round of my life with them was over. I then concentrated on my own needs, without much concern for anyone else.

One Sunday morning at the end of May, I was reading the paper when I saw a full-page ad for a 17-day cruise through the Mediterranean. OMG... one of my life's dreams. I had to go on this cruise. I felt it in my soul; it seemed like a once-in-a-lifetime opportunity I would never get again. I read and re-read the itinerary: Istanbul, Turkey; Ephesus, Turkey; three Greek Islands—Delos, Mykonos, Santorini; Sorrento, Italy; Rome, Italy; Florence, Italy; Portofino, Italy; Monte Carlo, Monaco; Aix-en-Provence, France; the Island of Mallorca; and finally, Barcelona, Spain.

Those memories of my 8th-grade history class flooded back. How I longed to visit those places when I was young, and now I finally have the chance. I never imagined it would happen, and he was my opportunity. I took a day to ensure I wasn't rushing into this decision. Deep down, I knew it was the right thing to do, but I felt I should wait one more day.

The next day, I woke up knowing what I had to do. I booked the trip right away. Luckily, I already had a passport, so I was ready to go. I decided I needed to talk to Ashlem about the trip and scheduled another reading with him, May 31, 2001.

Ashlem May 31, 2001

"May 31st, the year 2001. This is in an Akashic Reading for Tracey Renee Walker, by Bob Copeland. This reading is being done in person.

"I see a pinpoint of golden light appearing in the center of a picture. The golden light is expanding. Beautifully expanding. Filling the whole picture with soft, golden light. Now, a pinpoint of pink light appears in the center of the golden light. The pink light expands, blending with the golden light. This is causing a beautiful violet light to appear. The violet light expands to the fullness of the picture. How beautiful it is. Now, a pinpoint of white light appears in the center and expands rapidly and consumes the violet light. Leaves behind beautiful soft White Light.

"Now the images are forming in the White Light. Beautiful Angels. Magnificent Angels appearing. Seven of them. They seem to be small in like a shape of a rainbow. Underneath they appear. The Beautiful Blessed Virgin Mary. Mary is holding in her hand, a beautiful White Rose. How magnificent it is. The Angels begin to sing. Very softly. Beautiful music. Mary smells a beautiful White Rose. She begins to speak, and golden words appear, and the words say, *'And blessed art the among women also, to know your life within. To the horizons that are coming forth upon this time for thee that there be song in your heart and glory in your mission of life. For these angels will bring to thee love in your heart and in your body, and love for all things in the creative forms. But ye must believe. I come forth with thee. Here I hold your Christ Rose. I keep it close to my heart with many others. I am with thee always.'*

"*Appearing before her, a golden flame; a flame like a candle flame that flickers only at the top. The light is very bright and very fulfilling. As it grows in size and intensity, and now, it begins to soften and diminish. Ashlem is standing in the clay. Ashlem is wearing his beautiful white robe, his robe of simplicity. He has a beautiful smile on his face and his eyes twinkle. And the flame goes out in Ashlem bows lowly to the beautiful Virgin Mary. Then Mary hands him the beautiful White Rose. He accepts it and bows to her again. Mary disappears.*

"*The Angels are singing louder now. Beautiful sounds. Ashlem turns, and he sits upon the White Rock where all of this appeared upon. And the forest has appeared around. And the birds are singing. The Angels are singing with the birds, so to speak. Ashlem sits in a lotus position. He smells the White Rose. He bows humbly and wishes to speak through, I give my permission.*"

"**I, am Ashlem, known as Golden Image, I say to thee, 'Hail.' To many ways of life coming forth of this time, the Blessed Virgin Mary expresses to thee that she is still with thee of this time, and the Angels are surrounding thee into the spirit. Ye cannot always see him, but know that they are there with you. It is very important. If ye close your eyes at times and listen carefully, you will hear them singing. One who stands for thee into the Light of the Christ Consciousness with Love in their heart shall find love for their being of all time. Upon your pathway, as Mary has said, you have**

184

placed your feet, go thee hither and there and you will find that thee feel look for intensely. Now, there are many questions I will answer for thee. Please begin.

"Yes, Ashlem, thank you. I am going to Europe in a couple weeks and I'm going to seven different countries, and I want to ask a little bit about each. Of course, one is my safety as I go on this trip."

"If you walk careful, watch where thee walk you. You will not fall.   You're going aboard a ship."

"Yes, I am."

"Have thee been aboard a ship before?

"Not like this, no."

"First time for everything."

"Absolutely. An adventure."

"An adventure that thee will never forget the rest of your life. Let's us make it a good adventure. Before thee board the ship, say Mother Mary, please stand forth with I into this voyage. And bring peace in my heart and love, and I shall be forever indebted. Then board the ship. And upon the sea, ye will travel hither and there, and you will find love in your heart. There will come a time, a man will approach thee. Ye will be apprehensive at first. But the second time he approaches thee, you will begin to understand."

"Is this a romance?"

"Very much possibly, yes. Are thee not looking for romance?

"Yes."

"Let your heart open and feel assured.   There will be many choices upon this voyage. Make your

choices according to your destiny is that his destiny may flow into the same memories. The Angels will be there to protect thee upon this voyage."

"Yes. I have a desire, and I know that I'm going to go to the Hagia Sophia. Did I have any past life there? Did that play any importance in the Hagia Sophia? In Istanbul or Constantinople."

"There was a brief incarnation to that period of time that thee were with, into the region and area. It is so. But it is not relevant or important at this time into your life. But it is a romantic place, is it not so? It is a place of mystery and suffering. Never go down streets alone. Do you understand?"

"OK."

"Always be accompanied with one or more peoples. It is not the world's best place for women."

"Should I wear something that covers my head? Would that help? Because I know in the Muslim tradition, women are supposed to cover their heads and giving respect to them.

"Listen to the guides. They will instruct thee what thee should do or not. It is old custom. It is so, but there is much modern mating into Istanbul."

"Yes, yes. Another place that we're going is Ephesus. Which supposedly is the. Place that Mary passed. Is this true?

"It is so."

"Was I alive when she passed, or was I already passed myself?"

"Ye had already passed."

"When I go on this trip will past lives or things come forward to me?"

186

"It may come to pass to thee. Depending on your mind at the period of time. To receive a past Akashic of the place, you must meditate upon that place, and then you will see different things in your mind. Then thee will pass upon those things. To the real mission of your life, and feel comfort with them. Beware of the wolf in sheep clothing."

"Beware of the wolf in sheep clothing? Is that natives or is that people on board on the ship?"

"On the ship."

"OK. Another place that we're going is the island of Santorini, which again, I have such a pull to it. Is there an importance that that place will play into my life?"

"There will be a high place that thee will be intrigued with. Then, stand there and close thy eyes and feel the vibration."

"Is that the monastery that sits on the hill."

"I have spoken."

"Of course, we're going to Rome and Pompeii. And well, there are many places that we're going. Is there anything else that I should be looking for? In Italy?"

"Into the city of Pompeii. You will find a little bit of fear running through thee when walking through those ruins."

"Did I die in that eruption?"

"It is so. You are but a little girl. Do not fear it. Do you understand?"

"Is that why I'm afraid of being underground? Or is it one of the reasons?"

"When everyone goes to a place they have lived before, it is called deja vu. For ye know, ye have been there. It would be unnecessary for I, Ashlem, to speak to thee of their lifetimes, hither to there. But thee can recall it by merely meditating upon the existence to know of yourself of these times. Then that force will be with you of these experiences of time. It is the way life is of this period of time. But if one fears, then the fear manifests itself, does it not? But if one is happy and alert and attentive, they may find what they are looking for."

"In Rome, there are so many places that I want to go, and we're only there for a day."

"Will thee go with a group of people?"

"Well, I haven't quite decided yet because I want to the Vatican and Saint Peters Square and I want to get through the museum and see the Sistine Chapel. I would like to go to the Plaza, the Pantheon, and the Colosseum, but that is a lot and we are only going to be there one day. Can you give me advice as to which one I should maybe go to?"

"Go to Colosseum."

"I should go to the Colosseum?"

"You feel a vibration."

"Is that more important than going to the Vatican?"

"What is at the Vatican that thee would be interested in? Sistine Chapel?"

"Yes."

"Look upon the great paintings. It's all right, but it is not too far away to the Colosseum."

"OK. Is there anything else that I should look for?"

"Do not fear the Colosseum."

"Because I had a friend who passed away in that place?"

"Aye."

"Ok. I have to say that I did make up with my parents."

"This is good."

"I think we've come to an understanding."

"And your sister?"

"My sister and I are fine. It's her husband that I have problems with, and I haven't spoken to her since Easter."

"Does that cure the problem?"

"That I haven't spoken to her? I'm not sure if it cures the problem, but it doesn't agitate it."

"A person of the world stands forth with love and arms open for all peoples. If the Blessed Virgin Mary did not have her arms open to everyone would she have been chosen? Then open your arms for all peoples. Everyone has their transgressions. And thee also have them. Remember what he say upon the cross, 'Forgive them, Father, for they know not what they do.' It would be a byword for thee into your life; family and friends and relationships. Then you put a smile upon your face and continue with your life, and it will flow greater for thee, easier. But when you think of negativity with family, and think of negativity with others, even though they have stepped on your toes, you have to say, 'Forgive them, Father, they know not what they do.' Then you have to say, 'I forgive them, for they know not what they do.' Then you will understand, as they will in time, come full circle to thee. And you will find family love and

friendships endearing to thee. It is a matter of changing mind. It is not easy, but it is very good to do.'"

"I don't know what it was, but when I first met him, I actually jumped back. I don't know where it came from."

"I cannot make a comment of it."

"That is for me to find out later?"

"Do not fear him."

"I don't know what it is."

"It is a past experience. It is so. Into great China over a period of time. But it is not so of this period of time that thee should fear the spirit. Spirit does recognize Spirit, and this is what thee have jumped back about, as thee say. But the man is different."

"I want to ask you about my personal trainer, Brent. I have a very nice connection with him. He seems to be opening up to the Light and asking questions. When I was telling him about my trip, I mentioned Mallorca, which is an island that we're going to. And then the next thing he said was, 'Tell me more about Myopia.' Is he also from the planet? Can you tell me that?"

"There would be interference."

"That would be interference? Ok."

"Aye. But listen to your heart."

"My heart is telling me that he is, for him to have said it."

"He has not reached the part yet of opening himself up."

"I saw different lifetimes I've spent with him."

"It is possible that thee have spent lifetimes with him. But only dwell upon good lifetimes. Everyone has bad lifetimes and good lifetimes. It is how the experience flows."

"The only ones that I remember are just good ones. I've only seen flashes of them: in the Incas, probably in Chile. I saw a flash of being as a young teenager on the side of a riverbed and hiding in the weeds. He was coming to get me, but I felt no fear. Is that true? Is that a lifetime that I've spent with him?"

"It is so."

"The other thing is that being with him is very easy. He is, on the surface of what I'm looking for in a lifemate. Is he like my lifemate? Are the personalities or the traits the same?"

"He has many traits. He is a married man?"

"No, he's engaged."

Ashlem said no more about it, and I moved on.

"I was watching a movie adapted from a Russian novel by Alexander Pushkin. And the movie is called and Onegin. I saw a lot of myself in the main character. Being very restless and not finding fulfillment or pleasure in much. It was hard to see. Being that restless."

"Everything comes, for they who sit and wait for it. To review your Akashic is to merely relax and enjoy that which you review. But do not ever try to review negative happenings or even question about negative happenings. Sometimes the thought pattern brings it to the surface as thee continue of life of this time of yourself. Thought patterns, remember, manifest conditions. A person who is despondent in their life, finds no happiness. A person who is

apprehensive has a little bit of problems. A person who is optimistic with love in their heart and a smile upon their face, their life begins to flow. You have many lifetimes or despair of love. This lifetime, thee have had many encounters of love but yet have not encountered that one person. Will it come forth or will it not come forth? Put yourself and thought forth to say, yea, it will come first and whenever. And don't turn over any more rocks looking, for thee may find scorpions again. Be that beautiful person thee truly is. Allow love to flow."

"I also feel restless about a lot of different things. I get bored easily. And I don't feel challenged enough."

"Challenged? You need a challenge to find love?"

"Well, not love. I'm talking about in the work, if I'm not challenged or if I'm not busy. When I was earning my Master's Degree, it challenged me."

"I understand. Thee can challenge for yourself. The challenge being, 'I shall achieve and become greater into this position, no matter what it is.' Then you strive for that with happiness in your heart. Knowing that thee are worthy of it because of your intelligence, and bring forth your wisdom to guide your intelligence. This is what many people go wrong. They're highly intelligent but do not have a lick of sense."

"Sometimes I feel that way."

"Let your wisdom guide thee. There are many dos and don'ts in life, is not so? Do not do the don'ts anymore."

"One of the things that I've been feeling a lot is that I feel like people are touching me all the time. Like Angels are touching my face or surrounding me. I always feel like there is a bug. Something crawling on my leg. Is that their way of getting in touch with me?"

"Sometimes it is so. Listen carefully when thee feel you are being touched by Spirit. Maybe in your mind say, 'I am aware, what is it thee need?'"

"And they have been doing that a lot lately?"

"Yes. But thee do not listen."

"And because I do not listen, that's why they keep touching me?"

"It's because your mind goes so fast here and there. Then slow down."

"That's part of that boredom thing. If my mind is not going so fast."

"A habit of life, not Akashic of life or a Karma of life. To keep yourself busy before, thee had to be impressive. Speak fast. Work fast. Think fast. You are getting older, have more wisdom. Now you can slow down the thought a little bit. Thee may find it to be more acceptable for thee who are friends of thine."

"And how do you do that? Just say to your mind, 'Stop?'"

"This is so. You have to get out of the habit. When a person says, 'What did you say when you spoke to them?' They know that they did not hear thee because you're speaking so rapid."

"I have been trying to work on slowing down my pattern."

"Slow yourself down a little bit. Then it becomes a habit again. But slow down, but do not stop."

"I don't think I talk all the time."

"It runs so rapid that thee become lost in it. So you slow down your thinking to be more methodically, and you find a greater perfection into your life. Be careful what you say to some peoples. They are born of the material plane. We live the material plane. They do not look upon all things of heaven. They are orthodox, therefore. If you are not orthodox, you are not accepted. They are trying to see if you were a weirdo.

"The launching into the journey of life; a first time for everything. As thee will be upon the waters, you may find yourself to be ill. Take the Dramamine, what it's called for the motion sickness. When thee are upon the rail, look up or directly down, not at horizon for the first few days. Then the body will accustom itself to the up and down movement and the rocking, and you will not even notice it after that. Now, there will be many times, people will have parties and dances and so forth. Join them and do what thee can do. Be the beautiful flower. And it is how thee are going to be recognized. Your journey will be a good one for thee to remember. But not everything flows easily, does it?"

"No, never does."

"But if you put a smile upon your face where there is troubled waters, everything will turn up. There is a time, my dear, when you were a ship person of the Polynesians. And the ships were builded out of straw. It is a reed. And they were called rafts. And you were upon them. The sea is a transportation road. Is not all roads have bumps in them? Then worry not about it. And enjoy your way, your voyage. It will be alright. But thee must learn to relax a little bit. That is what it is for. You will find company in taking this trip for the force of love and peace upon thee of this period of time. Let love enter your heart. I want you to picture a beautiful pink heart. See a beautiful pink. Now the beautiful White Rose. It is laying upon the pink heart. Receiving the Christ into your body. Let the energy flow through thee at this time. Let us chase from thy being all negativity and cleanse oneself with this. Repeat I, Ashlem.

"I and the Father are One.
"I stand forth into the Light of the Christ.
"For I am Light. I am LIGHT.
"I AM THAT LIGHT.

"Breathe deeply again. Now the energy has passed in all. Negativity flows from thee, and the thoughts are beautiful enough. Peace and a heart of love. Mary will be with thee. And your Angels. I give to thee the sign of peace our covenant: Of the Father and of the Son, and of thy Holy Spirit, that the circle of God is eternal with thee. Never beginning, never ending, and never to be separated from the whole, and that is *thee. Very beautiful dove fly. Peace be unto thee, I take my leave."*

"Thank you, Ashlem. Thank you very much."

After the reading, I felt on top of the world. I will visit places I've only dreamed of and meet a lovemate. I feel like I hit the jackpot!

The cruise was just a month away, and I was busy getting ready for the trip. I called my parents and told them I was going on this journey. They were worried about my safety because they knew I would be going alone. They tried to stay positive, but I could see they were scared. They did their best to support my decision. I told them I would email them a few times from the ship so they wouldn't worry. I shared my itinerary so they could track my location.

I lay awake at night dreaming of meeting this soulmate. Would something I've been waiting for years finally come true? What would I do if he lived in another city? Would I move? Would he ask me to move in with him? What would I do with my house? What about my dog? Would she like him? These and a million more questions flowed through my mind.

The Trip of a Lifetime

On June 23rd, I boarded the Lufthansa flight to start my journey. The flight attendants served us breakfast before we landed in Frankfurt, Germany. I could barely tolerate the smell of breakfast in the middle of the night; I did my best to acclimate my body to the time zone change. I planned to visit the biergarten to enjoy a pint of German beer, as it was a bucket-list item. According to my internal clock, it was 2:00 am, even though it was 11:00 am in Frankfurt. I couldn't stomach drinking a beer this early in my day. So, I proceeded to the gate to catch the plane to Istanbul.

After we took off heading to Istanbul, my anxiety about this destined meeting halfway around the world significantly. How would I recognize him? How should I act? Will I meet him during a tour? At dinner? Or should I just go to the lounge? Do I need to join all the ship's activities, or will I meet him while looking out at the sea and feeling the breeze? These thoughts overwhelmed me, and as we drew closer to Istanbul, I became increasingly nervous.

Upon arriving, I headed to Customs and was shocked to see soldiers from the Turkish Army armed with AK-47s. They were stationed all around the airport. I felt uneasy. I had never been so close to an automatic weapon in my life. No such weapons were present at any American airport I knew. My thoughts drifted back to a movie I saw in the early 1980s called *Midnight Express*. It's a film based on the true story of American student Billy Hayes, who was caught attempting to smuggle hashish out of Turkey. He was arrested and later sent to prison, where he was beaten regularly and subjected to inhumane treatment by Turkish guards. After watching the movie, I swore I would never visit Turkey.

But here I was, in Istanbul Airport, face-to-face with soldiers armed with deadly weapons. I was afraid to move or answer any questions, fearing they could detain me. The brutality from the movie reminded me that I was no longer in the US. Luckily, there was no issue. I didn't have a record, and I wasn't carrying anything that should alarm the airport guards, but I didn't want to take any chances.

After completing all the required entry visas, customs, and baggage claim checks, I found the bus arranged by the cruise line to take me to my hotel. I was staying at The Marmara Taksim, which overlooks the Bosphorus on one side and the city on the other. It is a twenty-story hotel, and the top floor features a restaurant with 360-degree windows. The hotel boasts a unique blend of old-world charm and five-star elegance. I waited in line for my turn to check in and listened to the rooms assigned to my fellow passengers—rooms 801, 525, 638, and so on. Dread washed over me as I suspected I would be assigned a room facing the trash cans. I was traveling alone, and I couldn't understand why they would give me a room with a beautiful view.

It was my turn to check in, and I waited nervously to get my room. The gentleman handed me my room key and said, *"You are in 1901."* What? The top floor of the rooms. The bellhop assisted me in carrying my luggage to the room. He opened the door, and I looked out and saw the bluest water I had ever seen. I had the best view anyone could ever hope for in that hotel.

I could see ships coming and going through the Bosphorus, the Topkapi Palace, the Blue Mosque, the Asian Peninsula, and the Galata Tower. The view was incredible; it took my breath away. I watched the scene for hours and was mesmerized. I had no desire to leave the room at this point because the view was all I needed to experience the city's vibrancy. I heard the call to prayer several times. It was a beautiful sound, and for a brief moment, the noise of the city seemed to settle. I ordered room service and sat by the window to enjoy dinner. It was a fortunate start to my cruise. I prayed it would continue.

The next morning, I woke up early to join the city tour. Our first stop was the Suleymaniye Mosque, a magnificent mosque renowned for its Ottoman architecture and serene courtyard. It was beautiful, and the architecture is a style that I had never seen before. It was quiet, and you could sense the profound reverence Muslims have for their religion. During our tour, the guide told us they used ostrich eggs hanging from the ceilings to keep the spiders away. That way, they will never weave any webs in the corners, of which there were many.

The Hagia Sophia was next, originally a Christian church that was turned into a mosque. You could see the original Christian frescoes, painted around 537 A.D., peeking through the paint as the Ottomans covered them when they took control of Istanbul in 1453 A.D. Next to the Hagia Sophia stood an obelisk, the Obelisk of Theodosius, now known as the At Meydanı or Sultanahmet Meydanı. It was first constructed by Pharaoh Thutmose III around 1450 B.C. and brought from Egypt by Theodosius around 390 A.D. I was amazed. How did the Egyptians transport an 84-foot-tall stone obelisk all the way to Istanbul?

The final stop of the day was at Topkapi Palace, the former residence of Ottoman sultans, showcasing luxurious interiors and courtyards. There was a parade similar to the one held for the sultans between the 1460s and 1856 A.D. The architecture was truly stunning. The mosaics featured many vibrant colors, and the palace's structure embodied authentic Ottoman style.

The tour ended for the day, and the bus took us back to the hotel. I was tired from traveling the day before and stopped at a café to try my first Turkish coffee. If you've ever had Turkish coffee, you'd understand how I am about to describe it. It is very thick and bitter, perfect for waking you up in the morning. I had a sweet pastry with my coffee, and the sweetness balanced out the bitterness. The server at the café was very kind and polite. He made sure I was satisfied with the coffee and pastry.

I returned to my room and heard the afternoon call to prayer. Once again, I sat by my window and watched the sun slowly set over the city. I was fascinated by the culture and way of life here. The Turkish people were very warm, welcoming, and helpful—except when it came to their driving. Red lights seemed to be just a suggestion, and no one paid attention to stop signs. There was constant chatter and honking among drivers. I thought I was a crazy driver, but I'm not sure I could survive an hour on Istanbul's streets. The rule on the road was: the bigger vehicle has the right of way. I decided to order dinner again and sit by my window. There was no better view than the one I had, and I felt uneasy leaving the hotel alone. Dinner was served, and I heard the last call to prayer of the day. I sat there entranced. It is a soulful and peaceful song that sets the mood for reverence during your prayers.

The next morning was our last day in Istanbul before we boarded the ship. Today, we visited the Blue Mosque, an iconic mosque with six minarets and intricate blue tilework. This has to be one of the most stunning mosques ever built. The tile work is a masterpiece. The other mosques were beautiful, but this one was built for grandeur, and it showed in every detail. I decided to walk outside to an area where you could view the entire mosque. I was in awe.

A few minutes later, I started talking to an older man named Don, who was traveling alone on the same cruise as I was. He was friendly and polite, so we decided to spend the day together. He mentioned that he had cruised on this same ship when it was first launched many years ago, and he wanted to revisit it.

We then headed to the Grand Bazaar. On the way, the guide drove us past the old Silk Road Train Station. It was just as you imagined—very colorful. I longed to visit it. Maybe on the next trip.

Visiting the Grand Bazaar is a must when you're in Istanbul. The spices, food, music, carpets, and handmade crafts offer an experience you won't want to miss. The quality of the construction is something they take great pride in. Having a booth in the Grand Bazaar suggests that the quality is excellent. I couldn't pass up the chance to buy a Turkish rug. They wanted to haggle, and I am not a haggler, so I probably overpaid, but I didn't care.

I finished my shopping at the Grand Bazaar and stepped outside to observe the Turkish people. While sitting across from a mosque, I watched a man wash himself before entering to pray. It was a powerful scene—so peaceful and reverent. I could see his lips moving as he prayed through each step of the process. At that moment, I thought, *This is faith.* Muslims do not enter their worship space without first setting their intentions and cleansing their mind and bodies. I wish all spiritual or religious services would start like this.

After the tour left the market, they took us back to the hotel in the early afternoon. Don asked me if I wanted to walk through the streets with him to experience the real Istanbul, and I eagerly agreed. We wandered down alleys and areas most tourists don't visit. It wasn't dangerous or scary; it was just off the usual tourist paths.

We were hungry and decided to stop at this restaurant for a late lunch. The owners spoke English quite well and were surprised to see a blonde American come to their restaurant. The owner invited me to the kitchen to see how the food was prepared. However, I feel that he wanted his staff to meet a blonde American. The kitchen workers did not speak any English, but they kept asking me if I wanted to try some of their best dishes. The food was incredible; the flavors were unlike anything I had ever tasted before. I tried everything they placed in front of us, and I had no idea what most of it was. They were gracious and welcoming. I was falling in love with this city!

Don and I walked back to the hotel and wished each other well. Maybe we will see each other again on the ship.

I went up to my room and watched the comings and goings of the people in this city once more. I observed ships of all sizes entering and leaving the port, from large sea carriers to small fishing boats, all navigating the Bosphorus Sea. I felt like I could sit here for a thousand years, peacefully watching the scene.

As the sun set, I began thinking about the next part of the trip: the cruise and a fateful meeting with a love mate. I felt a mix of excitement and nervousness. Did I look good enough? Did I work out enough before the trip to have a nice figure? What does he look like? What does he do? All of these questions will be answered in the next few days.

The next morning, the buses arrived at the hotel to take us to the port where the ship was docked. I felt both excited and sad. I wished I had a few more days here to explore other parts of Istanbul. The city had over eighteen million people and covered more than 2,000 square miles. I am sure there was so much more history to see.

Boarding the Cruise Ship

Upon boarding, the ship took photos of us to remember our voyage. I was becoming more nervous. I felt like something was amiss, but I couldn't quite put my finger on what it was. I was escorted to my cabin and began unpacking my bags. We would be on the ship for fourteen days, and I didn't want to live out of my suitcases. After unpacking, we were required by the cruise line to attend a safety briefing in the dining area. They explained evacuation procedures and what to do in case of an emergency. Honestly, I didn't pay much attention to the meeting. What could possibly happen? We were in the Mediterranean during summer, not the North Atlantic in winter.

After the meeting, I walked around the ship to get familiar with it. It was a beautiful ship; although there were more modern ones, I preferred the larger cabins and fewer people than on newer ships. The feature that made it unique was the top deck, which was a 360-degree round room. It was the disco room, and it was not in use during the day. I thought it would be wonderful to sit up there in the quiet while we cruised through the Bosphorus Straits heading toward Ephesus. As I sat there taking in the sights, I began to feel a loud rumbling. Then it happened—the Turkish Air Force buzzed the ship with fighter jets. Since I was on the top deck, I was almost parallel to them. Wow! I didn't expect that. The entire ship seemed to shake during the flyby.

I sat there enjoying the scenery. I've never seen water as blue and clear as in the Mediterranean. I sat there captivated for a few hours. The area evoked a warm feeling of familiarity. I looked at the islands we passed and thought, *"This is where the Iliad and the Odyssey took place."* The nymphs. The sirens. Charybdis and the Scylla. Circe. And Calypso. More ancient history than I ever thought I would see with my own eyes.

After cruising for a while, dinner was about to be served, so I went back to my cabin, took a shower, and got ready. I decided to sit in the formal dining area instead of going to the buffet. I thought it would be better to meet people if I had to sit and have dinner with them. I was seated at a table of eight and was the only single woman. The food was delicious, and the atmosphere at the table was lively. We were all very excited about the trip and visiting the places we were about to explore. Everyone had their own favorite spots they wanted to spend time in, while I was excited to visit each place!

After dinner, I headed to the lounge area and had a few drinks, meeting some friendly and engaging women. No men approached me yet, and I didn't see any single men either. It was only the first day; I had thirteen more to go. After a few hours, I retired to my room. Each day involved a full day of touring, and I wanted to be well-rested for it. The next morning, I went down to the buffet for breakfast before boarding the bus to tour Ephesus.

I didn't know much about the Bible, and at the time, I wasn't aware of the significance of Ephesus. The tour guide met us at the city entrance and reminded everyone to stay hydrated. It was a warm day, and we would spend most of it in the sun. Living in Phoenix and accustomed to temperatures over 100 degrees, 92 degrees felt comfortable. I chuckled to myself, listening to everyone complain about the heat; they definitely weren't used to it.

I listened to the tour guide tell us the city's history. I could still see the wagon wheel etchings in the stone streets, and I noticed something else very interesting. The tour guide stopped and explained the significance of that etching. It was illegal to reveal the locations of the brothels to visitors, so a symbol was carved into the stone to guide them to those brothels.

Upon arriving at the Library of Celsus, which housed over 12,000 scrolls and was one of the most impressive structures in the Roman Empire, I felt as if my knees might give out. I don't know why, maybe a memory from the past. Usually, when I feel that way, it's something important or significant from a previous life. I did sense like I had been here before; there was a faint familiarity.

The last stop with the tour guide was the amphitheater. Here, we learned this is where St. Paul would speak to the townspeople and teach them about Jesus. Now, it sank in; the chapter in the Bible called Ephesians. I learned that the amphitheater was built with perfect acoustics and hosted rock concerts there through the early 1990s, featuring acts such as Michael Jackson and George Michael.

I returned to the tour bus and waited in the air conditioning for the remaining passengers to board after buying souvenirs. I looked up and saw Don. He was sitting a few rows in front of me, and I took a moment to say hello. He was happy to see me, and we chatted for a few minutes. We agreed to get a drink once we returned to the ship. I thought to myself, "This is the only man I saw traveling by himself. Surely, he is not the man Ashlem spoke about." Truly, he was a very nice and respectable man, but he was in his early 70s and definitely not what I was looking for. It was only day two, many more to go.

On the way back to the ship, the bus driver surprised us by taking us to the site of the Temple of Artemis, one of the Ancient Seven Wonders of the World. Only one pillar remained from the arson on the night of July 21, 356 BCE, by a man named Herostratus. He set fire to the wooden roof beams, motivated by a desire for fame and notoriety. Wow! I finally saw a Seven Wonder of the Ancient World! I thought the Great Pyramid was the only structure still standing.

The next morning, we arrived at the Greek island of Santorini. It's an island with almost no water, and the cities are situated on top of the island at an elevation of 1,100 feet. You can take a bus to the top or walk. I wasn't prepared to walk that distance, so I hopped on a bus.

The island is stunning. Every building is white with blue trim. The tour guide told us the reason: they are the colors of the Greek flag. It is a very clean island; there is no graffiti and no trash on the streets. I walked to the highest point on the island and looked over the bay. The tour guide explained how the island was formed. There is a historic volcano in the middle of the bay that erupted around 3,600 years ago in 1600 B.C., creating the island of Santorini. He explained that it was not a dormant volcano and that they knew it would be active and could explode someday. He told us that everyone living on the island understood this and accepted their fate. Someone asked him about drinking water. He explained that no one on the island drank water because it was too precious; they would drink wine instead. Due to the climate on Santorini, they produce high-quality wine.

Upon returning to the ship that afternoon, I had a sinking feeling that my love mate was not there. It felt like he missed the boat and was going to try to board at the Rome connection. I had hoped that was the case, as I didn't want to regret this trip. Although how could I ever regret visiting places I read about as a child and only dreamed of seeing?

The next day was busy. We planned to visit two Greek islands: Mykonos and Delos. Mykonos was famous as a party island with many topless or nude beaches. Delos was an uninhabited island that was destroyed and looted by Mithridates in 88 BC and again by pirates in 69 BC. The ruins of that destruction remain as they did 2,100 years ago.

Upon arriving at Delos, I began to feel strange. I stepped off the boat and had visions and flashbacks from a distant past. Walking along the beach, I could see myself dancing there in another lifetime. I felt like I belonged here. I noticed Don was on the same charter, and we decided to explore the island without a guide. The architecture and sculptures were stunning. I've loved art and architecture since I was a little girl, and America doesn't have anything that looks like this.

We wandered through the streets, and I instinctively knew where I was going without a map. We agreed to visit Cleopatra's house; he looked at the map but couldn't figure out where we were. I told him to follow me, and I made my way to her house without needing the map. When he asked how I knew the way, I brushed it aside; I didn't want to explain. I wasn't sure he would understand.

After we returned to the ship, I went to my cabin. It had been a long day, and sometimes recalling past lives or experiencing déjà vu can be exhausting. I relived all the sights and experiences from the past five days. The word 'incredible' kept echoing in my mind. Tomorrow would be a day at sea, a time to relax before exploring Italy. I was really looking forward to that part of the trip. Italy—one part of my family immigrated from there. My great-grandfather was born on the outskirts of Rome in the late 1800s. His family sent him to America to escape the fascists who were taking over. Unfortunately, anyone who stayed on the farm was killed by them. He managed to survive and carry on the family name. My great-grandmother immigrated from Florence when she was a little girl. This was the land of my ancestry and the land of romanticized history.

That night, all the passengers experienced a truly special event: Mt. Etna erupted as we sailed through the Strait between Sicily and the mainland, allowing us to witness the ongoing eruption. It was magnificent—how many times will I get to see this? The red and orange lava against the nighttime sky. Breathtaking.

I fell in love with Sorrento the moment I laid eyes on it. What's not to love? Beautiful scenery, the scent of vibrant lemons everywhere, lovely flowers blooming, and incredible food! There were so many tours I wanted to do while here, but I chose to visit Pompeii. When I arrived, I looked at Mt. Vesuvius and said to myself, *"Well, hello, old friend."* I immediately recognized the surroundings and once again felt at home. I followed the tour through all of the uncovered buildings. Walking the streets, I felt like I was transported back in time. I could almost see and feel what it looked like before the eruption in 79 A.D.

There were many unforgettable places, but the ones that stood out were the Houses of Vettii and Faun, the Stabian and Forum bathhouses, and a private garden with a glass mosaic. As I walked around Pompeii, a childhood dream flooded back to me. I had dreamed of a house with an interior garden and doors and windows that opened directly into the house. I now realize I was dreaming of Pompeii and my life there.

From Naples, we docked at Civitavecchia, which serves as the gateway to Rome. Many passengers disembarked, as they had only paid for the first half of the trip, while others boarded the ship to continue the journey to Barcelona.

This was one of the stops I'd waited my entire life to see: Rome. There was so much I wanted to do and see. The bus dropped us off near Victor Emmanuel's Palace, and I took the subway to the Colosseum. As soon as the doors opened and sunlight streamed in, the Colosseum stood tall right in front of me. I immediately got a chill and decided not to go inside. I stood there for a few minutes, processing my sadness—sadness for all the unnecessary death for entertainment's sake, and feeling the chill of the souls who passed there still lingers.

From there, I walked through the Roman Forum and was stopped in my tracks when I reached the Temple of Vesta. Memories flooded back at every turn. After leaving there, I walked to the Pantheon, the Fountains of Trevi, and finally the Spanish Steps. The tour bus would pick us up from there and take us to the Vatican Museums. I learned that Pope John Paul II was speaking to crowds in the Square, and I realized I wouldn't have the chance to walk into St. Peter's Basilica. I felt sad because I wanted to see it in person—the grandeur and the opulence.

The tour took us through some of the Vatican Museums and finally to the Sistine Chapel. There are no words to describe it. Everyone stares at the Creation of Adam, and it is truly breathtaking. The entire ceiling is stunning. I wished I had hours to take it all in. The ceiling in one of the Museums looked like it was carved in stone, but it was actually a painting. Suddenly, I felt an unkind presence there. I heard stories of murders and assassinations in the Church, and I dismissed those stories until now. Those souls were hanging around, and anyone sensitive can feel it.

My day in Rome was ending, and as I boarded the bus to return to the ship, I wondered if he might be waiting for me. I held my breath. Did he make the connection? Would he really be there?

That night at dinner, the ship's captain decided to join me at my table because there was an open seat. I had my answer; he didn't make the connection. I sat there heartbroken. I tried to put on my best face. After dinner, I met Don in the lounge, and we had drinks and talked about our day in Rome. Afterwards, I took a walk around the deck looking at the ocean and the stars. I softly cried. I haven't had any luck with love. I tried my best to keep the negative thoughts of unworthiness at bay. I walked back to my cabin, locked the door, undressed, and cried myself to sleep.

The next day, we docked in Livorno, located near Florence. Ah, Florence—the hometown of my great-grandmother. My heart swelled with joy. My mind wandered back to eighth-grade social studies class, and I remembered the conflicts between Venice and Florence. I always supported Florence, and I never understood why, but I was eager to find out.

The first stop on the tour was the Cathedral of Santa Maria del Fiore, also known as the Duomo. This church stands out because its exterior is ornate and colorful, while the interior is simpler. It has 463 steps leading up to the cupola, which offers a panoramic view of Florence. I didn't walk up there because it would take an hour, and I didn't have the time. The next stop was Michelangelo's Statue of David in the Galleria dell'Accademia in Florence. I stood in awe. The sculpture is so realistic it feels like it's breathing, almost eager for an upcoming battle. I was stunned and couldn't move; I'd never experienced that before. Finally, we arrived at the Basilica of Santa Croce. The basilica is the final resting place of many famous figures, including Michelangelo, Galileo Galilei, Niccolò Machiavelli, Leonardo Bruni, Carlo Marsuppini, and a memorial to Dante Alighieri, as well as numerous other notable figures in Italian history. I understood why I chose Florence over Venice. Once again, I stood there, recalling when I attended services here hundreds of years ago. I loved this church so much that the feelings I had over 500 years ago still remain strong. It was time for us to depart, and I didn't want to leave. I could have sat there for another couple of hours and still not quench my love and devotion to the church.

The last stop of the day was the Ponte Vecchio, a medieval stone closed-spandrel segmental arch bridge over the Arno River. It is the only bridge in Florence spared from destruction during World War II. I sat and watched the Arno flow for about an hour, feeling a sense of peace and gaining an understanding that could only be gained from actually visiting these places. My visions started to make sense, which took a bit to process. I also knew that most people would not understand it.

I returned to the ship and ran into Don. He asked if I wanted to take a walk to the shops by the port, and I agreed. It was a fairly long walk, but we had time before departing for Portofino. On the way back, we decided to walk on the beach to return to the ship. Unfortunately, we were running out of time. We reached the end, where gates surrounded the area, blocking access to the boardwalk. We didn't have enough time to walk all the way to the end and return to the ship. Anxiety started to set in. We looked and looked. Then Don ran one way to find a way out, and I went the other. We met again, and he said we would need to climb these poles because that was our only option. I was panicked; I didn't want to be left in Florence, not by choice. We approached the spot, and suddenly a wooden board with steps appeared. We looked at each other, and both said at the same time, *"This was not here before."* We paused for a few seconds in awe. A miracle unfolded right before our eyes. I climbed up, and once I reached the top, I yelled to the workers on the ship, *"Wait! We are here!"* They laughed.

Don and I did our usual, had a drink, and then went to our cabins to rest before dinner. I saw him afterward, and neither of us had shaken off the day's experience. He said again, *"That was not there."* I nodded and agreed. We experienced a miracle. It's a memory we will carry with us for the rest of our lives.

As the night went on, I grew more despondent. The main reason for this trip was to meet someone, and he didn't show up.

212

I became less interested in the places we visited until we reached Barcelona. During the tour, I saw several of Antoni Gaudí's works, including the Sagrada Familia, Casa Mila, and Casa Batlló. I realized that I was ready to go home, and I planned to do so the next day. I packed my things and prepared for the return trip. I said goodbye to the ship and thanked it for taking me to such wonderful places.

I needed to talk to Ashlem to understand what happened. Luckily, he had a time slot within the next two weeks. I was hoping to get answers.

Ashlem July 26, 2001

"I see a beautiful golden light. Light is emanating from a pinpoint of light expanding; gently expanding. How beautiful. Fills the whole picture with beautiful golden light. Now a pinpoint of violet light appears in the center, and the now the violet light expands. Now a beautiful orange light expands. Now, a blue light. And a green light. As the green light expands, it consumes, the other colors leave behind beautiful soft light green-light. Now, white light appears in the center of the green light and consumes the green light. Expands and leaves behind beautiful, soft White Light. The White Light is the All-Consuming Christ of Light and Creation. It now fills the whole picture with beautiful, White Light.

"Images are forming. It is a beautiful seagull. See it flying. There is a ship below on a large body of water. Seagull dives down toward the ship. Lands on the fantail deck of the ship. It is a cruise ship. No sails. Just a light-colored smoke from the stacks. The seagull sits quietly. And now another seagull comes forth. Lands down to the ship. It sits on the rail of the fantail next to the first seagull. They seem to look at each other and chatter. Then they move apart. About ten foot apart.

"I don't see many people on the ship. An Angel appears on this ship. A beautiful Angel. The Angel has long, light brown hair. Curly at the ends with a white gown on. Her name is Haleaiah. Now we come to an island. The island seems to open up. When the ship comes to the island, like it's going to land there. And now there is no ship. Just the island.

"A White Rock appears where the ship was. On the White Rock, a beautiful golden flame appears, a flame like a candle flame, that flickers only at the top. The light is very bright and very fulfilling as it grows in size and intensity. Now it begins to soften and diminish. Ashlem is standing in that flame. He was wearing his beautiful white robe, his robe of simplicity. There's a beautiful smile upon his face, and his eyes twinkle, and the flame goes out. Ashlem stands. The two seagulls are sitting in a tree. A male and a female. They seem to grow in size and in stature. Now they transform to Eagles. Beautiful Golden Eagles.

"Ashlem smiles. He bows to the Eagles, and the Eagles take flight together. And they fly up over the trees to the beautiful place in the forest with all the flowers, the pool of water. There is no ocean. They disappear from view, the Eagles do. Ashlem Looks down at the White Rock. He steps into flowers, parts the flowers. He finds a violet, a little small, violet. Picks it singularly. Brings it up and steps back upon the White Rock. He sits in a lotus position. Puts the violet in the palm of his hand. Covers it with the other hand. Bows his head. He takes his hand away from the other and ends his meditation. There is a beautiful White Rose in his hand. He smells the White

214

Rose. He bows his head and wishes to speak through. I give my permission."

"I am Ashlem, known as Golden Image, I say to thee, 'Hail.' To come forth into life is to fly here and to there. That is the symbol of the seagull, and the seagull is the scavenger at the time. But flies upon the ocean of time. Looking always for something to devour. Or to assimilate to itself. So, it is with life. Into its form. Let the form of the Eagle become one with thee of this time. And the realization of it. Now, there are many questions I will answer. Please begin."

"Can we talk more about what happened? In the very beginning, with the cruise ship and the seagulls changing into Eagles, the Eagles represent wisdom, truth and knowledge, right? And the seagulls you said are scavengers looking for food or..."

"Are not all peoples scavengers? Do they not always look for something to bring to their being? Spend their whole life with it. Are thee not looking for something?"

"I am always looking for something."

"Then could thee be the seagull? And thee have taken a journey, I said unto thee, 'Upon this journey, thee may meet one who could be your lovemate.' Right? And did not occur."

"No. Was he there?"

"No. Why was he not there?

"I don't know. Not ready for it?"

"Missed the boat."

"He missed the boat."

"Not upon his course of destiny. Do you understand? There's no control over this. When thee look here, and when thee look there, at the moment of time, not upon the course of destiny. They passed like two ships in the night."

"So that is done? Or will it...?"

"It's not done. It is what has happened."

"So, it is not done, it's just later?"

"You're going to ask, 'What about your love mate?'"

"Yes, I was going to ask what happened."

"Now do you know."

"Was he going to try to make it to the Rome connection and get on there? That came to me while I was on the ship. He was going to try, and make the Rome. But it didn't happen."

"It did not happen. Until this time, it was your anxiety of the period of time that did cause a reference of energies. He was trying to make the Rome engagement, but too many business problems. So, he quit."

"After we departed from Rome, I knew he was not on the ship."

"Does not mean it is over."

"I'm glad because I was upset about that, I thought that was my one and only chance."

"I know thee were upset. There's nothing we could do or I could do."

"No, and I didn't mean to. If I gave that energy to you, I didn't mean to. I was upset."

"I say, now, clear your mind of it. There's still loved ones coming to thee. Have patience. I cannot control these things. What I say to thee a lovemate has been placed here and there on the way to your destiny, to do this position. Did we enjoy yourself upon your cruise?"

"I had a wonderful time, more than. Words can even express it."

"It was not all in vain."

"No, it wasn't. I saw things that most people never get to see."

"That is good."

"And felt things that there are no words for it. I had a vision in Pompeii. I felt a deep peace. What a beautiful place. It was amazing. I love it so much that I could move there."

"At the excavations, did thee feel sad?"

"I did because of the destruction of life. I couldn't look at the people who were in the glass cases. That was a little hard for me. And I did feel sad because it was such a beautiful place, and there was so much love and energy there. I felt sad, but also felt happy because I was back once more to enjoy it."

"And when the warning came forth with the shaking of the ground before Vesuvius exploded, they could have been saved, but they cling to the material plane of that period of time. Consumed by the material plane, and they perished with it."

"Was I a young child at the time of the earthquake and eruption?"

"Ye were about five or six."

"What was the vibration in Santorini that I felt? I felt like the whole world was shaking, and I almost physically felt like I was shaking. Had I been there when that eruption occurred?"

"Not during the eruption, but you have lived there a long time before."

"I didn't know if I was feeling it because there is still a volcano underneath the bay. I didn't know if I felt the energy from that volcano."

"It is not an energy from the volcano that thee feel. But what thee have felt was the volcano of life that thee lived before the volcano exploded. Then Spirit remembers things. There was no vibration upon the ground, except thee felt it."

"How about in Delos? This is another Greek Island we visited. Did I live there because, as we were walking around the village, I knew which way to walk and which way to go to Cleopatra's palace?"

"It is a place ye have visited. A vacation place for Cleopatra. It is so."

"Who was the Angel Haleaiah?"

"She is looking over thee, in addition to Chaleaiah. Haleaiah is a traveling Angel."

"OK. Her name is like my soul name; many of my Angels have 'leaiah' in them. What does that mean?"

"It is part of your family incarnate group to speak of. It is like trademark."

"Where does it come from?"

"It comes from your own spirit. And spirits of your kind, gravitate to thee and become your family incarnate group."

"What was the small violet? in the very beginning of this reading?"

"My dear, I tell to thee these things, and ye do not wish to even try to figure them out. You want I to say unto thee. I say to thee, 'Work upon it.'"

"OK."

"What is a violet?"

"It's a flower, purple flower."

"What kind of purple flower? Where does it grow?"

"I want to say somewhere where it's dry."

"Not necessarily dry. It is a weed flower, is it not? That's all. Your other flower is rather taller. Then could that be a rose? Could it be, if one puts the energy toward it, then transforms it to the rose."

"OK. Which I have done?"

"Are ye ready to do in your life? Transform it to a rose?"

"Yes."

"Then be like the rose. Be a beautiful flower.

"Do thee have any more questions?"

"No."

"Then repeat I, Ashlem:

"I and the Father are One.

"I stand forth into the Light of the Christ.

"For I am Light. I am LIGHT.

"I AM THAT LIGHT.

"Breathe deeply again. Mary will be with thee. And your Angels. I give to thee the sign of peace our covenant: Of the Father and of the Son, and of thy Holy Spirit, that the circle of God is eternal with thee. Never beginning, never ending, and never to be separated from the whole, and that is thee. Fly, beautiful dove. Peace be unto thee, I take my leave."

"Thank you Ashlem."

I finished the reading feeling a bit better. I still had a chance to meet my lovemate. One thing did bother me; my anxiety at the moment caused a change in the energies, and our meeting was no longer part of his course of destiny. That bothered me a lot. I tried to push it out of my mind. I was not ready to deal with another mistake I had made. I had bigger concerns right now. I no longer had a job and needed to figure that out quickly.

After three weeks of applying to numerous jobs without receiving an interview request, I decided to reapply at QWEST Communications. I left the company through no fault of my own and had hoped to return. I applied and waited. I prayed I could return because I always did good work, the best I could. A week later, the HR department called and offered me the opportunity to return. I seized the opportunity. My start date was September 17, 2001.

Chapter Seven: The Day the World Changed

I started September by resting and reflecting on everything that had happened over the summer as I prepared to return to work. I am a natural night owl and usually sleep in. On the morning of September 11, our world was shattered.

I was sleeping and I received a call from a friend, and she screamed into the phone, *"Wake up, we were just attacked. Turn on the television."* In my state of sleepiness, I turned on the TV and watched in horror, as did all Americans. I was numb. I couldn't stop watching the events. While watching the TV, I saw the second tower hit. I was paralyzed, not with fear, but with shock. How could anyone think to do something so abhorrently evil?

While I watched every second of the coverage, my mind drifted back to 1987. It was my senior year of high school, and our class was going to New York City for the day. One of the stops was the Twin Towers. I clearly remember walking around the observation deck and feeling at ease. Not because the tower was swaying slightly, nor because the clouds were rolling in and out of the city, blocking the view from the tower. It was something completely different. I didn't feel safe. It almost felt like a morgue, and I didn't know why. Coming out of that memory, it suddenly made sense.

Not long after that, I saw the second tower collapse. Then came reports of the flight over Pennsylvania crashing into the ground, followed by reports of the Pentagon being hit. I watched people jump out of the towers from over one hundred floors. I couldn't understand how someone could do that. Maybe they accepted death and found peace in those last moments. It's likely they chose to fly and feel free rather than be burned alive.

Then, finally, the first tower fell. I felt the deepest sadness I had ever experienced in my life that day. I reached out to Bob later and asked if there were any openings with Ashlem for Thursday, and there was one. I took it. I was afraid of what was to come. Would this be WWIII? Nuclear War? How serious would the US response be? Do we start praying for our enemies? Or do we support the response even though it could mean more death for many, many people?

I arrived for my appointment, and everyone was still in shock and sad. There was a lot of anxiety. We knew we had to begin preparing for our purpose on Earth: to teach, help, and heal people through the Rapture and the Last Day. Was this the beginning of our mission?

I entered the meditation room, and Bob started his transition to allow Ashlem to come through. I would know the answer in a few minutes.

Ashlem September 13, 2001

"I see a beautiful golden light emanating from the pinpoint of light, slowly expanding in the center in all directions. And now, in the center of the golden light, a violet light appears, and it consumes the golden light. Expands. Fills the whole picture with soft violet light.

"Now, an image is forming in the violet light. It is the Blessed Virgin Mary once again who has been coming forth so often. With her is a host of Angels: Michael, the Archangel, and Gabriel are the two male Instincts. The others are beautiful female Angels. Mary is standing on the White Rock that

appears. Now the forest appears around. The sky, I can see now, is beautifully blue. Birds are flying here and there. Mary is holding in her hand the beautiful White Rose of the Christ.

"Mary smells the White Rose begins to speak, and golden words come forth. Mary has a tear in her eye. The words say, **"Blessed art they who have been of the innocence of life. And Blessed art they who rise forth into the hand of the Father. Blessed art they who have forfeited their life to save others, and blessed art they upon the Earth's Plane of grace and understanding. For thee, I come forth at this time. I am sorry that there is a sorrow in my heart, but when I see perpetrations upon the Earth's Plane of peoples who have maimed and killed each other, I become very sad. To come forth yet as that which I have described many, many years ago to the girls in the fields that they may understand. Those things are coming to pass today. My heart is with all who have love and peace within it. And blessed art thee among women, also, to know of your peace of life here. I hold your Christ Rose as I always will. For thee to understand that many things yet to come upon the Earth. Breathe deeply and let the peace settle your nerves of this time. The Angels speak with thee and of thee. And come forth to serve thee. Let us do this in love."**

"Before her appears a beautiful golden flame. A flame like a candle flame that flickers only at the top. The light grows in size and intensity. Begins to soften and diminish. Ashlem is standing in the flame, and he is wearing a beautiful, white robe. **He does not have a smile on his face.** He bows to the

Blessed Virgin Mary and accepts the Rose. Mary disappears, Michael the Archangel and Gabriel standing beside him as he turns and sits upon the White Rock in a lotus position. He smells the White Rose again. He asks to speak through. I give my permission."

"**To the blessedness of life that come forth, Mary's heart is sad of this time. But I am sad also, as thee are sad and many of the peoples into America are very sad of this time, have other parts of the world. Also peoples are sad over the occurrences that has come forth. And Mary has said this before into the Lady of Fatima and those letters that the girls have given and they would refuse to read to the peoples. If they were read, as they were supposed to be read to the peoples, then there would be awakening time. But now is the time for awakening. But thee did not come here to see and witness my tears or Mary's tears, but your own tears in your heart. There are there any questions, I will answer for thee. Please begin.**"

"Hello Ashlem. I have a lot of questions about what happened on Tuesday. Based on what happened on Tuesday, what can we expect now?"

"**I have said for the last decade of time what is going to happen. It will begin with America declaring war, as they call it, upon Arab nations. Some innocent peoples into the Arab nations will die. They call it collateral damage. But it cannot be helped. But they are to punish those peoples who have perpetrated upon the thousands of people into America who have perished, and they were all innocent of anything. One**" *wrong does not make it right. So, therefore, when America go forth, and they do bomb the other countries, and they will.*

"And they will weed out and maybe destroy that one who is called Bin Laden and his associates. They will then go after Gaddafi, and also Hussein. Iran will become very irate over this, and so will Jordan. And Jordan will make treaty with other Arab countries, and the countries will all begin to bind together against America for their own safety.

"The price of oil will skyrocket. Not because there is not a limited amount of oil, but because the oil companies into America will begin to extract their oil from the ground and want a great fortune for it. And the greed of the America come forth and show its ugly head. Then peoples will not be able to afford to go to work. They will ask for more money from their companies. Inflation will set in greatly. One hand feeds the other hand, does it not? And it is so of this period of time. What we have spoken of over a decade ago is now at hand. What more can I say?"

"Does this signify the start of World War III, as they would call it?"

"It is the beginning of Armageddon. Have three years."

"Three years before it's all over or three years..."

"Three years before Armageddon."

"Was Osama bin Laden behind this, or were there more than that?"

"Of course. He trained the peoples. He had his good training. Let's make him responsible for it. Then other groups who he has trained, are over the world of Earth, not just into Afghanistan or other places, but all over. They're binding together with greater strength. You will find the ganys into America will begin to bind together. As I had said 20 years ago, you'll find the hungry beast of man sticking its ugly head forth. They who have not listened, they will perish."

'People are calling for a military attack. A lot of Americans, out of anger, but is that the right thing to do? I mean, it doesn't..."

"How else can thee combat it? Its like fighting fire with fire. It is like fighting a forest fire. Fire with the fire eventually puts out the fire. Then you must understand at this period time of life what is happening here. America is fighting fire with fire. They are angry because innocence have come forth and perished in it. Children who went to the day school so that they parents may work for a living to feed and clothe them. They have died. That has not come forward yet, but it will."

"So, no matter how much peace that anybody puts forward, there's nothing we can do to stop it at this point?"

"It is a snowball, my dear. Rolling downhill. Did not know when it was to occur. We did know that it was going to occur."

"The country is rallying together. Will this incite?"

"It is good. It is good. Bringing strength, but you will find the businessmen of America who are greedy. They will come forth with their greed. Do you understand?"

"Yes."

"Farmers will decide they need more money to make their crops for them. And the middleman, he is the one who will raise the prices high. Do they know how to grow food?"

"I've done it before, yes."

"Better begin doing it. There'll be plenty of food. But could thee afford it?"

"No, I can't afford it."

"Could be afford to pay 5-6 dollars a gallon for gasoline to go to work with?"

"No. Is the president involved in this attack?"

"No. He was the recipient of it though. However, the CIA knew that there was going to be an attack but did not know when or where. They do now."

"So, the stories of Air Force One and the White House being a target were also true?"

"Possibilities. The plane that crashed into Pennsylvania was targeted for the White House. Plane that crashed into the Pentagon was targeted for the Pentagon."

"Will there be more attacks in America?"

"But of course. It is the mere tip of the iceberg."

"Will it be safe to travel?"

"Where are you going? It will be very shaky to do that now."

"I have been feeling extremely tired these past few days. Is the universe using my energy to help? I feel like I can't even get out of bed these past three or four days."

"Put hand upon heart. I only feel a great anxiety within. What is your problem? Besides America?"

"Well, I feel very stressed about a lot of the things going on. I'm stressed because I'll be going back to work, and I have classes four nights a week, and I know that I am needed to help get the book out and design the website and…"

"You have done well for us. Now ye must look at your personal view of life for thee to continue. Your direction and way. You have used your personal time here to help with the book. It is greatly appreciated. Now it is time to gather forth the loose ends in your life to begin to bring them forth. Ye must do this work, and you must go to school to do this work. Then do it. Do not sleep during class, but there may be some new things happening."

"Which you can't tell me at this point? With the book, or with school or am I not needed anymore with the book?"

"You are always needed in every and any place you want to be. It is up to thee."

"When we were in meditation, some of the Masters were coming forth, and I believe that they said that I would be involved further with the book. We are close to completion; it is mostly clean-up work now. Is that true?"

"It is possible. I cannot make a prophecy for thee. Let us see how the book is accepted."

"OK."

"It depends, and everything depends upon how the public accepts it. For the book is successful, according to the public, then it does not have to be number one seller."

"I guess I'm also feeling a little stressed because I feel I am leaned on a lot right now to get things done."

"But that is what ye have committed yourself to. You should not feel leaned on right now. It is not a simple task. So therefore, ye have agreed to it. Because you are being leaned on, it is being maybe over-taxed. You're doing a good job. We are pleased with you."

"Just so much is coming up, and if things are going to change with the job and the work, maybe that will relieve some of the burden."

"Release your energy of thought upon the book. The Angel come together, as they would come together, necessary. Put your things and thoughts upon work. Take the stress off of thee, so that thee can function fully upon the work. I have said, 'Do not sleep during class.' And that is something you have not heard before."

"As far as the website, should that be something that I kind of put to the side?"

"As well, you're going to have to put it aside. It will be put forth in time. Do not stress about it."

"I have been seeing a green and a pink light when I'm in class. It flashes around me, and I don't know what that is."

"The green light is a healing light. A pink light is a light of love, universal and impersonal love. Then why do thee question it?"

"Well, I didn't know if they were signs to me."

"You can see in front of your body? Bring it into your chest and bring it into your central nervous system. That is what to do when ye see that beautiful green and pink light. Breathe it in and feel the energy revitalizing thee. That is what it is for."

"So that's what it's being shown to me? When I was driving yesterday, I saw this huge golden light in front of me and next to me. It was with me for miles. Was that about wisdom?"

"Wisdom is good. Whenever you see golden light, you must think about wisdom. Now, whose wisdom is it? Is it your wisdom or the wisdom of Spirit? That is what thee must decide. Then let us say, to raise your wisdom forth, use your guidance of greater knowledge, especially when you're driving automobile. Your mind wander hither to there. Right? Most accidents are caused by the right foot."

"I have this friend Josh, and we've been speaking on the Internet, and I think that I scared him away with the information I was telling him. He was asking what I see. Is this the beginning of World War? I just said that everything I learned from the book could possibly be. The third world war will be nuclear, and the rapture could begin. After that, he was gone. I didn't hear from him, so I didn't know if I scared him away. I sent him a letter to apologize. I did not mean to overwhelm him with information."

"Has he answered your letter?"

"No."

"Put forth good thoughts. Have thee met this gentleman?"

"No, we just speak through the internet. He spent some time in the Himalayas to find himself."

"In the Himalayas, what was his position in the Himalayas?"

"He was at a Buddhist monastery. And I cannot remember the name of the city."

"Then thee did not frighten him away."

"OK. One night last week, we talked for six hours."

"When you meet somebody that is interesting to thee, before you continue a closer personal conversation with the person, say, please forward a picture of ye. I will forward a picture of myself. Then do it, just as you are, not as you think you are. Be yourself. Do not make stories up."

"Ok. There are a few things keep coming to me, and it seems to be important. Where did I come from before I came To Earth this time? Where was I last time?"

"Where do thee come?"

"Where was I before I incarnated on Earth?"

"Before this incarnation, you were in Spirit."

"Where in spirit? Was I on one of the planets or some other entity?"

"Just in spirit world. You were learning how to reincarnate again through your precious mother's womb. What were you were doing that period time? What do entities and spirits do when are there?"

232

"They guide and they teach."

"They guide and they teach, and they help each other. There are many Angels that ye would help of, and they have come to your aid of this period of time. They surround thee of this time. Then accept their love and make your own direction of this time. We have spoken many times, some of it intimately to thee about your personal relationships with men. If I said a criticism, would thee take it to heart?"

"No."

"Now, I'm going to tell ye something that thee may use as a tool for yourself. You are a very smart woman; greatly intelligent. And that is what frightens men away more than anything else; your intelligence, your business attitude. Great intelligence. It sounds into your voice. It is why businessman look upon thee with great wisdom and say, 'See, there is a woman who knows what she is doing.' But a lover does not want that. So ye must learn to change the tone in your voice. Listen to this recording and then begin to realize the softer tone of voice makes it more sexy, more desirable for men. Sharp business tone is not good for love. Think about what I have said. I am not criticizing.

"I'm giving you a tool that ye use to increase your own personal being. Ye must listen to it. You may not hear what other people do hear. But thee are a good, beautiful person and a very beautiful woman. I have seen men, ye have spoken to. After ye have spoken to them in person, they disappeared. Because

*ye have overwhelmed them. Because of your
intelligence. A man is stupid, but he wants to be
thought of as bright. But when there is an intelligence
above him and he said, 'I don't think I could cope with
this.' Then he turned his face.*

*"Now to set a trap for a man. Set your voice
softer from your talking normal. Just simple talk. And
leave the business mode away, and then define
yourself. That is your true being I am speaking of. Ye
have stepped into what is called a business rut.
You're great to do the business, but do not treat your
lover as a business partner. Treat your lover as a
friend and as a lover."*

"And that's why there have been so many men who have
come in to help me with that?"

*"Aye. And as ye begin to understand what I'm
speaking of, ye listen to your voice on this recording
and other recordings. Lower the tone of your voice.
Take the sharpness off. Let it mellow and roll. Then
thee will find this to be a good habit. When thee are
talking to men, they will come to thee like flies to
honey. Then ye must want to remain and maintain
that attitude. When you are in business, be that
businesswoman. You are a good businesswoman to
them. Make a difference between each. You'll be
happier that way."*

"OK. This goes back to the other thing I was asking
about. Am I involved in any of the space travel that happens? A
teacher of the Brotherhood of Light?"

"Oh, ye have taught many peoples in the Brotherhood of Light. This is what you were trying to get at when you asked me earlier, where was I? Here or there? You were here in the spirit world, working upon coming through your mother's womb. But in between the incarnations, often ye go to the Brotherhood of Light and to various planets into Coresus, Antunosus, Antoria, and too many other planets throughout the cosmos you have never heard of before. There ye teach and find happiness and wisdom for peoples. Different humankind, but still humanoids. That is what the Brotherhood of Light is; dedicated to helping humans all over creation. Spirit work with thee carefully."

"In meditation one night, my arms spread out to my sides, and I pictured myself standing on a cliff, and I heard the words, 'You Are Moses.' And I did not understand that."

"What did Moses represent?"

"A leader of the Israeli people to bring them into safety."

"He was a handmaid of God. And who is God?"

"That is us, all of us; The Creation."

"Then you are to be a leader of those within, by the authority of the Grace Consciousness working with the Brotherhood of Light. Where did Moses end up? With the Brothers of Light. Did he not ascend from the Earth into the clouds?"

"Then he did not die..."

"Then thee are of the Moses of Life. You have wisdom. Use it wisely. I have given to thee a little bit of thought to think about personally for yourself, and

expanded into other realms of your life, and ye will find greater happiness."

"Was I with Moses at that time. Do you know that?"

"Ye were a little girl in that period of time. With the Exodus. Your name was Anima. You were seven years old. You were a very hardheaded little girl. Mother told thee to stay upon the wagon. Ye wanted to push the wagon. Disobeyed. Jumped off the wagon and the wheel rolled over thee and killed thee. What is it called today, collateral damage."

"I have always had a yearning to see the Ark of the Covenant. And I don't know if I saw it as a child. I had a dream last night, and when I woke up, there was a white rose in front of me."

"It was protecting thee; the Christ."

"Did someone give it to me?"

"You never lost it."

"I don't know if they had given me another one."

"Mary keeps your Rose; your Christ Rose for thee. And she give it to I, Ashlem. I keep it for thee, and I will give it back to Mary. But it is always yours anytime you wish to image it, it is there."

"Did Mary put it in front of me to remind me?"

"There are always reasons for everything."

"People sense that my psychic abilities are opening up more right now. And it seems my wisdom is increasing. But how do you know how to answer those that ask? For instance, Josh asked me about a woman he met and was wondering if I could see him with her."

"Answer some of the questions without interfering. Understand my love, how to answer the question, you just say, 'I have seen thee with many, many thousands of women. Which one do we speak of? I am not a psychic. I do not see the one you are speaking of.'"

"I said to him, 'It's not important what I see. It's what's important what you see.' I just don't know how to answer people like that. I understand what you mean, and I don't want to interfere in their life. It's their life."

"Put everything into self, my dear. When a person says, 'Do you see I doing this or doing that?' Ye say, 'I don't see anything. I have my eyes closed.' You're speaking of the Spirit. Then listen to your own Spirit within to see what thee think. Thought is the creative force, and it is a projection, and then tell them to begin to project their thoughts of goodness, and their Life will become good."

"How do people who read cards..."

"How do they contain who is right and who is wrong? If the shoe fits, wear it."

"If they tell someone that they don't see these two people together, and that person walks away. If they listen to that person, and walk away from the other, and their lessons are not completed between the two, is that interference?"

"No, it is not interference. They say, 'I do not see these two people being together again. They should not be talking about people who are not sitting in front of them. In other words, it is none of your business if Jane and Joe over here are together and will not be

together forever. If you personally say, "Is Jane and John going to be together?' Ye say, 'I don't know. Ask Jane and Joe.'"

"But if they're talking about the person whom they're reading, isn't that interfering?"

"If a person asks, 'Am I going to be with Joe for this long period of time?' Then their answer of wisdom should be, 'Is it not up to thee and Joe?' In other words, sidestep the issue of what is prophecy. Otherwise, a fool speaks. There are many good card readers, who are not reading the cards, but they are reading your mind, reading your mind of your desire and by your desire they can arrange what is. You're going to do it because you have this great desire. In other words, a seer say to thee, 'I see ye with tall, dark man. Is your heart not looking for a lover?' Then they may know this, and they say to thee, "I see thee with this man who is tall, because you like a man who is maybe taller than thee or stronger than thee. You like a man who is a man. So, they pray upon that and say I see ye with this man. They are 50% correct and 50% wrong. It can't be any other way. That is how they work. So, if they cost a lot of money, their prime purpose is money and making you happy so that ye spend more money. They will tell ye whatever thee wish to know. But is that true prophecy? Then the greatest prophecy is thee within thee."

"My higher self.

"Your higher self and your ability to go forward and to create your destiny. When you are quiet and

238

not filled with anxiety and other bubbling desires, then ye are quiet to listen to your higher self. It will guide thee. When you are sad, you bring forth sadness, is it not so? When you are happy, you bring forth happiness, is it not so? There cannot be any other way. Do not be sad at the world. To be totally sad, this is written into the archives of Time, long time before you were even a glimmer in your Father's eye."

"Were those people lifted? From the planes before they hit."

"Those people who died, who are innocents, they will come back again with greater love in them; period of the Seventh Day. Many of them cried terribly before they perished. But when they knew they were going to die, they were at peace.

"They sit at the right hand of the Father. Cry for they who remain upon the Earth's Plane, not for those who have already gone."

"I'm sad because I know what's going to happen to the Earth, and more people are going to die, and it's not going to be pretty. The next couple of years, there's not going to be much peace."

"Let me ask thee, 'If I could raise my hand, and wave it to stop all this, do thee think I should do that?'"

"No, I think it needs to be done."

"And what would it end? What would be its purpose if I had the power to simply raise my hand and end of all of this negativity and bring nothing but peace upon Earth?"

"That would be the best."

"It would? It would be best for a time later on and then for peace, but then people would not have learned their lessons or completed their karma. They would have to come back and do it again. Then I would be interfering with their choices of life, would I not?

"Now do ye understand when the healing comes forth. When you put your hand to heal someone and they are not healed, you cannot interfere with the freedom of choice of destiny. If it is their karma, then you cannot cure it. But with divine love, ye began the Healing Force. That is what it's about. And that is what Jesus taught people. Put his hand upon them and said, 'Through the Father, let the Light come forth.' And He image himself as the Light. And the Christ came forth, and surrounded him, and healed. Did he not? Thee have the same power. But ye look for the miracle. He did not look for the miracle. He already knew."

"So, I could put my hands and if, I truly believe it, that I could heal, and it is their karma, it will be done."

"It is so."

"I guess I believe it. But I guess I'm not to the point where my whole heart is in it. Do you know what I mean?"

"It is so; you are human. You have been told you're nothing. Then ye become nothing. If you are told from the beginning of your beginning of life here, that thee are a great healer, and ye will heal peoples, and you will bring forth the Christ Light, and you will put your hand forth, and you will become a healer. I say unto thee, 'I heal peoples". I do not let them look

*for a miracle to heal. I put my hand upon their heart,
and let that energy of the heart begin to do the healing
work. That is what it's about. If ye need to be healed,
then thee must put your energy also there and feel the
energy coming, and the more ye feel of it, the greater
and stronger it will become.*

*"Americans are so sensitive about their own
personal self. Open up to the greater oneness of God. I
am sorry these people who perpetrated they called it,
Jihad, Holy War. There's nothing holy about it. It is
their own ignorance. They have not the right to take
life in the name of God."*

"That's why I'm trying to send as much love and
peace..."

*"Do not send love to a murderer. He would not
receive it. But send thoughts of goodness to his
perpetrators, who he perpetrated upon. To pray for
their spirit. Pray for the spirits of the people who have
gone forth. They are the Holy Ones. They were the
innocents. For the mother and the father who went to
work that day, and the child who was put into the
daycare center so that they could go to work, and now
they cannot even leave. Pray for them. Their spirit be
accepted with great love and thy karma be ended, so
they don't have to come back again."*

"In the Bible, Jesus said love thy enemy as well."

*"If you love your enemy, there is no enemy. That
is what he was teaching."*

"OK. So, if I send love to Bin Laden, then he is no longer
my enemy."

"Best way to send love to Bin Laden is to say, 'I forgive thee. Maybe, God forgive thee also. Let it be so.'"

"As well as the other people involved in this? His allies or his people he trained?"

"It is their karma. Ye cannot take it from them."

"Are they young souls?"

"That would be something I would not look into for thee. They might be stupid people.

"Start growing food and herbs. Will find it will be beneficial for your financial status to grow food into your garden. Tomatoes and onions and foods that they can put upon thy table. Foods that you like to eat, do not grow foods you do not like to eat. The foods you do like to eat, and then you supplement your table, which keeps money in your pocket. Then you will enjoy eating the food that thee have grown. At first, it will cost as much to grow the food as it would to be purchasing of it. In time, you will learn tricks of the trade, as ye call it. You will find it is easy to grow food. Once ye know how.

"Then let us give to thee a healing here upon your heart at this time of life now. Bring the love forth here upon thee. Picture a beautiful pink light. Breathe in the pink light now. Feel it entering your body. Then expand your entire body. Feel it coming forth here into this center. Here is where it is centered your central nervous condition is here. As ye bring forth into your body that love, pink love, it begins to grow that love upon thee at this time. To fulfill the Light for thee and

242

through thee. You are one with that Light now and one with the peace. Feel the comfort coming into your body. Breathe the love forth upon thee. Deeply. It is a growing effect of light for thee. A peaceful love. Into your solar plexus, the beautiful kelly green light. Breathing in the kelly green light. Breathe it in deeply. Now let this energy of the kelly green light expand upward into the heart chakra hither. Feel it coming forth. Expanding.   Feel the energy rising into your right lung. And your right breast. Breathe it in. Into your left lung and left breast. Breathe it in. Feel this energy rising forth to thee. And the central nervous system hither.   Healing as it comes forth. Into your throat chakra, blue light. Bring the light down through your body. To the solar plexus. Feel the healing coming forth. To your solar plexus, as it guides thee upon the Light. Feel that energy rising for thee.

"We have talked about energy, and the feeling of the energy. Produce it; bring it forth into your hips and your thighs, your knees, calves of your legs, your ankles, your feet, your toes as it goes downward through your body. Let it flow and begin to heal. Feel the tingling into your toes that brings up into your ankles, to your thighs, to top of your legs, to your knees, into your thighs. Bring it into your root chakra. Let it come forth and feel that healing coming there. Bring it up into the organs through your spleen chakra. Feel the healing beginning there. Entering all the organs of the body as it heals. Coming upward

through the body through the solar plexus. It is the center of Creation here upon your own being. Create here, from your own solar plexus with your healing. Let it expand there and let it grow widely into your entire body. To feel the energy rising forth. It is that force of Light that is important. Into your heart, breathe beautiful White Light. Through the White Rose I have given to thee. Now repeat after I:

"I and the Father are One.

"I stand forth into the Light of the Christ.

"For I am Light. I am LIGHT.

"I AM THAT LIGHT.

"Breathe deeply to receive the Christ into your body. Feel it radiating through all cells of your body, expanding from the tip of your toes to the tip of your head to the fingertips. Radiating the Light Christ that you have proclaimed your heritage. Call this into your heart. This is where your heart is, to its' whole value of life. Upon the goodness of life for thee. Continue to bring that Christ Light into thee everyday of your life. Do not look for fallacies.

"When you are speaking to a gentleman that thee are interested in, walk softly. Speak softly. As I have guided ye now to do these things. Then ye may meet a man upon what they call internet. Before any commitment is made, see if each other are appreciative of each other's view or image. Then thee may meet with a person, make it public place for a short period of time. Not upon a date. But for a period of time of getting to know each other. When you get to

244

know each other, you may find a greater love that will not bring to thee the tears in your heart. I have spoken to thee how to attract.

"For a person who images a woman to be a model, he is only looking for sexuality. Person who is looking for a friendly companion and a lover, you will find as ye walk upon the Earth's Plane. Beautiful one. We are pleased with your work. Care about yourself. Listen to yourself. You will see what I, Ashlem, are saying. Then slowly begin to change your attack. I don't mean attacking person, you understand? I mean, your verbal attack. You will find I have talked to thee the truth. And it will begin to be the honey that captures the honeybee.

"Then, remember to continue this for rest of your life. You are not the way when you were into school. But you gained that knowledge because of your I AM. You began to be the person that thee are: of great wisdom. It is a lonely world. So now showing the world, be humble. But do not lose your wisdom and your intelligence. Use it when you need. Learn how to use it wisely. Use it when it is necessary. Blessed be thee upon this Earth's Plane. Peace be unto thee, I take my leave."

This was the hardest reading with Ashlem that I have ever experienced. I could sense his sadness, Mary's sadness, and the heaviness of melancholy in God's realms. I knew Ashlem sensed my sadness and tried to lighten the mood when we discussed topics other than the attack. However, he sounded angry about the events. That was the first time I sensed something other than love and happiness in him. Still, his words and wisdom regarding the need for this unveiling to humanity— so we can learn our lessons and pay our karmic debt—helped put it into perspective.

It was difficult, and looking back at those events still feels painful. I had hoped that all of humanity would learn from this and never face such violence again. How many more tragedies would it take? I knew the answer: as many as necessary for humankind to turn their hatred and anger away from each other and learn to love and accept one another, to respect each other and not take advantage for money or power.

These words came to me: 'It is only the beginning.'

For the next four days, I sat in front of my television day and night, watching the rescue efforts shift into recovery efforts. I saw the country put its personal differences aside and come together as one. The days that followed were a mix of beauty and sadness, turning into anger over this attack on innocent people. The quote from Tora! Tora! Tora! by Admiral Isoroku Yamamoto came to mind: *"I fear we have awakened a sleeping giant and filled him with a terrible resolve."*

Chapter Eight: A Return

On September 17, 2001, I restarted my career with QWEST Communications. There were many welcoming arms, and I was glad to be back. I wanted to focus on doing well and rebuilding the success I had before. I was determined not to let any manager treat me that way again. The leadership was aware of the past, and they tread carefully to ensure no impropriety or hint of impropriety occurred.

I developed a simple routine: go to work and come home. Once I felt comfortable again, I decided to learn about herbs. I wanted a degree in licensed herbalism and searched every program I could find. All of them were certificate programs, but I rejected each one. I knew that pharmaceutical companies, governments, and healthcare organizations could use their power to limit practitioners who didn't have a license to practice herbs.

One day, I discovered a program at the Phoenix Institute of Herbal Medicine and Acupuncture. They offered two Master's degree programs: Oriental Medicine and Acupuncture. I asked about just the herbal program, but I was told they did not offer it. To pursue the herbal program, I would need to enroll in the Oriental Medicine program, which encompasses both acupuncture and herbal medicine.

I thought carefully about the program. I didn't want to do acupuncture. I wondered who would actually want needles stuck in themselves. And who really enjoys sticking needles in someone else? I couldn't do it. So, I turned my attention to another profession: teaching.

I enrolled in the University of Phoenix's Master of Education program. After three classes, I realized I didn't like the formal teaching style. I observed that there is a significant amount of political involvement in the education system, which I believe is not in the best interest of the system. I changed my major to a Master of Business degree because I knew it would be more useful.

I started considering opening a healing center, and I wanted to ask Ashlem's opinion on whether it was a good move for me. I believed I had the business background to make it succeed, but I lacked the money and the skills needed for growing foods and herbs. However, I knew I could hire people to assist with that. The bigger question was: where would I get the money to make this happen? On January 31, 2002, I attended the reading. I was very passionate about this healing center, but I had no clear plan for making it a reality.

Ashlem January 31, 2002

"I see a beautiful pink light. The pink light is expanding horizontally. I can see the vison of the darkness with the pink light separating. Now the pink light seems to be radiating upward like the curvature of the Earth or a planet. Now that pink light slowly begins to turn to a beautiful soft golden light, as it expands upward. And, now on the edges of the golden light appear violet light as it keeps expanding upward. It is a sun rising like. But the sun is different. The sun is like our moon, when the moon is full. Soft white. Yet, it reflects these colors upon vapors because I can't see clouds. But I see light coming forth now. It is bright. Upon the planet of the Ancora. It is the crystal energy of Ancora, that causes the reflections of the sky

of the Ancora. Something that most of Brothers of Light come to witness.

"We seem to be in a meadow with some very tiny, beautiful, pink flowers and some very large orange flowers. They look something like tiger lilies, but they're very large; 7-8 inches across. And the crystals that grow out of the White Rock there. The energy is so beautiful.

"A little white unicorn comes forth, and it bounds into all directions. The gravity upon Ancora is very light for the unicorn can leap a long distance like a gazelle. How beautiful. Everything seems pristine. And now with that light, I will call the sun. It is high and there is warmth radiating from it. And now a beautiful multi-colored bird. The multi-colored bird is about the size of a dove. Beautiful colors: blue, and green, and red, and white. It flies around one of these spires. The bird is called an emituhua. And now it lands upon a spire that has an opening about four foot across.

"There are seven spires on this crystal cluster. It lands on a short one. And now in the center appears a beautiful golden flame; a flame like a candle flame that flickers only at the top. The light is very bright and very fulfilling. As it grows in size and intensity, it begins to soften and diminish. As always, Ashlem is standing in that flame. Ashlem is wearing a beautiful rainbow robe. It is beautiful, reflecting through those crystals. Ashlem puts out his finger, and that bird comes to his finger. The bird is speaking another language. I don't know what the bird is saying. Ashlem speaks back to it, and the bird takes flight. The bird flies to a large bush, almost like a tree; beautiful flowers. It seems to pick one of those flowers and flies over to Ashlem. There is a fluid in that flower. Ashlem takes the

250

flower and raises it, and a few drops of the fluid goes down his throat as he raises it above his head. Then the bird takes the flower back, and flies away. A unicorn comes forth, and Ashlem reaches out and scratches around its single horn. Then Ashlem sits in a Lotus position in the middle of that White Rock. Ashlem bows his head and wishes to speak through. I give my permission."

"I am Ashlem known as Golden Image, I say to thee hail. Bringing forth the energies of Ancora always stimulate a person into the force of life and understanding of that force. And the beautiful birds there. There are many hundreds of thousands of them. They love to serve the Brothers of Light and Spirit and Humankind, even upon Ancora. The nectar is collected within the flower, and the flower is then separated from its place. When the nectar is full enough, and the birds may drink of it or they may bring it unto thee. It is a very stimulating drink. Thought you would like to know the existence of that period of time.

"As we come forth to know, the robe of life that I wear here is your signal of life for thee at this time, and the arrangement of a new coming era. It will come into your life soon to come. We have summoned thee forth that we may recognize of your existence. The beautiful planet of Ancora described to thee. Now I want thee to meditate upon it when thee retire into this evening. And take it where I have shown to thee, and see if it does not say to thee of great beauty. There are many questions I will answer for thee, please begin."

"Thank you Ashlem. The book is coming to a close, and with what is happening in the world, a feeling came over me to build or manifest a healing center. We would grow and sell herbs and organic foods; have polarity healing and stress relief; meditation, etc. It feels like it's what I was born to do."

"Are thee speaking of a non-profit clinic?"

"Well, I haven't gotten into that far to determine if it should be nonprofit or for profit. It feels like I should be going that way."

"But of course. There are many peoples, who have same attitude and thought of it. The people are not ready for this. Many have gone for too often, and many have used all their resources, and then have to go back work for their standards of living. But if there is a position to come forth, where people will come, and be able to grow the herbs necessary, and the foods as I have said for over a decade of time. This will occur soon, very soon now. Man will have to learn to grow their fruits again to survive. So, therefore, I have said to them, to learn how to grow food, and no one pay attention to I, Ashlem. That is their choice. But I say to thee of this time, they will regret not paying attention, for they will become hungry, which will formulate what is called the hungry beasts of man.

"They will begin more burglaries through banking, robberies, and so forth. And more peoples will die. And gangs will rise up for survival attitude. If there is places for people to go to grow food, many of them will do this. Not the one who walks upon the street on this day and days of plenty. But they who

have had plenty will not want to be without of it, so they will begin to grow foods, so they can rally into the force of life.

"It is occurring. At this moment of time. But this is not just an American problem. This is a world problem that is happening. So, your position and your thoughts are proper of this time. But right now improbable.

"Soon to come forth another, now, that Robert has water. It is not totally perfected yet, but will be, and there will be growing. If people wish to come out to grow foods there, they may do so. Otherwise, Robert is instructed to grow fruits, and donate it to the food banks, to the best of his ability. That you and other peoples who wish to come out there, and work on your off times, then he will be pleased of this. And the work is to be garden work. Robert wishes to sell the property. But it has not appeared as such yet. If people do not come, first to rally around him and help him, then we will allow the sale to go forth."

"I guess that's why we talked about how it would be such a good base for the nonprofit or the healing center in the future?"

"It was what it was supposed to be. But monies forfeited it. And peoples did not wish to come. Now they will see hungry times. They may change their minds."

"Will there be a time when a healing center will manifest itself for me? I'm doing a business plan and at least getting the ideas down on paper."

"It might be so in time. Let us see how the economy goes in America. If people, as I have said upon that recording of 2001, ye call New Year's Eve, then if people listen to what I say, and begin to keep spending their money and time investing, and so forth, then the economy will rise up again. But if they begin to hold their monies, then it will fall down and become greater recession. Companies are gearing up for it. That is why they are laying everyone off and going bankrupt."

"So that's why you instructed me to grow food. I'm having some difficulty with my house and how to do it."

"What is wrong with your house?"

"I would need to give up the grass that I have."

"Do not have to give up anything."

"So how would I do that? "

"Grow it in pots. Can the grow tomatoes in pots. You can grow carrots in pots also, and you can grow all vegetables in pots."

"I understand. My current financial situation is not good for going out and buying all that stuff right now."

"For pots, Robert will give thee growing pots. They are disposable growing pots. They are good enough. Go to nurseries."

"Ashlem, I have not been feeling well lately, and I was thinking of doing an intestinal cleanse."

"The intestinal cleanse is excellent for thee, and the liver cleanse. Do it once per year. That is good enough. Maintain your digestive tract. The nerve endings here. (Ashlem touches my stomach.) The nerve endings come down to the coccyx, to the autonomic, and into the sympathetic nervous system. Intrude the pericardium. And there are alarm points that are caused by anxiety. And they are the ones that you are speaking of. Through all of this and around your breast. This is the sympathetic nervous system. It is sympathetic to the autonomic, which is down your spinal column and points to all directions Here upon your back, your shoulders to your entire body. They are known as Chakra points. Therefore, if working that direction for thee, then it releases these alarm points for thee and releases the stress.

"It is called Shiatsu. It will help thee, if you find a massage therapist who do Shiatsu. Stop being so stressful. You must control your immediate anger. You let little things anger thee and then they began to hurt here." (Liver and intestines)

"I met a gentleman who seems to be interested in learning, and he is my chiropractor right now."

"Is he married?"

"I do not know."

"If he is or going to divorce, turn your face and walk away from he."

"OK. I was going to ask if this a good relationship for me?"

"But all relationships are good for thee because you learn experience from. Or maybe you become very despondent when it ends. It's good to have friendships, even intimate friendships, but do not disturb another woman's husband. So therefore, at this time, if a man *is married, he only is looking for one existence from thee. Then you must make that choice of yourself. Do they want to become part of a triangle? Then you must learn to say nay. If the man is interested into thee or he is interested, thee must ask the questions to him. Do not be afraid to say. 'Is he married?'"*

"Will he tell me the truth?"

"I do not know."

"OK. Can you tell me if I had a past life with him?"

"To Machu Picchu ancient times. In the little village of Acuva, outside of the great Machu Picchu, you were a little girl. Of that period time, of 13 years of age, grown to be women of that period of time. And he had his eye upon thee. And he was at that age of 28. Ye did not want to be with him. Your father asks thee if he would go and live with this man. Whose name was Toma. And ye say, 'Toma seems to be a gentleman, but I do not want yet to leave thee father.' And he say, 'When do they think ye would leave I and the family?' Ye said unto him, 'But I do not know that.' Toma became despondent with thee, and he married another girl that was younger than thee. It was proper at that time. Then thee were angry with yourself for not listening to your father."

"When I was over in Rome, you told me to go to the Colosseum, because a friend had died in there. Did I watch him die?"

"It is so."

"Will I know this man in this lifetime?"

"It is very possible."

256

"When I do meditation, I keep seeing an older gentleman who's writing on scrolls, and he lives alone at the top of the mountains. He hasn't spoken to me yet. He just continues to write, but he knows that I'm there. Who is that?"

"It is Rebezar Torres."

"Was that a past life, or is that something that's happening?"

"It is something that is happening now."

"And I also saw myself as being a young child, reading a book, and he was still writing on the scrolls. It wasn't the same setting, but I was a young child reading a book, and he said, 'Where's the book?' I didn't know, but it felt like I opened up another book."

"It is the opening up of a life, not a book. Opening up to your life story."

"And that's what they're showing me now? Why would that be important now?"

"But you're the one who wish to know what is happening into the future. From the book, you may project to the future, but first ye have to understand the present in order to project to the future because the present wants the future. So therefore, it is a moment of moving of time upon Earth. It is measured by your existences. Then, I have said to thee before, you might run helter-skelter down thy course of destiny. Do not turn over rocks looking for love. May find slimy worms, or snakes, or scorpions. So as ye walk down this pathway, let love come to thee. Then recognize an interest as we have spoken of. And let it grow. Do not push, and when it is then offered, you make your

decision: yeah or nay. And then receive that energy of love. No matter how long it lasts. It may last for one moment, for one day, for one week, for one year, or for one lifetime. We do not know. But always wherever it is terminated, that is when thee must say, 'I have learned goodness from that relationship.' And not why did it quit? What did I do? What did he do? That means you blame yourself or others."*

"Something I heard in meditation, and I'm not sure who said it, but they said, 'Watch out for the white elephant. Look for the white elephant.' What is that?"

"What is the white elephant?"

"I don't know."

"White elephant represents wisdom. Or it could be a wise man. Or a wise person? I should say, or could it be something that is worthless?"

"Something that is worthless? A white elephant?"

"Did you not hear the symbolism of man who have purchased a white elephant?"

"I've never heard of that. What is it?"

"Something that has no value now, but, could have value before."

"So, it was a warning?"

"It very well could have been."

"In the last meditation, a Master named Ikena, came forth. The vibrations were so strong that night. Who is he?"

"He has been mostly a silent one of the Spirit, but wants to come forth to counsel peoples, and will gather together spirits into his circle of Light and help

them. He was a Master upon the Earth's Plane into Tibet, an ancient time ago."

"So, he came forth because of our Light, and we were open to it then?"

"Aye."

"Why do I change every green amber crystal that I have to a golden color? I bought a ring and not more than two months later, it was golden."

"It is energies of the Earth that changes it, not thee."

"So, this one was given to me at Christmas last year, and it was very dark. And now it is becoming very light, and it's almost like an olive color. One part of it is dark and the bottom part is very light, almost like this is a crystal I have on. I brought the Light of the Christ through it. Is it changing because of Earth as well? Some people have said maybe my energies that are changing it."

"It is the Earth."

"I have two more questions. I had met a gentleman on the internet, and we are just friends. His name was Josh, and I think I told him something that upset him. But I told him the truth. He asked my opinion about a woman he met. He thinks he is in love with her. But every time I say, 'go for it', there's always an excuse. Either that it's not the right time or something else. And I said, well, then let her go and live her life. And if you come back around, then you come back around. He has not spoken to me since."

"Ye hit the nail on the head. He's not ready for a close relationship."

"Yes, I very much understand. He has a lot of growing up to do."

"Seeking of love sometimes brings strange bedfellows. Seeking of love brings different vibrations of Consciousness. What would thee have in common with him? Are ye not seeking of love? Ye are not ready for it, so get ready for it."

"Last question I had. Another gentleman, my friend Brent, was married in December. And he emailed me last week, and he wants to get together tomorrow night. He said he wants to talk. And it is very surprising to hear from him."

"Please send to him, 'Then I will meet you in this public place, like restaurant or something.' Do come alone and leave alone."

"Why? What is the connection? What does he want?"

"All he wants to do is to have a little bit on the side."

"He's not happy with his marriage?"

"Has had nothing to do with happiness. It is to do with conquering."

"He had his chance before him, but not now."

"And he say unto thee, 'Why don't we get together again?' Ye say unto him, 'You have made your choice. Your choice is honorable, and I honor it. If ye were not married like beforehand, that would be different. But ye was married already.'"

"I told him I can't go down that path. He even asked me before he got married to try to talk him out of it. Did he not want her, or did he not want to get married?"

"He wanted ye to think that he did not want to get married. And when ye said I won't go down that path, and ye had nothing to do with whatever his decision was. He would still have married.

"Walk down this pathway of Light for the goodness of your Creation. You are upon your pathway now. The road will become bumpy. Grit your teeth. Do not become angry. Then keep your eyes open for the life of this period of time to live your existence and Christ Consciousness. I want you to picture the beautiful White Rose. Now the White Light from the White Rose. Feeling it penetrating your central nervous system here. It is now penetrating your central nervous system. Expanding. It is calming your central nervous system. Reenergizing and vitalizing your being. Into the heart it comes forth the energy breathing into your Christ Light penetrating thee through your vascular system, into every cell of your body. Begins to radiate into your colon here. Feel the energy passing through your colon. It is healing, revitalizing, and strengthening. Feel it coming forth at this time. Repeat after I, Ashlem:

"I and the Father are One.

"I stand forth into the Light of the Christ.

"For I am Light. I am LIGHT.

"I AM THAT LIGHT.

"Breathing again, now, the power of God comes radiating through your entire being, expanding into your aura. A smile radiates your aura of goodness. Smile more. There's no reason to be angry. Place hand

upon ye forehead. I have opened your Veil. Anger has solidified it. Stop being angry. Let love come to your heart, for the force upon thee and through thee of this time. You will find your way. Do not become despondent because it does not happen tomorrow. It is often said in sports, 'Roll with the punches.'

"You feel like you are rolling with the punches for a long time. Walk into the Light. Have peace unto thee."

"Thank you, Ashlem."

After I finished my reading, my mind wandered to Ashlem's parting words, *"Roll with the punches."* Haven't I been doing that my entire life? Hasn't life already handed me many truckloads of lemons? And how many more would I need? My friends marveled at how I endured so much yet continued.

It wasn't easy, but what other choice did I have? I learned that if you commit suicide, you'll need to come back and do it all over again. That was the last thing I wanted; I had already endured enough heartbreak, sorrow, sadness, disappointment, and tribulation to last me three lifetimes.

A Fresh Start for Everyone

I settled into a comfortable routine for the next six months. Then I received news that my sister was moving back to Pennsylvania with her husband and child. They planned to stay with my parents until they could find stable jobs. My sister believed it was best for many reasons, including moving Dean away from his longstanding drug contacts and having my

262

parents there for support. I agreed, though I wasn't sure my parents were ready for the chaos that would come. They didn't believe me about half of the things that happened. I hoped they wouldn't have to endure what I did, and I hoped Dean would get his life together — for my sister, my nephew, and mostly for himself.

They moved back, and it didn't take long for the antics to start. I learned from my mother that things were not going well, and they decided to move out on their own. I was worried and began to think about how I could help. However, I realized that everyone involved had lessons to learn and experiences to have, but none of those involved me. It wasn't my business, and after careful thought, I decided I didn't want to get involved. These are choices made by adults, and each one bases their decisions on what they believe is best.

My life went on without much drama or stress. Finally, the pendulum of my life paused, and I found myself sitting in the middle. The perfect place to be after the storms of the past. Nothing to learn right now; to enjoy the lessons of the past without reaching for new ones in the future.

In November 2002, I decided to join our local union's committee to advocate for fairness and equity for everyone. I wanted to give back for all the help they had provided over the years. I was a union member, and I felt safer in my job as I became more involved with the union.

I enjoyed being part of the committee and valued the camaraderie it provided. The local elections were approaching, and everyone was discussing the man running for vice president. Gary was a field technician who had worked for the company for several years. He was causing quite a buzz among the longstanding officers. One day, while working, a union representative dropped off his election flyer. I felt a shiver all over. I read his campaign promises and goals for change in the union, and I was hooked. He was very convincing, and the passion he expressed for his convictions was clear. Then I looked at his picture and immediately thought, *"I'm going to marry that man."*

The election was over, and Gary was elected Vice-President. There was excitement and dread. The union members looked forward to change, while the established officers were very cautious. If Gary got his way, many traditional ways would be altered. The union needed fresh ideas and had to become more adaptable to future demands. The movement against unions was growing, and they had to change to stay effective.

Not long after the election, Gary and I met. I felt sparks immediately, and he seemed genuinely interested in me. We formed a friendship after seeing each other at different union events. When he called, we talked for hours. We had a lot in common and understood each other's perspectives. I longed for those phone calls. Finally, I felt wanted and respected by a man.

He was a huge hockey fan, just like me, and we often met up for Phoenix Coyotes games. Naturally, when the Philadelphia Flyers came to town, I wouldn't miss the game, and I always wore my orange and black—true, die-hard Philly fan indeed.

The more we met and talked, the more I got hooked, and I found myself falling in love with him. I was addicted. I would change my schedule to meet him, talk to him, do anything for him. The love I felt for him was like an earthquake and a bomb exploding simultaneously. It was becoming a love that chains and binds you, rocks you to your core. You feel helpless to resist it, and you realize you really want to do everything to be with them. You give up your identity for them, so they can be in your life. You don't consider your own well-being. You're always a little nervous and unsure of yourself and where this relationship is headed. Addiction. That's the best word for it.

And then, just as quickly as it started, it was over. I didn't hear from Gary anymore. Not long after, I met a man from Italy. We started to date right away. He took me to all of his family's celebrations and dinners. I felt at home, and they were very welcoming. Giuseppe and I planned a weekend trip to Sedona at a lovely resort, and as we checked in, he told me that he didn't have any money for the weekend. He said his ex-wife called and needed money for the children, which left him short. I felt trapped. What was I supposed to do? So, I paid for the weekend.

The next weekend, he said he had to do something with his family, and I couldn't be there. I knew something was wrong. Saturday morning, I drove to his apartment, and there was another woman with him. Needless to say, that morning was the end of our relationship. I was angry and hurt. I thought to myself, "I should be accustomed to this by now."

On my way home, I listened to Joni Mitchell's song called "*Cactus Tree.*" I don't think I've ever connected with a song as much as I do this one. The song is about a person who meets man after man, and no one is the right one for her to give up her freedom. Her heart is still full and hollow.

My heart was both hollow and full. I yearned for Gary, and I filled the void with someone who didn't even deserve a second glance. Giuseppe kept calling me and trying to explain himself. He missed me and wanted to reconcile. I knew the truth: he was seeing other women, and I wasn't going to be part of his rotation.

Not long after this breakup, I became very sick. No doctor could figure out what was wrong with me. Every week, he gave me a different prescription, and it made me worse. He thought I had a fatty liver, so an ultrasound was ordered. It came back negative, and when the doctor reviewed the results, he tossed it aside and said, "I don't believe it, I think you have a fatty liver."

I was flabbergasted. He had the results from imaging in his hand, and he didn't believe my liver was healthy. That was my last visit to the doctor's office. I decided it was time to meet with Ashlem, and he would be able to tell me what was wrong.

Ashlem May 29, 2003

"I see a beautiful pink light emanating from a pinpoint of light expanding slowly. And now, in the center of the pink light, a violet light appears. Both the pink and the violet light are expanding rapidly. As they expand, they seem to blend together with each other. This causes the pink light to be very radiant. Magnificent. Now, a pinpoint of white light appears in the center and expands, like it were exploding. Blends together with the other lights, causing the White Light to be very radiant, yet soft. The All-Consuming Christ. The Light of Creation fills the whole picture now.

"Now images are forming in the picture. Shrubbery. Shrubbery has little violet flowers covering them. A forest appearing everywhere. Trees. Some of them are very dense areas. There is a pathway. The dirt pathway. It's about two foot wide. A doe deer comes running down that pathway. Now

266

the doe deer suddenly stops. It stands and shivers for moment. Then it eats the sweet grass on the right side of the pathway around the beautiful flowers. On the other side of the pathway, there are thistles with their beautiful violet-colored flowers blooming. But she seems to know they are thistles. She walks down the back way now.

"Suddenly, a lightning bolt strikes a tree, and she runs down the pathway, wildly in same direction she was going. There's no more rumbling. The trees become less dense, more sunlight. She quietens down. She comes to an intersection of another pathway. These pathways intersect each other. Then, they begin to run parallel. She stops and waits at that moment on the pathway, looking in all directions. Then she walks on slowly. Eating the sweet grass again around the flowers. A buck deer comes down the pathway from the opposite direction. They stop and gaze at each other across the flowers that are blooming between the pathways as they are running parallel to each other now.

"He, the buck deer, steps across the flowers, being careful where he steps, to the pathway she is walking on. She nuzzles him with his nose and her nose. She wags her tail wildly. He wags his. And they walk shoulder-to-shoulder down the pathway in the direction she was moving. You can still see the parallel pathways. They come to another intersection. They both stand in that intersection. The buck deer turns to the right and goes up on that other pathway. But does not go down it. And he turns around. He comes back to the doe deer that is standing very forlorn now. They both turn shoulder-to-shoulder to the left, and go down the pathway at that intersection that leads away from the parallel pathways.

"It enters into a beautiful clearing where magnificent flowers are growing. That beautiful clearing. It is so bright and cheerful; bluebirds singing beautiful songs, flying from tree to tree. Little animals running hither and there. They begin to eat the sweet grass in the meadow. They come to the White Rock. Stands by the pool of water being fed by that waterfall. They walk around the White Rock, then follow the stream down. They disappeared around the bend.

"On the White Rock, appears a beautiful pink flame, a flame like a candle flame only at the top. The light is very bright and very fulfilling as it grows in size and intensity. Now, it begins to soften and diminish. Ashlem, as always, is standing in that flame. Ashlem is wearing that white robe, the robe of simplicity. He has a beautiful smile on his face, and his eyes twinkle, and the flame goes out. Ashlem stands looking down toward the two deer that passed around the trees and can no longer be seen. He smiles, steps from the White Rock. He bends and picks a beautiful White Rose. Comes back to the White Rock. He sits in the lotus position, holding a single White Rose. It is in full bloom. Now, he meditates upon the White Rose. It is grown and become pristine. Perfect. Then, he smells the White Rose, bows his head, and wishes to speak through. I give my permission."

"I am Ashlem, known as Golden Image, to say, 'Hail." I come before thee of this period of time to express to thee, a new pathway of life that thee have chosen at this time, though thee have not been aware of it. It is emotional, and also physical of this time. Ye had been down many pathways in your forest of life. Ye have eaten many thistles in the forest of life, but

268

thee have learned not to eat the thistles anymore. But the sweet grass, that is always available to thee. You are lonely deer in the forest. But there is abundance of life around. If one would look at it, all pathways lead to the clearing of life, and ye have discovered in time yet to come. Let life begin, and the healing within begin stronger. Now there are many questions I will answer for thee, please begin."

"Can I ask you about the image that you gave me? So, the gentleman who was in my life a couple of months ago, he was thistle?"

"Ye have already been answered that question."

"Yes, but he keeps trying to be friends and come back into my life."

"Do you need to eat more thistles?"

"No, believe me, no. Can I ask why I met him? I saw the Light in his eyes. Why would I see that?"

"Because you're looking for any sparkle, of any kind of Light. Isn't that so? Out of the loneliness. Out of desire. Which ye have continued down the pathway, being sure not to eat the thistles. As ye passed down here, ye will see the pathways parallel."

"I've been reading my cards, and the Deception card keeps coming up for him. Is it my deception in my thinking of him, or is he trying to deceive me in some other way?"

"Passing down your pathway, let the trees you passed, let them be. Elst thee eat more thistles."

"I don't want to go through that again. One of the biggest reasons that I've come here today, is that I've been really sick for eight weeks."

"But thee have made own self sick."

"I made my own self sick? From the stress of everything?"

"It is so. It is your anxiety and stress. Doctors say they find nothing wrong."

"They think they did. So, there's nothing wrong with my thyroid?"

"Except they're only in emotionally imbalance. There's nothing."

"Is there anything wrong with my sugar metabolism. That's what they're looking at now."

"Do you have fainting spells?"

"I haven't fainted, but I felt weak. I get sick if I don't eat."

"Blood sugar might be a little bit high or low. But I think it is controllable. Low at times. It is up and down. Into thy heart, there is still nervousness in your central nervous system. You have to let go of that nervous energy created by association. Remove yourself from that existence. Picture blue light. Breathe it in. It is bouncing your thyroid. Ye have been overactive, which causes that faintness. It is coming forth to the central nervous condition. I find no great disorder. The thyroid has been a little high, which is causing the nervousness, and then the stress, and the anxiety of the past only compounds the issues. Your anger. You're doing better now."

"But I was not. I was jealous and I was being deceived."

"Aye. I will give to thee healing of this day to increase the value of your energy."

270

"I've been doing my cards, and the God of Water card keeps coming up. Do you want me to read this? It says the God of Water speaks to a successful, intense man with dark hair and eyes, who has keen perception. Seeks to help and advise you to be open to the emotional rewards offered by influential older men. Tightness and liberality are emphasized during this time. Giving or receiving emotional comfort. The God of Water brings generosity, personal commitment, loyalty, unconditional love and divine report. Is this the buck deer that we were talking about?"

"Your courses of destiny will cross, then decisions have to be made. He will have to make a decision."

"So, our courses are running parallel and intersecting?"

"They have not crossed."

"Is he the one from the boat, the cruise that I took?"

"Your pathways have not yet crossed. What's your rush, my dear? Is it not relevant. Do not all the decisions have to be made into life down each intersection and each pathway? Do not thee have to make decisions? I showed thee a pathway; it is up to thee to put your feet upon it."

Hopefully, I can go in the right direction. I think it was good. My relationship with this one. It showed me that I'm much stronger, and I don't need to put up with that."

"Then you have learned a lesson, yes. And the lesson was the reason for the relationship."

"Can you tell what past life I have with him, if I had any."

"Past life with him, what is his name?"

"Giuseppe."

"In your lifetime in India, a relationship. The lusting was upon his part, not upon thine. You were already spoke for by another man. And the tribe sit back and watched. And the other man won your heart which ye gave to him freely, which broke the heart of the other who return into your life, for that message of wisdom that thee now have gained. Your pathways do not run parallel."

"I would hope not."

"Be more open to helping peoples along the way. For when you help somebody unselfishly be along this pathway, it leads and ripens up to a higher degree. But be honest and truthful with them and helping them and making friends along the way. That leads to the pathway of success."

"I've been trying to do that a lot more in this department. Trying to get along with more people. I have become very close to the team leader. So, I'm hoping that I'm doing well, but I don't know if that is where I'm supposed to be."

"Then let it flow with these dream state of being. Bring it into reality with that force of expression, universal love, that thee experience. Thee will be strong. Anger is your enemy. It will never go away. But ye can control it. Then, realize you're the captain of your ship. Guide it well through the waters. The waters are not always smooth."

"I was thinking about the world today. Is there any advice you would give, knowing what the economy could be like and possibly another war?"

"They are going to be real troubles, my dear. Terrible troubles yet to come forth in America. The world has always been in great turmoil. You will see it upon the shores of America."

"Are there places that are not safe to go, or can you travel freely?"

"Do not go to California. Grounds are very unstable. Armageddon will appear in time. I do not know when. It depends on the decisions of mankind. They are already making first step with war upon Iraq. They have found out that if you go to a country, you cannot kill all of these insurgents. They're finding what Saddam had said to be true; many Americans will die every day. It is not a war of Holiness, as they would like to say it so. America is not trying to tell the Muslims or whoever it is to worship their way. They are saying the oppression of the peoples is a sin. Because their religion does not look upon it that way. That is why they call it holy war."

"But they are saying it was really for their weapons of mass destruction that were supposedly there."

"They are there. Of course, they are there."

"Are we going to find them?"

"In time. Are there any more questions?"

"No."

"The White Rose that is usually brought forth by Mary, I pick for thee a new one in the forest. It is the

273

same Rose. Close your eyes and picture of it. Repeat after I, Ashlem:

"I and the Father are One.

"I stand forth into the Light of the Christ.

"For I am Light. I am LIGHT.

"I AM THAT LIGHT.

"The energy is filling. The Christ Light is becoming stronger. To every part of your body, reverberating. It is cleansing and healing. Breathe into thy solar plexus, the beautiful kelly green light. Expand it, release it. Feeling its reverberation through all your body, and all your limbs. You feel it?

"Now, bring it down through your heart through your internal organs. Feel the healing taking your place. Into your hips. Feel it healing. As it slowly passes down your thighs, through the tops of the legs, through your ankles. Leaping to the toes. Passing through the knees, into the hips, into your hips. Into your solar plexus. Breathing into thy heart. Feel it into your throat. Into your central nervous system. Feel the White Light into your crown chakra. With the energy flow, in and out completely. Covering your entire body. From your head to the tip of your fingers. And the healing is complete. I'm opening the inner eye greater and brighter.

"Beautiful one, it is time you realized the power within. Ye have this power. Be kind, and loving, and gentle. Ye have come a long way in this period of time since we have spoken. I have occasionally watched thee.   It is good. You are losing the weight that was

put on thee by anxiety. Now it is coming off. Ye will
return to a beautiful figure, and as ye reach this
pathway, another pathway will cross your course of
destiny. Ye will see. Remember all that thee have
learned on this great pathway. Ye have wandered
down aimlessly. Bumping into the trees and thistles
along the pathway. But each one was a learning
experience. Then let it be so, the wisdom within.

"There is a child spirit that is standing nearby.
A female. She's standing there smiling.

"I give to thee the sign of peace, our covenant: Of
the Father and of the Son, and of thy Holy Spirit, that
the circle of God is eternal with thee. Never beginning,
never ending, and never to be separated from the
whole, and that is thee. Fly beautiful dove. Peace be
unto thee; I take my leave."

"Thank you, Ashlem."

I already felt so much better after the healing Ashlem
gave me. Now, my mind was clearer, and I could reflect on the
reading. A new man is coming into my life, and we will walk
down the path together. But it was not Gary. Why can't I get him
out of my head and heart?

And who was this little female spirit standing nearby? I
recall from a class Ashlem taught that the child spirit brings its
parents together. Maybe that's why it is close to me. I looked
forward to meeting this man. However, my past cautioned me
not to get too excited. I'd been down this road before.

As summer turned into fall, I got an unexpected call: it
was Gary. And just like that, I was drawn back in. He called

every day, and we talked for hours. He listened to me, comforted me, laughed with me, and made me feel wanted. Remember how I described my feelings for him: addiction. And here I was again.

I waited for Gary to call me, and I felt anxious when he didn't call during his usual times. When he had time, he would call. I listened as he complained about the Arizona Courts and how he couldn't get a fair trial for his child custody case. He was obsessed with gaining custody of his boys. He accused her of everything possible. I sat there and listened. I tried to be someone I wasn't. I supported him, consoled him, and said everything that would make him feel better. I had a feeling that most of what he accused her of didn't really happen. I waited and waited for it to be over. However, when one case ended, another one began.

During one conversation, he told me he was moving to Avondale, which was seventy-five miles away from me. He was moving in the wrong direction. I tried to be understanding; he said the house he bought was a steal, and since Phoenix was expanding in that direction, he would make a lot of money on it when he sold it.

As the holiday season arrived, I didn't hear much from Gary. He was busy with his family, and especially his children. The holidays were always quiet for me. I know most people felt sorry for me since I had no family here in Arizona and no family of my own. It became easier and easier with each passing year.

My life became quite routine: work, home, calls from Gary, and school. After my third semester at the University of Phoenix, I decided I had had enough of their MBA program. I hadn't learned anything; it was a waste of time and money, so I dropped out. I knew I wanted to pursue an herbal program to become an herbalist, but I still hadn't found the right one. I considered acupuncture school again or even earning a degree in naturopathic medicine. The naturopathic school sounded worse: I would be performing IVs and minor medical procedures. No, that's not for me.

One day in May 2004, I received another unexpected call. This time, it was my sister, and she was moving back to Arizona with Dean. She didn't explain why and wanted to stop by when she arrived, since they were already on the road. I had a sinking feeling this wouldn't be good news. But I remained silent and waited for her to arrive.

When she arrived in town, they invited me to dinner; even worse, I knew it was going to be bad news. When I got to the restaurant, I noticed she was a little swollen around the middle. She told me she was pregnant again, and our parents were not supportive at all, so they decided to go back to Arizona. Dean worked in construction, and there was a lot of building here compared to what was in Pennsylvania. Dean could easily get a job and support them. They had already leased an apartment and were happy. She asked me to be happy for her. I told her that I was happy if she was happy, and I would be there to support her decision.

When I arrived home, I received a call from my parents asking if she had told me, and I said I had. I told my mother, *"It's her life and she needs to do what is best."* After we hung up, I thought to myself, in three months, she will be at your door. I was wrong; it only took six weeks.

Chapter Nine: An Unexpected Return

One Friday night, I was at the movies with friends, watching *The Secret,* when I noticed my cell phone was ringing nonstop. I answered it, and it was my sister, angry and hysterical. She had come home from work after 9:00 pm to find her three-year-old alone on the couch, and her husband locked in the bedroom, high on drugs. She decided she had had enough and packed herself, the baby, and her dog, heading over to my house. I told her I would leave and meet her there.

After we settled in, she told me a little bit about what was going on. There was no money for rent or utilities because he was spending it all on drugs. I asked her if she wanted to move in, and she agreed. She was about five months pregnant, and a new baby would be arriving. Her situation was about to become even more dire.

The whole world had turned upside down. My sister worked in the evening, and I worked during the day. I had to be a mom until she came home. My oldest nephew was three, so it wasn't as tricky as caring for a newborn. He was a good boy, listened, and didn't really act out. The other responsibility I took on was the financial one. She wouldn't be able to help much with food, utilities, or other expenses. She still needed to handle the responsibilities she and her husband had.

The following week, she returned to the apartment, packed her belongings, and moved them into my house. Luckily, I had two extra bedrooms that were unused. My nephew seemed to take things in stride. I never heard him say he wanted to go home; although, he might have spoken to my sister.

Dean tried his best to win back my sister. She held her ground for a while, but Dean insisted on seeing his son. My sister felt it was the right thing to do, although she would supervise the visit. One day, we returned to the house, and I sensed that something was amiss. Tasha, my Akita, was acting a little weird. I walked into the kitchen and noticed that a box of protein shakes was open, and food was missing from the pantry and refrigerator. I went up to my bedroom and did not see anything missing. My sister swore, and I ran into her bedroom. Money had been taken; money saved for food and my nephews' care.

I knew it had to be Dean. He crawled through my large dog door for my 75# Akita to get inside the house, and Tasha recognized him and let him in. Otherwise, she would have attacked the intruder. Who else could have broken into the house without my Akita stopping them and only taken my food and my sister's money? He knew he wouldn't be prosecuted for the food, and since my sister was still married to him, that money was community property, and he had every right to it.

I was furious. If he needed food, I would have given it to him, but don't enter my home without permission to steal. Later, I noticed that my SSN card and my first marriage certificate were stolen—both items necessary for identity theft. Months later, I received a demand letter from a few utility companies for non-payment, and I had an address on my credit report for a house in the West Valley. I never lived in the West Valley and had owned my home for years before that address was reported.

My parents tried to calm me down, saying, *"It's only food."* But to me, that wasn't the issue. My home is my castle, and I don't let anyone in to steal. I will give, but don't take without asking. They had been trying for years to settle the animosity between Dean and me, and they always seemed to take his side. Even after Dean keyed their truck and stole from them, they wanted peace and expected me to go along with their approach. That is not me and never will be. I forbid Dean from ever coming to my house again, or I will have him arrested for trespassing. My sister was contemplating divorce. I knew she still loved him and felt it would be a failure in her life, even if it was the right choice.

As summer ended, my anxiety grew. The baby was expected to be born in a few months. I wasn't sure how I could handle being a step-in-parent. I didn't have children for that reason. The second reason was that the baby was due on November 2nd, which would make him a Scorpio, and we all know the volatile emotional nature of water signs, such as Scorpios. Very different from this Air-Fire-Fire girl.

I decided it was time to talk to Ashlem. I knew this new development was unexpected, and I wasn't sure how to handle it. I also wanted to ask about Gary again. He seemed like he was making his way back to me. Perhaps, he decided it was time for us.

Ashlem September 23, 2004

"I see a beautiful pink light. The light is oval-shaped. The light radiates energy from the center out. Beautiful waves of pink light. And now, in the center of the pink light, a golden light appears and does the same, expanding. And now, in the center of the golden light, a green light appears and does the same, expanding. And now in the center of the green light, a violet does the same, expands. And now, a pinpoint of white

light appears and expands in the center, consuming the other colors, leaving behind beautiful, soft White Light where the White Light is the All-Consuming Christ, the Light of Creation. Now, fills the whole picture with beautiful, soft White Light. Images are forming in the White Light. It is a flock of white doves. There are eight beautiful white doves. They are flying like eagles over the beautiful forest below. And now the leader of these, always leading in front, dives down, and the other doves dive with her.

"They come down to the beautiful clearing. The wildflowers appearing beautifully magnificent. Roses are among the wildflowers growing. The spring of water that comes out of the forest, and the waterfall, and the spring that waters the little stream that runs again down to the forest. Again, how beautiful. Everything is pristine, magnificent. Now the doves are below the treetops, flying around this beautiful clearing.

"The White Rock appearing, standing above with flowers. The first white dove, leading the other seven, lands upon the White Rock. An oval shape of White Light appears. The other doves fly around the clearing. Now, before the White Light, a candle flame appears: a golden flame. The flame, like a candle flame, that flickers only at the top. It begins to soften and diminish. As always, Ashlem is standing in that flame. Ashlem looks at the White Light that is oval-shaped in front of him. And he bows to the White Light.

"And now images are forming in that oval-shaped White Light. It is the Blessed Virgin Mary. Mary has in her hands a beautiful White Rose, the Rose of the Christ. Now, the other doves come forward and seem to hover behind Mary.

And they turn into beautiful Angels. First very small, then, they expand. Very etheric. They begin to sing beautiful songs. Each Angel has a pink heart on their gown. How beautiful they are. Ashlem ends his prayer and bows to the Blessed Virgin Mary, and I notice on his white gown, he has a beautiful pink heart embroidered over his heart. Ashlem is wearing his beautiful white robe of simplicity, expressing simple love.

"Mary begins to speak in golden words, come forth and the words say, **'Unto thee, my friend, Ashlem, forever we have been together. It seems of this time, you have served, I, with great honor and love, and I appreciate your service. You have brought forth they who I have spoken to in this life. And there's still more to come.'**

"She turned sideways, and hands Ashlem the beautiful White Rose, she says, **'Ashlem, this is Tracey's beautiful White Rose of the Christ. Bring it within her and return to I, when you are finished. I am always with thee, also, with love and peace.'"**

"Mary fades, but the angels remain singing, Ashlem takes the White Rose, and he sits in a lotus position, and smells of the White Rose. He bows his head and wishes to speak through. I give my permission."

"I am Ashlem, known as Golden Image, I say to thee, 'Hail.' The Blessed Virgin Mary has come forth once again as She has so many times before to express the love and peace of mankind here upon the Earth's Plane. And her unto thee, that you have not been forgotten. Of these periods of life here, She brings to thee, your Christ Rose, that she has planted in her garden. I will return it to She, and She will replant it

282

in her garden again, forever and forever. One who follows the Light within has patience. They find that which they need, for love blooms everywhere, like the flowers of the days. Let the love come forward at this time for thee. Now there are many questions please begin."

"So, Mary brought my seven angels to me?"

"Aye."

"And the heart on their gowns, what does that mean?"

"What does it mean to thee, my dear?"

"To me, they're showing the love that I have for people, and it's on their hearts and they're giving..."

"But is it the love of others also?"

"Yes.

"Then are thee in store for love?"

"I hope so."

"Why do you think we have brought the hearts to thee? You should."

"Yes, I know. I want to talk about that a little bit later, but I think what's really troubling me a lot is my sister. I really need help with my home situation, which is with my sister, and my nephew, and the new baby coming."

"Is she divorced from her husband?"

"No."

"Where is her husband?"

"He is here, living in Arizona?"

"Is he living with thee also?"

"No."

"Is she going to divorce him?"

"I don't know. She said yes, and then she doesn't do anything. Then she changes her mind."

"It is up to thee my dear. Remember, you are the captain of your ship. Your ship is also your home, is it not? You are the king of your own castle. The queen of your own castle as it is said. Then treat it as such. Are thee responsible for your sister's work? And her way of life. Is she working?"

"She is working."

"And you are caring for her child? Is she paying thee rent?"

"Not really."

"And why not?"

"She doesn't make a lot of money. She's just starting to go back to work. But the husband has a drug problem, and he does not have money for her."

"Does he pay child support?"

"No."

"Why not?"

"Up until about 30 days ago, he was, but now he is taking that money and using it to buy drugs."

"Then she must force him to pay for his child, and she is going to pay half, also, and the newborn come forth. Are you going to raise this child yourself?"

"I don't want to."

"Then say the word nay. For they come through your sister's womb, for the family incarnate group of this period of time. They did not come through her womb for thee to raise them. Let us make that straight. Do you understand?"

284

"I feel very responsible."

"That is because you are a responsible person, but is there an end to someone else's responsibility?"

"Yes, I feel that's the case. I feel like I'm using my guilt, and because I care about my sister and these children. I don't want anything to happen to them. But I've just been overwhelmed by it. I don't know where that fine line is."

"To understand this life force of this time, you are here to help her get on her feet. Set a time limit, with reasonable things, and keep to it. Any if she is not gone by that period of time, and when she has not put the effort forth, show her where the door opens. My dear, for this period of time, you have to clear your slate, so to speak. There are changes coming in your life. Changes you have been asking for. If you do not have time to entertain these changes, they will pass like two ships in the night. I have nothing against your sister. She is a good woman. But she will take all that you have. She must be responsible for her life. She married the gentleman when people told her not to do, but she ignored them, and now she is in trouble again. Your mother and father have turned their face on her? How much would it take for thee to do the same?"

"I know. When I heard that they decided to move back to Arizona, I knew she would be back at my doorstep. It didn't take a very long time. And it has been very draining."

"And thee say to your sister, 'I love thee, but I have put my life on hold for thee to be here. It is time for ye to put your life on hold and let me live mine.'"

"Would it be good to set a time frame like, after the baby is born?"

"Of course, ye want to help her. It is good to do that. The baby is born, and then you set a time limit for her to find her own place, her job. You cannot afford to support her and her own family."

"I never wanted to do that but that's all I feel that I have been doing. Do I have anything that I need to do with these two children other than being an aunt?"

"You will be their aunt and advise them as they grow up in different ways. You will still be members of the family, but they have chosen their mother's womb to come through, their father's seed. They have done it for a purpose and a reason. They may see their father's inability to be a man and make them be to come forth at this time. They are old souls."

"We're talking about my situation with my parents, which is really not good. They want to come out for Thanksgiving or Christmas. I'm just trying to do the best for everybody. But in the middle of everything, I don't even want to be here."

"I understand. You have to say to mother and father, 'I have so many people in my household now. It is not big enough.' Say to them, 'If my sister moves out to find her place, then, it would be delightful to visit with thee and father.' Then let them be the judge of it. If your sister is still living here, it would be a burden upon thee."

"I don't know how to deal with my mother about things. When I tried to talk to her about them, she becomes so angry and she doesn't want to listen."

"What is she angry about?"

"In my opinion, she's just angry that she can't control the situation. And no one is listening to her or doing what she would."

"Then you say to her, 'Mother, I will do it my way.'"

"I have done that, but then she doesn't speak to me, and she is not speaking to me now."

"It's alright."

"It's just difficult. I've got so much going on in my life. It's just one more thing I feel like I have to fight."

"You don't have to fight it, you have to learn to say no. It is what you have to say. 'No, I cannot do it. I love you. But I cannot do it.'"

"And my father speaks to me. He's actually very understanding. He makes it easier, but it's just not easy for a lot of things.

"I have a big question about Gary, and you said I've been waiting for a while. I always had the feeling that maybe he was my life mate, but we had some trials..."

Ashlem shakes his head no. **"But you care about each other, and do you get together occasionally?"**

"I see him occasionally, but I talk to him much more."

"You do not date him anymore?"

"No."

"Who are thee dating?"

"I am not dating anyone."

"Then, we have spoken to you so that you realize you need to clean your household. Then you can go back to your relationships to find the loved one that is to come forth soon."

"So, it's not Gary then?"

"Certainly not. You have decided that before."

"That he was not my love mate?"

"Of course you have."

"I didn't know that. So, there is someone else coming?"

"Of course there is. You have looked into the eyes of Gary, and did you see the Christ shining there? Did you find him to be purity of love and peace? Did you find him to be gentle and caring?"

"He is gentle and caring."

"He is demanding also, is he not?"

"Yes."

"That is not your love mate."

"He was just another lesson to learn?"

"Aye."

"So, there's another one coming. Can you tell me anything about him? Like where I will meet him? Is it through work or through people or a different type of thing?"

"It is not written into the Akashic's where you're going to meet him and how you're going to meet him. But only that the course of destinies will cross forth soon. So, you keep working and stop turning over stones, looking again."

"OK."

"Just work. Do the things you need to clean your household. To understand the force that is within. Be

288

open and ready for love to come your way. Then let it come your way. If the person is only interested in your body, then let him go upon his way. The person comes into your life, who is willing to work with thee, and is interested in your body, also, and he's ready to work for thee to make your life more pleasant, then that is the one you look closely at."

"OK. I am concerned with the world today, and what is going on with the election, wars etc."

"I have been telling people, and I do not care one way or the other myself, but I say to thee, if Mr Bush is reelected into the office, there will be Armageddon soon. They call it World War Three. It is inevitable because he has angered all the Arab Nations. They are making secret treaties with each other. Something they have not done in 4,000 years, and they'll be against oppression by America and Israel. Then North Korea will sell nuclear weapons and the ability to launch them to a third-world country. That will begin WWIII or Armageddon.

"If Mr. Kerry is involved, in other words, to become President, he will first stay by his negotiations with the Arab Nations. He is not stupid man; he is wise man. The political situation that is being done upon America, are very childish. But they do not know any difference of this time. But that is what my opinion is of this time. Then, you will find into your news pattern to come forth, some crop circles into Nebraska. The wheat fields into Kansas and so forth into that area.

"The Brotherhood of Light is going to increase the communication with Man upon the Earth's Plane, Americans also, to see and let them understand that it is going to be. They will interpret one of the crop circles as a message to be, 'Let there be Peace reigning upon your planet.' You begin to understand that there have been some crop circles already, but the government keeps them quiet. Do not want people to think The Brotherhood of Light is here. Mr. Bush has refused the Brotherhood of Light, as every president has been visited. He refuses to go with the Brotherhood of Light or to entertain them. Therefore, they have wiped the visitation out of his mind."

"Are we going to see more of what happened in the 2000 election?"

"Terrorists? It is so. It is very possible at this moment of time, as we are speaking, they are preparing an atomic weapon in a suitcase."

"For the United States?"

"That will be exploded in the United States."

"Are we safe here in Phoenix?"

"It's not in Phoenix; it has no strategic command posts. They are going to put their efforts where the people are most: New York and Los Angeles."

"Did you say it would be a nuclear bomb?"

"It will be a dirty bomb."

"So, there will be many fallouts from that..."

"Many illnesses."

"There are many hurricanes happening..."

"That is not caused by Saddam Hussein's peoples. That is caused by the changing of the Earth, which is called shifting of the poles at this time. The great trenches in the Pacific Ocean, are opening wider, causing superheating of the subterranean waters as they have already found that the oceans are warmer than they were before. Therefore, they are melting the polar caps, and soon the oceans will rise 20 feet. There are many seaports that will be underwater completely. These are things to come forth yet. Will the polar caps move across the face of the Earth? Nay. They are melting."

"I completely forgot, but Atlantis was located off Florida, right?"

"It is part of the Floridian area. Of course it is. Bemini being part of it. Atlantis was those islands out there. As was Cuba part of Atlantis, before the sinking of it. But Poseidon is the area that is off of Florida. Bemini is where the Fountain of Youth was found. It is still there."

"Ok. I don't have any more questions."

"Of coming forth of this Earth's Plane, it is important to pass peace along your way when you are talking to peoples. It is not proper to say, I do not think that this President is doing us any good. People are buying into his money by making money. The rich person is going to work for Mr. Bush because he has been promised more money from his money. So, he's going to work for Bush. He does not care if the world is going to be destroyed. So, it is difficult to

understand that. When you speak to the people who are not rich, and they begin to understand. If there is enough of them realize what Mr. Bush is doing to United States, they will not vote in that direction of he, but into the direction of the other. We do not say that Mr. Kerry is a great President. He has to prove himself like other peoples do. But of this time of life, he has to find of himself. You already know what Mr. Bush is about; you do not know Mr. Kerry. Some people say it's best to keep the devil you know than the one you don't. And that's sad."

"I wanted to ask about my life work. Am I still on my path?"

"You are walking on your path, but you have not grown the herbs we have spoken of."

"No, I have not. I have a lot going on."

"Aye. I understand. When you screw your head tightly upon your shoulders, you begin to realize what I, Ashlem, have said. The urge will come unto thee greatly. You will not be able to ignore it. That is when you have to do the herbs. Do thee understand?"

"Is it necessary to take a class on how to use the herbs; how to mix them? Is that going to come to me? How do I get that knowledge?"

"Read books. Read the books on herbs and how to heal with them, and what compounds to use. How to find the herbs to use of this time. You say this herb does this and this herb does that. You combine the herbs together. They work on the same organism of

the body. For the same disease as you're combining together to make compounds to use in that matter. Talk to health food stores about the herbs that you need. They have places where you can go to classes.

"If a person charges a great deal of money for their service, their service is not worth it. But if a person is working with other people to learn, and to express the need of the herbs of this time, then that is the person you must go to. Then learn about the herbs and how to use them. Using experimentation upon yourself and others, but I say to thee, do not say to the people, 'You take this herb for this and this herb for that.' You would say, 'If I had your illness, I would use this herb and that herb for this purpose.'"

"Why would the government pick on little old me?"

"They're going to try to shut down the herbal industry, my dear. Why do you think I am expressing to people to grow herbs? Then if you wish to work upon the internet over herbs, you may do so to start a program of barter upon the internet with herbs. Then that would be a good service. No money exchanged. You can then pass it through the mail. Use what is called the plastic peanut butter jars. We have experimented with this and found it is very inexpensive. The jars do not weigh very much at all. And the herbs will then be sending through the mail.

"If someone requires a great amount of something, then you have to say to them, 'Then, it will cost, I, X amount of dollars, will thee reimburse, I, for the herbs?' If they do not have herbs of which you need this time. So therefore, you may get herbs that grow into Texas or herbs that grow into New Jersey or ones that do not grow into your area.

"You can give to them chapparal. That can be craft-harvested; wildcrafting. You go forth into the desert and can pick the chaparral. You cannot sell it. But there is no law against giving it away. And that is what the government is going to try to shut down. They have shut down chaparral from being sold into your herb houses. So, they cannot sell chapparal because people do not know how to use it. But they, who do know how to get it, know how to use it.

"Chaparral grows wild into your area of Arizona. It is the bush that thee call, creosote. The leaf is called chaparral. It is the Indian bush of medicine used for many different things. Study it and you will find you have to merely go out and cut the branches into small areas. Put them into buckets. And leave them sit. It is best time to harvest them, is when you see it's essential oils are on the leaf. You can see it; they glisten. Do not pick it after it has just flowered. But you do this when the essential oils are readily upon it. Then you put them in the bucket and let them sit and dry. When they are dried out, you take the small pieces of stems, and with your fingers, you break the leaves off. And what other stems drop into the bucket, you need to take them out. But after you have harvested this, you take the stems out of the bucket and throw them away. And their leaves, after they have dried up, are very small powdery things.

That is your chaparral. Take all the stems out. It is good for removing tumors. It is good for people who think they have a breast tumor. It will start dissolving the tumor if it is caught in time. If the tumor is too big, it will not do much for it."

"Would it be beneficial to try to speak to an Indian medicine man?"

"If you have the opportunity to do so, then certainly do that, for they have the knowledge. When you speak about herbs to other people, it opens the door. Then you will have knowledge from speaking about it. Then you ask them questions like, 'What good is marshmallow?' I believe it is good for feminine disorders. I think it has something to do with menstrual, I am not sure. I am not an herbologist. But I do know that the herbs are going to be essential. Soon to come forth. Look at men's greed in the pharmaceutical companies.

"Take hand, put upon thy heart. Mary bring to thee your White Rose of the Christ. Close your eyes and see the beautiful White Rose of the Christ.

"I and the Father are One.

"I stand forth into the Light of the Christ.

"For I am Light. I am LIGHT.

"I AM THAT LIGHT.

"Breathe deeply, receiving the Christ into your body. This is the Hand of the Father upon thee. Feel the energy and the power of the glory of the energy passing through thee. Entering your body, expanding into every cell of your body, through your vascular

system. Feel the power of God rise up into thee. It enters every atom of your body and into nuclei of every atom of your body where the Christ truly lieth. Then by your proclamation, you bring this Christ Light unto yourself of this time. For the experience of life into thee and through thee. It is important to remember of these things of being always.

"At this time, you must dedicate yourself to the Christ each morning. Do not forget it anymore. It is important to do this, because it shines around you, and people see your aura of purity of love, and then you are welcome greater into the higher places that come forth. You turn away the negative people who surround thee. It is how to do this. You are then more of a loving person yourself, and your lovemate will look for the Christ. Is it important to understand of these things.

"Place hand upon forehead. (Ashlem sings a Tibetan prayer). *Let us lift your Veil and open your inner eye wider. Then let the greater wisdom come through. We open your crown chakra to be one with the Christ of this lifetime.*

"We are pleased with your progress, it is certain. When I call of thee, come forth. For you know here in your heart, when I call of thee to understand that force of life in this period time, for that experience of oneness to thee. It is important of this time. There are many things coming forth into your life. You must live your life. You must be the captain of your ship. The Queen of your Castle. Then it is not being rude of

this lifetime, my dear. You have gone through your pains of suffering of life, and your financial things, and your mother and father has become angry with thee over them, isn't that so? But you say to them all, you have to conduct your life to whatever your financial needs are. You love your sister and your nephews of this life force to come forth of this time. You love your family, but it is time that they go upon their way to stand for their own two feet. So, you can stand on your two feet.

"I give to thee this sign of peace. My covenant unto the Father, and of the Son, and to thee, thy Holy Spirit that the circle of God is eternal. Never beginning, never ending, and never to be separated from the whole, and that is thee. That is where life begins at this time. That is true love, universal love. You have cared and you have shared. You do not have to be washed down the drain. Walk into the Light. Peace be unto thee; I take my leave."

After leaving, I laughed to myself. I didn't call for Ashlem; he was calling for me.

I realized I had a lot of work ahead of me. I needed to talk with my sister about making plans to move out after the baby is born. I also needed to establish boundaries with my parents. Additionally, I had to clean my house to prepare for my lifemate to enter my life. Wow. I took on more responsibility than I thought I could handle, and now I have lessons to learn about prioritizing myself. My father had repeatedly called me selfish, and now my actions would reinforce that. I felt like I was in a dilemma. I invited my sister to come and live with me, and now I have to ask her to leave.

Ashlem encouraged me to do this because it was a lesson for the family to learn, and no one really wanted to learn it. My sister didn't want to learn how to stand on her own and raise her boys, my parents wanted to control and guide our lives, and I didn't want to reinforce the idea that I was selfish.

I postponed those lessons and discussions because they felt overwhelming. As October progressed, my anxiety and nervousness reached a peak. Early on a Friday morning, my sister knocked on my bedroom door, came in, and said, *"Today's the day."* I took a deep, shock-filled breath and said, *"Okay."* Then, we headed to the hospital. My new life was here, and whether I was ready or not, it was changing.

My Second Nephew Arrives

My second nephew was born without complications. I was the second person to hold him. I had never seen a newborn before and wondered why his hands and feet looked so blue and purple. The nurses told me this was normal and would change in a day or two. I was more involved with this baby than with my first nephew, and I knew I would need to learn how to change diapers, feed him, hold him to give comfort, and be a step-in mom, while my sister was at work. I wasn't sure if I could do it. Thankfully, she had six weeks of maternity leave so I could learn from her.

The day she came home from the hospital, I was worried about how my Akita would react to the baby. My sister set the baby carrier on the floor, and Tasha came running over. She

298

sniffed the baby everywhere, which made the baby fuss and cry a little. Tasha pawed at the baby to ensure it was okay, and that was it. Tasha now had another one to care for and protect. She guarded the two boys day and night, sleeping in their room and constantly staying beside them. She understood they were members of the pack, and she took her job very seriously. During those days, she barely spent any time with me, nor was she outside like she usually would be.

After my sister went back to work, my real anxiety and stress started. I worked during the day while she worked the second shift, so someone was always there for the baby and toddler. After a full day of work, I would pick up the children from the babysitter, and my responsibilities would begin. Feeding, changing diapers, entertaining the toddler, giving baths, and getting them to bed. Most nights, the baby would wake up screaming around 10:00 pm and wouldn't calm down. I would pick him up, and he would scream even louder. I was at my wits' end. Many times, I called my sister and asked her for advice on what to do. Most of the time, she said he would settle down if he was held – not by me, though.

I set my alarm to wake up at 1:00 am for his next feeding, and my sister would come home around 2:30 am. Then I would go back to sleep until 6:00 am. The next day, it would all start over. I was still managing a team of twenty-one people, dealing with all their personalities, and handling the demands of that group—some understood my situation as being an unprepared step-in mom.

One night, when it was quiet, my dog came into the house and howled, then went back outside. She did this several times, and it was the first time she had ever done it. The third time, I went outside and found her lying against the cement fence. She looked miserable and in pain. I called my sister, and immediately she said, *"I think her stomach is twisted. I watched many of the emergency vet shows on TV, and the symptoms are the same."* She told me I had to get her to the veterinarian right away because we didn't have much time.

I packed up the kids, and Tasha and my sister left work immediately to meet me at the emergency veterinarian's office. It was almost 11:00 pm, and they confirmed she had a twisted stomach, and we had very little time left. I didn't have the money for the surgery, so I called my parents, which was 2:00 a.m. in Pennsylvania. They agreed to pay for the surgery, and I told them I would reimburse them.

The vet techs quickly whisked her away to the surgery room, and I was panicked. Tasha was my saving grace, my companion, my protector, and most of all, the most loyal and reliable thing in my life. They instructed me to go home, and when the surgery was over, they would call me. As I drove home, I recalled the day I bought her.

The breeder had two litters of puppies for sale. I'd estimate about ten to twelve puppies running around the enclosure. I walked around it three times and kept my eyes on two others. A friend was with me; she bred the Pomeranians I had and pointed to Tasha, saying, *"This is yours. She's been following you the entire time. She's picking you."* I looked at her and bent down to pet her. My friend was right; this was my puppy. I paid the fee, and we left, and Tasha has been loyal to me ever since. She's always belonged to me, and I've always belonged to her.

For the next three hours, I couldn't relax. Tasha was my girl, and I wasn't sure if I could handle another loss in my life. At 2:00 a.m., the vet called and told me we were lucky; the surgery couldn't have happened any later for her survival. When she opened Tasha up, some tissue had turned black, which was an ominous sign. She untwisted her stomach, and the tissue turned pink. She would make it. I thanked God for the mercy He showed to Tasha. She wasn't ready to leave me, as she hadn't finished her mission with me.

During my conversation with the vet, she said she would need to keep Tasha for three days to ensure there were no negative effects from the surgery. I could pick her up on Monday evening. Around 4:00 pm that day, the vet's office called me and said, "Please come and get her. She won't lie down, she's pacing, and with all the activity, she could cause the stitches to open, and it would be the worst-case scenario for her." The tech mentioned it was obvious that she would be better off at home with me. I smiled and thought, *"That's my girl."* She has a job to do, and a 'little thing' like a twisted stomach wouldn't stop her.

I received strict instructions: no jumping, no running, and no stairs. I placed the baby gate at the bottom of my stairs and locked the doggy door so she could not go in and out as she pleased. When we arrived home, she was so happy to be there. She was jumping up at me, and she leaped over the baby gate to run upstairs to check on the baby. I tried to limit her activity to no avail. She was going to do what she wanted, and I smiled and thought to myself, *"That's my girl."*

Tasha healed quickly. Her will to live was stronger than anything I had ever witnessed. I realized I learned another lesson: the power to heal yourself comes from the strongest desire to live. No matter the odds of surviving a sickness or accident, if you believe you can heal yourself and it's not your time to return to spirit, you will survive and thrive.

I took a deep breath, another crisis averted. Now it was time to focus on my home situation. The holidays were approaching, and my parents were coming to visit. At least I would get a break from caregiving, and I desperately needed it. Some women are not meant to have children, and I realized I was one of those. My parents, on the other hand, were not convinced and started pressuring me to have children. They loved being grandparents and wanted more. When they brought up the subject, my response was, "*If you want more, then you need to talk to my sister.*" My father didn't like that response and responded to me, "*You are being selfish.*" To end the conversation, I replied, "*You're damn right I am.*" And that was the last time I heard anything else about giving them grandchildren.

On December 26, 2004, a 9.3-magnitude earthquake shook the Indian Ocean tectonic plates, which caused the greatest fault rupture ever observed, and an ensuing tsunami with waves reaching 100 feet hit Thailand. I felt like it was 9/11 all over again. I was sitting in front of my TV, watching videos of the tsunami approaching. I watched as the survivors wailed for the safe return of their loved ones. I saw people travelling on foot from one makeshift camp to another to identify the remains of their loved ones. Once again, I cried for hours.

It is the deadliest tsunami in history, the deadliest natural disaster of the 21st century, and one of the deadliest natural disasters recorded. It killed approximately 228,000 people across 14 countries. No nation was spared, as many

Europeans and others vacationed in Thailand during the Christmas season. If this were a sign of what the future holds, I was fearful for the Earth and its people.

As Spring 2005 arrived, I felt like I was drowning. This wasn't the life I wanted. I was so unhappy that my mental health started to decline. I wasn't sleeping, and I was gaining weight. Gary and I spoke occasionally during this period. He loved children and understood the challenges of raising them, having two boys himself. He would give me advice on how to handle things, but most importantly, he was my lifeline. Those conversations were like a life buoy to me.

I needed to find something that would bring me happiness, and I wanted to start herb training because it was vital to my future. One day, I woke up and thought, *"Go to acupuncture school, learn herbs. It'll be alright. You can stick needles in people."*

In May of 2005, I started my classes. My first course was Oriental Theory and Point Location. From the very beginning, I felt like I was the dumbest person alive. The theory was so unfamiliar to me. I couldn't quite wrap my mind around it. I struggled with it. My teacher would ask me, *"Why are you so hard on yourself? This is new, and you are in school to learn it. You weren't born with the knowledge. Give yourself a break."*

I wasn't sure of myself at all. The more I tried to comprehend, the more frustrated I became. And I didn't need any more frustration; I had my managerial work, my sister, my nephews, my house, and now my schooling. I felt like I was going insane. I woke up one morning and couldn't handle any more. I was broken.

I went into the office that day and spoke privately with one of my employees. She was a union officer, and I needed her help. I wasn't a union member, but I truly needed her advice. After I explained all the aspects of my life to her, she said, "*I now understand; you have too much on your plate. No wonder you are a bitch.*" I laughed for the first time in months. She shared the name of a counselor I could speak with and urged me to take a leave of absence. She was right. I was about to have a mental breakdown.

Chapter Ten: A New Beginning

Things got tough right from the start of this new life. I left QWEST Communications and took on temporary work to cover my bills, but there were a baby and a toddler in the house, and they weren't included in my budget. My sister did her best by getting EBT and WIC, and by working, which helped a lot. My mental health was better in many ways. School still challenged me, but I was able to focus more now that I had a less demanding job.

The good thing was that Gary and I spoke every day, almost all day when we had the time. He made me feel normal, and it was a burst of happiness and joy in my day. I felt like we were turning a corner in our relationship. I could only hope this would continue.

On a fateful day, August 28, 2005, I sat in front of my TV, once again in shock. This time, it was Katrina—the hurricane that devastated most of New Orleans. I watched as interviews aired, showing people going to the Superdome to shelter from the storm, following the instructions of New Orleans officials. I was terrified for their safety. At one point, a reporter interviewed a couple who had gone to New Orleans to experience what it was like to live through a Category 5 hurricane. I remember thinking they were crazy – yes, I made a judgment, a lesson Ashlem had been trying to teach me for a long time.

As Katrina descended upon the area, I couldn't believe my eyes. Once the levees broke, widespread devastation followed. It looked like the Great Flood of Noah. Rescue teams were going from house to house. Helicopters were circling to help. People were crying desperately for rescue. The despair on their faces and the fear in the way they carried themselves and their children were evident. I cried and cried and cried. Less than a year ago, the world watched the tsunami in Thailand, and now Katrina. Instinctively, I knew it was only the beginning. This would be repeated time and time again.

Gary called in the afternoon as usual and asked me what I was doing. I told him about the hurricane and how I wept. He was in shock; he hadn't heard about it because he was out in the field working. He asked many questions about the situation. We were on the phone the entire afternoon and that evening. I was emotionally drained and didn't have the energy to do much. I, once again, was glued to the TV for days.

I knew it was time to talk to Ashlem about this new direction of mine and the Earth's. I took a big risk by choosing school over my profitable career; I hoped I had chosen the right path for my future.

Ashlem September 22, 2005

"I see a pinpoint of green light appearing in the center of the picture. The green light is slowly expanding, very bright, and very soft. As it expands, fills the whole picture with soft green light. The light of healing. And now a pinpoint of pink light appears in the center of the green light and expands. And now in the center of the pink light, a violet light. And now in the center, a blue light. All the colors of the rainbow coming forth from the center out in beautiful waves. And now a pinpoint of white light appears suddenly. It expands rapidly and consumes and blends with the other colors, causing the White Light to be very radiant and beautiful. As it fills the whole picture, images are appearing in the White Light. Beautiful butterflies. Very

large butterflies, but beautiful. Multicolored. Now, behind the butterflies appears the forest; The trees, the flowers, the streams of water, and the beautiful forest appearing.

"The waterfall. The stream at the end of the pool. The pool of water. How beautiful. it is. Complete now. The butterflies are flittering here and there. The White Rock appears and on the White Rock appears a beautiful pink flame. A flame like a candle flame that flickers only at the top. It is very bright and very fulfilling as it grows in size and intensity. Now it begins to soften and diminish. Ashlem is standing that flame. Ashlem is wearing his beautiful white robe of simplicity with a pink heart over his heart. We call this his robe of simple love. Ashlem stands with his hands in front of his face, like in prayer.

"Now appearing beside him, is Michael the Archangel on the other side, Gabriel. Now, a beautiful butterfly, a white butterfly with gold trim on its wings, comes flittering over to Ashlem and lands on the White Rock in front of him. Instantly an oval-shape of White Light appears. A great energy. Now an image is forming in that White Light. As always, it is the Blessed Virgin Mary, who has come forth as a butterfly. How beautiful She is. She's holding in her hand the beautiful, White Rose of the Christ. The other butterflies take their places above Ashlem, Gabriel, and Michael. They are very etheric but can still be seen. The butterflies turn into beautiful Angels. Magnificent Angels, and the Angels begin to sing celestial sounds, not words. Beautiful tones in perfect harmony.

"Ashlem is bowing to the Blessed Virgin Mary, as he always does. He stands forth, and Mary smiles at him, touches his cheek, and says, **'My dear friend, Ashlem, this is her** beautiful White Rose that I had taken from my garden. I will replant it in my garden if you bring it back to I. It'll be there forever and ever. I thank you, my friend for working with I.' *She turns sideways and, says,* **'The Angels sing your praises of this time of life. Let the flow of God flow within thee always, and know the purity of your being. There are many things yet to do upon the Earth's Plane. We are sure you will be able to do it. Peace.'**

"She has handed Ashlem the beautiful White Rose, and She fades away. The Angels sing louder. Ashlem sits in lotus position on the White Rock with that White Rose. Michael and Gabriel become more solidified now, merely standing like sentinels. Ashlem bows his head and wishes to speak through, and I give my permission."

"I am Ashlem, known as Golden Image, I say to thee, 'Hail.' The blessedness of Life come forth to they who bring the grace into their heart by love and peace of these times. Of this period and your desires to come forth at this time, the Blessed Virgin Mary expresses to thee of your wisdom. And of your beauty and of your grace, and is going to replant your Rose into her garden again. It will be there forever, She say. Now, there are many questions you have, please begin."

"Ashlem, last time we spoke about my lifemate, and you said that we may pass in the night like ships, and I was just wondering if we did."

"He is still on his way. He's had a little bit of difficulties with prior portions of his life. But he is

upon his course. But it will not be too long. Do not turn over rocks looking – remember what I said."

"OK. Because I was, I was always concerned that he did not come, because I did not get my sister out of my house."

"You will in time. You are being good to her of this time of her life. She does understand and is truly appreciative, but she does not have full control of the situation, but she will. In time come forth, upon her own, and she will always remember this. But that does not mean she has to bow down to thee, but she will always respect it."

"Well, let's talk about Gary. I was concerned that my lifemate had passed, and my relationship with Gary has intensified."

"Very good, very good. Now to understand, what is the plight of this situation? Is he waiting for thee? Very good. And to this life force, work it out, whatever it is. Enjoy it for what it is. Even if it is for what you say, fun and games."

Even though I love him, is he not the mate for me?

"Very good. Treat him with respect."

"Tell me about a past life with him because I feel such a connection, and I don't know where it comes from, and I don't want him out of my life when another comes in."

"We were always friends into the period of the time of Qin Shi Huang, as we spoke about before. Where we worked upon the China wall. You were there also, and there, thee and he were good friends, and occasionally lovers we thought, when the mood struck at that period of time. You were very petite of

310

that period of time, and he would always watch. Always ready to make sure you did not overburden yourself with the stones you were carrying upon your back. If you had too big of a stone, he would take it from thee, and you would become angry with him because you want to pull your own weight. It was all volunteer work. There was no slaves in that time."

"Is that why I don't want to walk away from him?"

"Aye."

"It's so easy to be with him."

Ashlem was quiet and waited for me to continue.

"Since we last spoke, I started growing herbs and vegetables, but it did not go well. It was my first year. Everything started blooming, and then the sun just killed my vegetables and my herbs."

"To prevent that, use a sunscreen or sunshade over them. Stretch it good and tight after what is called end of May and beginning of June. And then if you can do it, put misters to keep the plants to keep them cool. If you put misters out there, you could mist them, and it does water the plants also, but mostly it makes them cooler."

"Since the last time we spoke, I am going to a school that teaches Chinese Medicine – herbs and acupuncture. Is this a good step for me?"

"Very good. Did thee ever order the book The Complete Book of Shiatsu by Toru Namikoshi? You find the meridians of the body, and you can use acupressure or acupuncture. Learn acupuncture from a person."

"But they're teaching that at the school. In my second class on meridians, and one class actually teaches about the energetics of each point."

"Very good. It would help thee into all different degrees of the body, to the mind, and to the working positions of the muscular tissues and the body, all working together with the mind. And that is important."

"They also teach Chinese herbs, and I know we talked before about herbs..."

"Search upon internet to find chat room that speaks about herbs and expressing about bartering herbs. Ask questions about different chat rooms until thee find people who are interested into herbs and therefore, you can learn to barter herbs upon the internet. Never sell herbs upon the internet. The Government will come down on thee, it is certain. Use washed peanut butter jars and send them through the mail. Ask them to return the herbs in the same peanut butter jar. It is a trusting system; we work upon trust. If you do not honor the trust, then we will address your name so that others will not work with thee. Because there are going to be some people who would say this, 'I will need this chapparal.' And they will never send that which you need. They would sell the chapparal. So, you have to say that is OK if they want to sell the chapparal, but you cannot sell to a store. You cannot sell it over the internet, it must be bartered. They have no law against bartering herbs over the internet."

"But they do not have the laws yet to sell herbs?"

"They are going to. Right now, they are trying to control all herbs. Especially the price of herbs. But you can share and trade things with each other. It is not against the law. You trade ounce for ounce. That is how to work with it. May go on to White Rose program into Korea, where they would have different herbs, also, especially your China herbs. For American herbs, ask Robert to give you Nicholas Weed's name and his address, and you may contact him about herbs. And maybe upon the internet, you may work with his things. He has an herbal company. He is doing it to make money; he is not going to barter herbs. But he would tell thee what kind of herbs to use and so forth.

"So, I can substitute the Chinese with the American?"

"Aye. Horsetail grows wild into Colorado."

"I went to a conference last week and one of the speakers said that you can heal someone by sending healing thoughts and being positive about it. Maybe touching them, which has its own merit, but if that is the only way we need to heal someone, why do we need to do herbs and acupuncture?"

"But not everyone can realize the energy of the Spirit. But the truth of the matter is, that herbs cannot heal anyone unless they believe into the herb. You will learn soon. The same thing with energy transference. If someone believes not into this energy transference, you cannot heal them. But if one believes strongly into that energy transference, then by energy that they accept, then it begins to create that substance of life to

313

heal. And then the body begins to take upon it, those needs and then the body becomes healed. Because the mind is saying, 'You can heal this way,' So that is what the difference is. But you do need herbs because everyone is different.

"Mankind, especially Americans, have to have visual aids and physical aids to believe into anything. So, therefore, it is why the herbs are there, and the herbs have special properties into them of healing properties. The body is then consuming these herbs, and that energy. And the energy is the healing energy that they believe this will heal I. Then it is so."

"So, it's really just a matter of a person believing it?"

"Of course. You eat meals everyday? Do you know you don't have to eat to survive? But you have to have the memory of Breatharian. To breathe in the energy of the cosmos to your body. If you truly believe into this without a doubt, your body will begin to breathe in the expression of the cosmos into your aura, your chakras, your body will be healed, and your body will work. And you will not have to worry about eating anymore. You will stay young.

"But mankind cannot feel this energy of third dimension of light, so they have a problem with it. Into the First and Second Day of Creation upon Earth in the third orbit, Man were Breatharians. They could merely breathe the air, and the air was pure, and the air was good. And they did not need to eat.

"You have heard of the Garden of Eden and they talk about the apple in the Garden of Eden. And there

314

was a fruit there, that they would eat, and they would have all the supplements that were necessary. Just one thing. They called it the apple, but it was not the same as the apple of this day. So, you begin to understand. If I said to thee that, you're going to gain the energy you need to function for this next month that you do not have eat anything, and I hypnotize thee, then thee would be Breatharian. And your mind would create all this energy, and it would take and supplement your body. In a month's time, thee might have lost a few ounces of weight, but you would be healthy the same. But if the mind is saying, 'You have to eat every day, and if you don't, you will die.' You will die in a month's time. Then it begins that way. So, it is mind over matter. That is most important to realize of these times of life for thee."*

"That is hard for people to realize."

"Aye."

"Here's another one they talked about at this seminar: 'Whatever we want, the Universe has to provide.'"

"Excuse me. 'Whatever thee want, the Universe has to provide it?' Wrong wording. Whatever thee want, can be provided by the Universe, does not mean it has to present it to thee."

"That is what I was thinking. There are many times I think, this is what I want, but that doesn't mean it is going to be mine."

"Depends upon how much you want it."

"Well, if I say I want to win the lottery and be a millionaire."

"Then you have to play the lottery."

"If I believe in every cell of my body that I am going to win, that doesn't mean it will happen. It may not be my path."

"It may not be your path in your course of destiny, but it would be a beginning, would it not? Do you understand what I am saying to thee? The thought creation comes forth. You put a desire, 'I have a great desire to win this lottery, and I need the numbers to do this with.' So, your mind begins to work with numbers of the etheric realm. You write these numbers down, and you go to the lottery. You play this lottery for this time. That doesn't mean the numbers you got were not good numbers for that lottery. It might be two weeks or a good way that you're going to use that same number for. And then it would pay off. But your mind is going to reach the higher thing that you need when your desire says, 'I need this to function with because it is going to be part of my experience here upon the Earth's Plane.' Then there is a need. If you say I want this, because I don't want to work anymore, then you may not get it."

"I would like to have it..."

"You cannot say you would like to have it, you have to say I need it..."

"Do I need it? It would make life a lot easier, and it would help me get through school..."

"But would people benefit from your knowledge and your wisdom?"

"If I am going through school and getting through it quicker, then yes."

"Aye. Many times, we have offered peoples such as thee with the greater finances, winning the lottery, and suddenly they became rich, and they forgot their mission. And then the mission was then destroyed because of their vanity and their greed."

"My mind is that I would love to travel. And one of the things they spoke about at the seminar was to write down your heart's desire, and I would love to travel the world."

"It may occur before you pass into the Spirit."

"But first I must get the herbs and the healing done."

"Aye. I express this to people I have told for twelve years. To grow herbs and dry herbs and store herbs. Only a few out of the thousands that I had spoken to have done it. You are one of them."

"I have tried."

"But they have not even tried. Soon, there will come a great revelation to them of what I, Ashlem, was saying to them. They will not have medications because of cataclysmic changes or great pharmaceutical companies controlling everything. They're going to try to control herbs that way also. But they cannot keep thee from growing herbs and then trading herbs. And that will keep the pharmaceutical companies from getting bigger and controlling everything you do."

"Well, let me ask you this. When I'm healing people, and I am giving herbs like a tea or a formula to use…"

"You do not do it that way. If they have an illness, they have a stomach problem and there is a tea that would satisfy the stomach upset. Then you would say to them 'If I had that stomach upset that you have, I would use this chamomile tea in this mannerism and that mannerism, if I had it.' And if they said to thee, 'Are you telling me to use this chamomile herb tea to cure my stomach problem?' You say, 'I said that is what I would do.'"

"Will I become a full-time healer and get my income from that?"

"It is very possible as you work with it. Would you like to? I say you speak to Nicholas Weed. He has pure herbs that he grows them pure. And you will become interested into his work over the internet. And therefore, you will find out what he is providing to homeopathic doctors. Then you may ask him questions about how to grow, and what to do. Then you say to him you have spoken to I, Ashlem, and have said for you to contact him. If you know of a homeopathic doctor that would be interested, then you turn him onto Nicholas Weed for he is one of the few who have taken my advice and began to investigate and learn about herbs. And he is very well-read on it. And he knows. If you have a license to sell herbs, you can sell them."

"So, when I've gone to school and then taken my boards, I'll actually be licensed and certified to do herbs."

"Very good. Then you will be able to prescribe if you have a license."

"And that's what I was concerned about. We talked about that before, and you said that I'm never prescribing anything."

"You say, 'This is the best thing for you.'"

"So never say prescribe because the government will be all over me?"

"Aye. It is the pharmaceutical companies and the doctors that are controlling this. It is all about money.

"And then I can use the acupuncture, acupressure, and cupping, and gua sha as well."

"If you pass the board, you can become an acupuncture doctor. Then thee will find clientele to work with. You would need people such as Nicholas Weed and other people who would say, 'For the people in Arizona or other areas, go see Tracey. Doctor Tracey. She will help thee. And that is how it is done."

"I want to ask these things because there are so many things on the Earth that are coming to pass. The Mayan calendar says the world will be over in 2012."

"It's not so. You have much more time. Everyone is going crazy. Could it be that the Mayan calendar ceased because they got tired and ran out of room? No one knows how long it will be before the pole shift. It could come tomorrow, could it not? But improbably not. It could come a year from tomorrow, but probably not. But if you are going to live your life in fear, then you are going to be doing nothing. So, you live your life day-by-day, projecting forth for tomorrow, to be the goodness of the person that you truly are. And you worry not about the great future. For it will come if thee are here or not. But to work with yourself is important. To work with others and

help others. I always say if you take a person and you take a pain away from them, even for an hour of time, how can you say you are wrong? So, therefore, is not that hour important for the person out of pain?"

"If they are in pain all the time, then an hour would be a blessing. What about the Earth and the horrible hurricanes? Like Katrina?"

"They will get stronger and more of them. As the Atlantic Ocean has already become a degree hotter in the last decade of time. That is what is stemming these hurricanes, as thee call of them. The Pacific Ocean has raised its heat a lot more than that. It is why it is working that way. The polar caps are breaking away and floating away in the ocean."

"Is that from the global warming or the pole shifting?"

"The global warming and the trenches into the Pacific Ocean, and that is superheating the water is the same thing."

"Is it from the Earth tilting?"

"It is part of it. It's all working together, you understand. That is what is happening. The waters are being warmed by the core within Earth putting forth volcanoes under the sea. It is superheating the water, and water goes forth and it must circulate around. It runs from the North Pole to the South Pole and become hot and cold. This is what is causing these disturbances, as you call storms. Wind, when it hits the warm water, it is coming forth. It causes the winds to become stronger. It is not that God is angry with New Orleans, or Galveston or any place else in the

320

World. It is not God doing this. It is the Earth
movements. They will continue and get stronger. You
will see Category 6 hurricanes soon."

"You taught us that people who hold onto their material
possessions will perish. It was no more obvious than down in
New Orleans with Katrina. They didn't want to leave. That is
another question for you. I have rice and beans stored, and I
have strike anywhere matches, but what about water?"

"No, my dear, it is not necessary to get the
water. It is necessary to learn how to purify bad
water. You boil it. You may vaporize the water
through distilling. You take what is called six-quart
pressure cooker and take off the weight out of it and
put in the place of it, a fitting with quarter-inch copper
tubing. It is inexpensive. Then you put the water in ¾
full into the pot and put it upon your stove. At the end
of the coil, you put a pan that could hold hot water,
because it will be hot coming out. And you then, as it
cools, it becomes water. It will be pure water. And
then you have to clean your pot from the calcium
deposits and so forth. Impurities, you understand.

"You will take this purified water and seal it.
Then, thee will have a long time of water. If you are
going to take tap water or water they say that is not
purified, then it will not last long and will become
disruptive to thee. And if you drink of it, then you will
become very ill. So, learn how to purify water. There
will be ample water, but not clean water."

"I will boil my water for bathing if it is like Katrina,
because of the disease that is there, and they will find diseases

that they did not think about there. It is because of the human bodies in the ground that have not been found yet?"

"They have decayed, causing disease. It is all about money, my dear. The Cities of New Orleans knew that their levees would not hold better than a Category 3 Hurricane. We never get anything bigger than a Level 3 hurricane. Until now, they have found that their levees would not even withstand a Level 3 Hurricane.

"What about the greed of the companies and our government?"

"Can you stop them?"

"But there is another hurricane bearing down on Galveston where all of the oil is. It's like it is karma?"

"Can you think of any reason why it is so?"

"The oil into Galveston and that region is not even used by the United States. So, they are going to charge us $5/gallon of gas, and it is not even for us?"

"Most certain! Of certain, it is to be so, very soon. That means you will not be able to go to work because you can't afford to drive your automobile there."

"So, I will need to hit the lottery, so that I can go to work!"

"How about you and other ten million people? Even if the oil does not go to us, the companies are still greedy, and they will use that to sell overseas. Most of them sell their oil overseas."

"So, they sell the oil overseas, and then we keep taking from the Middle East, and then we develop in Alaska. Is there a lot of oil in Alaska?"

"They are taking very little oil out of Alaska. There is enough oil in Alaska to last one hundred years."

"Does that not destroy more of the environment up there? Animal lives?"

"It is not causing a disruption to the animal life up there. That is a fallacy caused by people who are so alarmed. This poor little spotted owl here, is going to be disturbed by a big pipe running by its tree. Don't be foolish."

"So then, it is a good thing they drill in Alaska, but only if they use it for the United States. But they won't."

"My dear, into California, they have oil reserve places, thousands of acres of oil wells that has never been capped or never been used. Yet it has been drilled and set. There is enough oil in America, for America, to use twice as much as it is using right now for over one hundred years."

"So why did they not capitalize on the oil that is here?"

"Because they want more money for it. They buy the oil cheap from the oil cartels and sell back to you. It is why they invaded Iraq. To make the Arabs angry with America to raise the oil prices. The American oil men want this to occur so they can raise the oil prices with any excuse. Do they really need an excuse? They do it anyway, don't they? As you have seen, soon after Katrina hit, they raised the oil prices

high. But the oil was not coming from Katrina. The oil coming to Arizona is coming from California. There is nothing you can do about it. But it is the downfall of America. Inflation is going to run rampant. But, part of that, is that China and Korea own so much of your national debt."

"Will we see that when China decides to call in our debt?"

"Of course. China is a sleeping giant. But this is not a great China that existed thousands of years ago that ruled the world. They will rule the marketplace of the world. They do not want to run the countries. They want the money."

"So, it is completely different than the Great China that had all of the inventions, and all of the herbs, and built the Great Wall. It's more of a materialistic China than the spiritual China that we once knew and loved."

"It is so."

"Why do I feel it is harder to be with most people? Let me explain. When I went to that seminar last weekend, there are people, who are open-minded, but it's getting harder for me to be within peoples energies. And I know it either has to do with my energy changing or their energy. Does it mean that my energy is being raised or is it being lowered because of the things I've been through in the past year?"

"If you allow your vanity to take hold of thee my dear, you will not be comfortable any place. When you are in the company of other peoples, respect their energy. Whether it is lower than thine or higher than thine. You respect the energy level and then exude

324

into thee, yourself the energy that is coming forth of good energy to build yourself greater. Then you do not have to question whether this person is good or is this person not good? For that is a judgment. Then what you do, is you listen to what this person has to say. If you find that it does not fit what you believe, it is very good to let it pass, and then be on your way. Find something that does assume thee, for your truth."

"I need you to explain what you meant by the vanity. When I'm talking to people, it seems like they have to prove themselves. They need to prove that they have the knowledge, and that is so wearing. I have a harder time going to seminars where there are open-minded people because they just want to prove themselves."

"Aye. That is what it is about. But you say, 'If they raise the consciousness of one person, how may you say they are wrong?'"

"I agree with that. It's me trying to..."

"Then you have to say, 'I understand where that person is coming from. God bless them.' Let them be upon their way. Ye do not have to associate with them. It is not your belief. Ye are higher above them into beliefs, then go upon your way with people as high as thee are."

"I didn't feel comfortable being around others, and maybe this is where vanity comes in since I have much more knowledge than they do."

"Everyone must start at some degree."

"That is true. I had to go through a lot to learn this knowledge. It's hard for me but I know that I need to learn how to do that."

"You will find it. It is called humility."

"So, you back down and say, 'I understand that. I recognize it. I respect it.' And then let it go."

"Aye, let it go."

"I feel like people just look at me and judge me, like it's jealousy."

"If they come to thee and say, 'I understand you grow herbs. I'm interested in growing herbs too.' And you say to them, 'What kind of herbs do you wish to grow?' They say this and that and this and that, and you say, 'I have grown them. How could I help you?' And they would say, 'I don't know how to grow.' Then you say, 'This way is to begin a little at a time.' And you do not charge them for that information."

"The last thing I wanted to talk about is my sister."

"You need the burden off your back. But give her a little bit more time. As long as she is working and endeavoring to better herself, then stay with her. You do not have to support her."

"I know she's going back to school, and that's a wonderful thing. She's learning she wants to be a teacher, a high school teacher, or a child psychologist."

"Can thee support her that long?"

"I don't want to, but the government's been giving her money to go to school. So, we talked about her moving out in January."

"It is good for her to get upon her own and organize her life herself. But you say, 'I love you, sister. I want you to stand upon your two feet. But if you fall down, please call me, I will try to help as much as I can.' That is good friendship of siblings. You have done much for her. But, you do not have to do that all your life."

"I feel pretty good that my sister has learned how to be stronger by being with me."

"Aye. We are pleased with your progress at this period of time. Do not lose hope for yourself. For each time you are changed in a different direction, it is for a purpose, and more doors are opened up for thee. As long as you have a positive direction, a positive mind, you will continue that way. And you put your feet upon the pathway you have chosen, and you find that which you have come to do – to heal."

"There has been a whirlwind of change this year, but this is my 35th year. So, this is my 7th year cycle."

"We are pleased with your progress of this period of life. Remember the Virgin Mary is with thee always, when you call upon her. Michael and Gabriel are standing there for support to thee. Michael is a Defender of Truth. It means that you are upon your pathway of this time, and he is standing by to protect thee. Gabriel is a Healer of Light. You will need his energy into time to come forth. You merely say, 'Gabriel, my Blessed One, give I the strength and the energy to do this.' You will do this going forth. And you will see the body suddenly change.

"I have given to thee this beautiful White Rose of Mary. Your Christ Rose. Remember it always. Close your eyes and see of this energy. Repeat after I, Ashlem:

"I and the Father are One.
"I stand forth into the Light of the Christ.
"For I am Light. I am LIGHT.
I AM THAT LIGHT.

"The Hand of the Father is upon thee. Feel the reverberation of the energy passing through your body to the Light of the Christ. As it enters every cell of your body, it becomes one with thee. It enhances all the movement of your vascular system in your body. It stores itself into every atom of your body and the nuclei of every atom of your body. So, remember always to place the Christ Light around thee every day of your life. If possible, if you can remember it, do it again. It will help thee. The Christ Light is the protection of life for thee.

"I lift your Veil and open your third eye wider. Opening the crown chakras. I have energized your psychic awareness chakras to open the meridians of life for thee. It will begin to grow; don't be frightened of the things you may see. Just say, 'Thank you, Father.'

"I give to thee the sign of peace, my covenant to thee that we have not forgotten. Of the Father, and of the Son and of thee, thy Holy Spirit. That the circle of God is eternal within. Never beginning, never ending,

and never to be separated from the whole, and that is thee.

"Beautiful Angel fly. Peace be unto thee; I take my leave."

I left that day more determined than ever to finish my education in herbs and acupuncture. Ashlem provided me a wealth of information about healing with herbs and hands-on techniques. And he was right, Americans needed a prop to help them heal themselves, although it wasn't necessary. Tasha's recovery reinforced that.

I had to smile to myself; Ashlem finally revealed the story of the life we shared together, working on the Great Wall of China with Gary. He explained that, like most others building the Wall, he thought Gary and I were lovers—companions, and friends supporting each other, and when the mood struck, lovers, just like now.

My sister and I started arguing quite often in the fall of 2005. It was the right time for her to move out, for both of our well-being. She felt she was being used, and I felt the same. It wasn't healthy for either of us. We were both financially strained, which only increased the tension at home. At Christmas, she told me she was moving back to Pennsylvania. She was moving in with my parents, who could provide the environment for the boys that I couldn't. It was a relief. I felt like Atlas, who shrugged the boulder off his shoulders.

My New Year began with a quiet, empty house. It was just the two of us again: Tasha and me—no one else. Not even Gary, as he disappeared once more.

Chapter Eleven: Turning the Corner

While 2006 began with peace and quiet at home, my work life was falling apart; in fact, it was nonexistent. I no longer had any temporary jobs and applied to many others without success. I knew I couldn't be a manager at that time. It was too stressful, especially since I was in school and found it very demanding. I needed some Divine Intervention. Ashlem and my Angels had, in the past, sent their energy; I hoped they would be willing to help me again.

I arrived at the reading once again, armed with many questions and feeling as if I needed to ask for help. I don't live with regrets and have no regrets about any decisions I've made so far. I did the best I could with the knowledge I had at the time. If nothing else, I learned a few tough lessons along the way.

Ashlem February 1, 2006

"I see a beautiful pink light emanating from a pinpoint of light, slowly expanding. Fills the whole picture. And now a blue light appears, etheric blue light. And now a violet light and the colors of the rainbow are coming forth. And now a White Light comes forth. Beautiful. Radiance. Intense. The All-Consuming Christ. And now images are forming in the White Light. They're beautiful flowers. They are not like flowers, like the forest. There is no forest here, just flowers and plants of different kinds; a garden, as I keep pulling away from it. It is a beautiful garden. There are walls made of stone, like river stone, with mortar in between them. Ivy-like plants are

growing on the walls. The sky appears streaked with fluffy clouds. The sun is peeking over the horizon, casting a flickering light upon those clouds, turning them to hues of purple and orange and red and yellow.

"And now appears a wide spot in the middle of this garden, a pathway. In the middle of that pathway appears a beautiful golden flame. A flame like a candle flame that flickers only at the top. It is very bright and very fulfilling as it grows in size and intensity. Now it begins to soften and diminish. Ashlem is standing in that flame. Ashlem is wearing his beautiful white robe of simplicity with a pink heart over his heart. We call this his robe of simple love. Ashlem has a smile on his face, and his eyes twinkle, and the light goes out. Now Ashlem stands in prayer with his hands in front of his face and his head bowed.

"Now beautiful butterflies appear; very large, etheric, pastel-colored butterflies. And now one butterfly, white with golden wings, flitters in front of Ashlem. It turns into an oval shape of White Light. In that White Light, appears the Blessed Virgin Mary, who always comes forth in a different way. How beautiful She is. She has in her hand the beautiful White Rose of the Christ.

"Ashlem is bowing to the Blessed Virgin Mary. Her oval shape of White Light, recedes to her aura, and Mary begins to speak, and golden words come forth, and the words say, **'My dear friend, Ashlem. We come first to serve again, all of these people, for they who have dignity and love for each other. So that they may find the true peace within that I, and my Son share also. I thank you for your service to us.'** She turned sideways and says, **'Dear one,**

*this is your White Rose of Your Christ, that I have
planted in my garden. Ashlem will return it to I, and I
will replant it again in my garden with the thousands
of others that I have there already. I have a most
beautiful Rose Garden. You're part of it. Find peace in
your heart and glory upon yourself. Call my name,
and you will smell the Roses. Peace.'*

"Mary fades. Ashlem has in his hand the beautiful White
Rose. Ashlem turns on this pathway and sits in a lotus position.
Ashlem smells the White Rose and bows his head. Ashlem
wishes to speak through, and I give my permission."

**"I am Ashlem, known as Golden Image, I say to
thee, 'Hail.' To the blessedness of life, one comes forth.
The Blessed Virgin Mary comes forth, and I have
created for her, and for thee, the garden in which she
was put upon the Light of the Christ Creation, of that
period of time, into the temple of the Essenes. It is a
beautiful garden of all types of energies, especially
herbal energies. Because of this life, the peoples in the
Essenes Temple, who are well-healthy peoples by these
herbs. We have waited for thee to come forth again.
Now there are very many questions I will answer for
thee please begin."**

"Ashlem, I have many questions. I am very confused
because there have been many changes. I am studying herbs
and acupuncture to be a Doctor of Oriental Medicine, and I am
enjoying it. But the difficulty I am having is with my job. I've
had a few jobs over the past couple of months, and nothing
seems to be going well."

"Why did thee leave your last position? Do you not work at the phone company?"

"I left that in July of last year. I was not enjoying it, and I was very sick all the time. Between the stress and pressure of managing a team of twenty employees, going to school full-time, and helping my sister with her two children, my body broke down. I could not think straight, and I cried all the time. I was angry due to the stress and pressure of having to do it all. I supported three additional people along with work and school."

"What you have to do is go back into a job of communications."

"Like telecommunications? The telephone"

"Not telephone. But communications companies to work for them into the office. It is not for thee to make calls for them. There is not enough money into it. But you have to learn to be impersonal to people's problems. For everyone has a different opinion of problems. And also, their character. You have to look at their character and let it go and not keep it within thee. It causes thee to become very anguished. So, you have to learn to be more impersonal to people's lifestyles, and the ways they do their work. That is most important. That they do their work, and that you are supervising them. But this is important for thee to realize. Then you are able to work with peoples, and not become too personal with them."

"And that's why I figured I'd be an assistant to an Executive, but they feel threatened by me. Many of my former managers feel threatened by me, and I don't even try to do

anything to deserve being fired. Other than do my job as well as I possibly can."

"Because of your intelligence, they think this is a woman who is climbing her way up to the top, any way she can. And that is what their thinking was. Of course, then they start to fight against thee without even any problem."

"Yes, that's exactly what had happened."

"It is the business world. There are lots of ladies who do it; achieve their position to higher states on their backs, and so to speak. And this is the predominant problem in the business world of this time. There are ladies who will do that to get ahead. They think first, of the monies, second of the job opportunity. But of this period of time, you were then what ye would you say, marked in that way. So other peoples were against thee to get rid of thee, and that's what it is about. So, into a new position, you go to work. You will find a position soon similar to one you had. You will be able to supervise some people. Dress properly and dignitatively, so they cannot say those words."

"They're very hurtful and it's not even something that I do."

"I understand, but they think, because they do not know thee, that they're trying to make it with all the male people there. It is what it is about of this time. But you will find your way at this time of life also. As you go forth, be more modest in the delivery of yourself. You will have to dispel those things, and

people will then say that she is a beautiful woman, who has great intelligence. Let your intelligence shine forth. It is alright of this time of life. You have grown great knowledge since a few years ago. And now you will find yourself to be better equipped to conduct yourself in this business world. You're learning to be a businesswoman for a purpose, and a reason. Do you understand? It is important that thee realize that is to come forth of your future. That is coming forth. We have steered ye into the herbs, and that will be your future in time yet to come. You work with this energy of this time, and after you have become, let us say, the boss, you will not have to worry about those people."

"And that's my goal. And that leads me to one of my last questions. To go through the schooling about the herbs and to get a license, so that I can do it legally and properly and open a business, it's gonna take three or four years."

"You have to learn to mark time into life. You are still a young woman. You still have a lot of opportunities to go before thee, as you are learning quickly, that is important. Then you will learn many other lessons about the business, especially in the herbal business. And then you will be able to set yourself further upon this roadway of life. You are studying to be an acupuncturist. Study more to the herbal. Acupuncture is important. You will find you can use acupressure equally well, in the same meridians you're working with the body. The difference is actual acupuncturist can be sued for

335

malpractice, where a herbologist cannot. It is all taken from Shiatsu, the ancient art."

"So, stick with the three or four years of schooling?"

"You will do well. Do not rush. The fastest train is not always the one that gets to the station first."

"I wanted to ask you about a dream I had. In my dream, I was with a man, and I don't know if we were a couple, but another man came into the picture, and I grabbed this new man and would not let go of him. And the first man said that's fine, I have someone else for fun on Tuesdays. Then he left. What did that mean?"

"I don't understand the 'Tuesday.'"

"I don't either, that is why I am asking."

"It has nothing to do with sexuality as you think it does. It has to do with working and proper work, and so forth. Appointments like. You are still looking for a companion. The new companion that you grabbed onto."

"It was my friend, Gary, and he came back. He was the second man. The man who I was with, I don't know who he was. Gary came back in, and I did not let him go."

"Because you did not let go of him, because he is your friend, and you have security with him. The person you were with is something that you were not sure about. So, you were looking for an island of security. And you manufactured this friend to come forth. But there is another person you will call a friend who will come into your life."

"My lifemate?"

"Very possible."

336

"Which is the one I've been waiting on."

"Very possible, since you have put your feet upon the right pathway. You will see many things changing. Stop worrying about so many things. Continue to do your work that you are trying to do, to study, to be an herbologist, and a good one you will be, in time. Are there more questions?"

"I wanted to ask about Gary."

"Do you really want Gary to come back?"

"I really love him, and he is a support for me."

"Then why is he not with thee?"

"Because of his ex-wife and children."

"I see. Why is he wrapped up in his ex-wife and children?"

"Because there is always something going on. He is always with his children because of the abuse from the mother."

"She is not abusing the children."

"Because of that, he is always in Court trying to win the custody of the children."

"It is he who is not letting go. When he has learned to let go, he may return. But you do not want him until he returns in that way."

"That is true. I don't want that drama in my life. But there are so many things that he makes me feel good about, and we can talk for hours without a loss for words or a break in the conversation. We agree on so much, and we so much alike in many ways. He called me at 10:30 p.m. to see how I was doing with my temporary job. I know that he cares."

"Then continue your friendship and keep communication lines open with him."

"So, then I should not remove him from my life, so my lifemate can come in?"

"**He may be your lifemate.**"

"Gary is my lifemate?"

"**It is not impossible.**"

"I always knew that he was my lifemate. But you guided me that he was not. I am very confused."

"**But my dear, let's understand something. When a lifemate is coming for thee, if he is not upon his proper course of destiny, he cannot be your lifemate. If he steps upon his proper course of destiny that aligns with thee, and collide with thee, then could he not be your lifemate? So, a lifemate depends on the course of destinies.**"

"So, if he does the right things, he could be my lifemate."

"**He would have to give up all ties to that family. He has to give up his vendetta against his ex-wife.**"

"The very first time I learned about him was when he was running for office in our local union. A representative from the union was handing out his election flyer, and I looked at his picture and immediately thought, 'I am going to marry this man.' And I thought I was wrong because things have not worked out, and it's been over three years since we met."

"**It is very clear.**"

"Then I want to ask you about that cruise I went on a few years ago, and you stated that I would meet my lifemate and I didn't because he never made it to the ship."

"**Could be, could not be. Do you understand?**"

"No."

"I said ye would meet someone. Did you meet someone?"

"No. Well, I met someone, a friend only."

"Then you begin to understand what I said to thee. Did you learn lessons?"

"Yes."

"Very good. Then that is what it was for."

"Oh, and here I thought I was supposed to ask every man that came into my life, 'Were you supposed to be on a cruise in Turkey, and missed the boat?'"

"Are there more questions?"

"I wanted to ask you about selling my house."

"Why do thee want to move?"

"Well, Gary is moving out way farther in the West Valley, and I would not see him much. It's 70 miles from my house. And with all of the people moving to Phoenix, and they are moving into the West Valley. I would be able to get more business out there."

"Then do it. Why do thee ask I, of things that you have already felt within thee to be of the way to go? You have to trust self."

"Yes, I do need to trust self. I've made a lot of mistakes in my life, and I'm kinda gun-shy about making those decisions."

"I understand, but thee must learn to trust thyself. You will find it very beneficial to move into that area. It is newly developing, and you will make twice the amount you purchased the house. Are there other questions?"

"I wanted to ask you a medical question. I read that allergies can cause autoimmune diseases. Like your lupus. Is that true?"

"It is a degree to be certain, but I say to them that autoimmune diseases causes allergies. But allergies are caused by Consciousness and thought out of fears. That is what triggers allergies. The body reacts to many emotions, and these emotions are the ones to cause the challenges. If you're going to work with the allergies, then you have to attack this system to say, or to calm a person's body, and to keep the nerve centers healthy. Then you can find the immune system can be helped by that way."

"So, you're talking about the energy. When I was reading this book, they say every meridian was affected by an allergy, and they cited different causes, which I was really amazed by. I did not expect the meridians to be affected that way."

"But of course they can be affected. The entire body can be affected by any allergy. But I say, there is no such thing as an allergy. It is an existence that is created by the mind, out of fears, anxieties, and so forth. It becomes a disease. It affects all; the whole immune system breaking it down and what not, out of those fears. But to work with the mind, to recreate, and to sustain a calmness in the body. Get rid of the thought about the allergies, and the allergies will go away. You may tell the person, 'You are not allergic to this.' So, they have been allergic all their life to Bermuda grass. And you make test upon them and say, 'I find no allergy about Bermuda grass; it will not affect thee.' And you will find that the patient will not have any more symptoms. Because the mind changes, to 'I don't have it,' and so it is done."

"Now I have noticed that I feel like I've become more allergic to dairy and wheat. Then in Chinese medicine, they're saying that those two cause dampness in your body."

"We have some ancient theorems, you understand, that are still unproven."

"So, they could be incorrect, is what you're saying?"

"Of course. There is nothing that is perfect. If there was perfection into all theorems, and things working upon the Earth, there will be no illness. So, the human body is what people are working for, to help create these illnesses. You will find your pharmaceutical companies are not interested into the cure, but to treat the symptoms. If they cured the disease, they would be out of business. Let us face the issues into Oriental Medicine. Also, the properties of the herbs grown. Have thee began growing with fish oils?"

"No, I have never thought of it."

"Then study and look into fish oils into growing that region. There are certain kinds that can be used for certain different herbs. It's a fertilizer, and then, that will give a certain property to herbs. A better property. It is what the ancient oriental herbologists used the fish oils. Because fish was staple so, they use the oils from the fish and for the fish itself, and to growing foods."

"Bob told me about this fertilizer. And, at this point I cannot remember the name, although I can see it sitting in my house."

"Wachters?"

"Yes, Wachters."

"It is not a fertilizer; it is a growing nutrient. Learn more about the herbs."

"I wanted to ask about winning the lottery, and we spoke about it last time. Is it my destiny to win?"

"I do not know. Do you have a crystal ball?"

"No, but isn't it part of your destiny?"

"Your destiny in this lifetime is to make your way to learn to grow herbs, to be an herbologist, and to work as a counselor. The money is secondary. If you are good with your business, and your wisdom will come forth, you will be a wealthy herbologist. But if you are mediocre, then that is what you will be. Being rich is not part of a destiny."

"I was thinking it would help me on my way."

"Then keep that thought of helping yourself and others equally. Do not forget the others equally. On a long journey, one must put their foot forward, first foot forward, and then the second one to follow. And when they follow the first foot, as it follows the second foot, and the second foot in the third step is following the first step. As you continue in this way, it is how life is. You have put your foot forward, and take a first step. Now is the time to take the second step. Each step brings a learning process of wisdom. If you run down this roadway, you're going to trip and fall."

342

"And I did that many times."

"Aye."

"Ok. I have a few questions about the world and what is going on. I'm concerned that the Constitution and the Freedom of Rights that we have in the country are being violated, and more businesses and more corporations take it over every day."

"Is that not the way of American life, right now? Are you going to stop it?"

"Well, I can't stop it by myself, but I can certainly plant the seed."

"It is good to have the voice and speak the voice, then go back upon your way and stop worrying about it. We cannot control it."

"But what about our rights and the changes on the Supreme Court. It is becoming more conservative, and the new judge is the swing vote for the installation of very conservative values."

"Very good. Then his power lies with him, his Consciousness. And what he does, he will pay the price, yeah or nay."

"But those decisions affect millions and millions of people."

"Very possible. But they have already fought this out into the Courts and in Congress. Then let them make those decisions. It is like I say to not vote for a certain person to be President. And he was re-elected. I did not have control over it. Neither do you. You begin to realize what is happening. You are a pawn in a great chess game. If you play chess, you will begin to find that pawns are expendable. So, therefore, in this

life force, make yourself to be a queen and not a pawn."

"How do I make myself a queen?"

"With your wisdom and knowledge. You have gone forth of this period of time. We're talking about the value of the queen, not the position of the queen. Then you'll be a queen on a chessboard, which is very valuable. And that is what you're striving for, to be the best of your ability, into that situation you have chosen to be. Then you have the power to work with you. If you're going to go into politics, then you will be concerned. But you are not into politics. But you will see your wisdom that has been put to thee, at this time, will reflect the time coming forth where the government will try to regulate herbs. I can outline a passage for thee to say.

"You are in the right direction. Hold your head high and continue to walk down your pathway. Carefully. Do not run. You're searching hither and there to find a position that can afford thee. Gather all your ducks in a row and know where those ducks are. Then, continue down your pathway for you will find everything will fall into place when you are in the right direction. I cannot point the direction for thee, you already know that. But, what I say to thee, you're in the right direction. Now, at this time, continue with your herbal medicines and teachings. The material plane is the world of your work.

"I have said to thee look into fish oils for fertilizer like that of the ancient times. And how they

344

grew the ancient herbs; it was more difficult in those days. Look into the White Rose Program. There are many wise people there who still remember the ancient ways.

"Feel the power of God rushing through your veins, the power of energy. Breathe it in deeply and slowly. It is the Creation that you must find. It is your chi/qi. You work upon this, and you will find it, and you will increase your qi.

"Breathe in green light and feel it expand. Learn to use this system in your sleep before you retire into the evening. Very important that you bring it into your heart, and you feel the power, and the glory rising through your body as it expands. It radiates into your aura, so that people will come to know your divinity, and your grace, and be fulfilled by it.

"Anxiety must go away for greater love to come forth. Let God flow through thee at this time. Not in a pious mannerism, but the reality of health and goodness. You will go forth and find your pathway. Remember always the Blessed Virgin Mary and the Butterfly.

"I give to thee this sign of peace: my covenant unto thee of the Father, the Son, and thee, thy Holy Spirit. Remember unto thee the circle of God is eternal: never beginning, never ending, and never to be separated from the whole, and that is thee. It is the force of life.

"Peace be unto thee; I take my leave."

"Thank you Ashlem."

Ashlem encouraged me to keep searching for a job in communications. I realize how helpful that will be in the future when I become a counselor and a herbologist. I didn't know where else to look anymore.

Not long after this reading, I found a temp job at a real estate firm in North Scottsdale. I worked with some great people there. I felt comfortable for the first time. I learned quickly, kept quiet, and tried to maintain a distance from the men. I worked, studied, and went to happy hour with them on Friday nights. I enjoyed the quiet and the mundane. Still, my mind kept drifting back to Gary. It had been a while since I heard from him. I decided to call him; there was no answer. I left a message. Days and weeks went by with no response. Why can't I pass by this man? Why do I still want him, even when he leaves me behind without a care, and then comes back when he needs something? Why can't I have a greater self-worth than this? Those questions continue to haunt me, year after year.

I was sinking into a deep depression; the walls felt like they were closing in on me. I felt utterly alone in the middle of the sea with no hope of survival—no life raft. I didn't want to go on living like this anymore. I was ready to leave Earth; I thought I had nothing left to give. I had been in survival mode for years. I only experienced brief moments of happiness, and then they were gone. Gary was gone. My family had once again turned away from me because of my sister and the terrible things they believed I had done to her. I didn't have much contact with my sister or my nephews. They were busy adjusting to their new reality and thought I didn't care about them. But that was far from the truth. I was working full-time and attending school full-time. I didn't have the energy to spend hours on the phone listening to drama from home. I felt like I had nothing to give anyone, and I ended up becoming the villain for a different reason.

I made my way back to Ashlem. I wanted to find out if I could leave Earth and what the cost would be. It had to be less than what I was paying, over and over again. I was less than a month away from my 36th Birthday. Another very special year. I suspected another challenging year, as this was a spiritual year.

Ashlem May 31, 2006

"I see a beautiful violet light from a pinpoint light expanding slowly in the picture. Now, golden light appears on the outer edges of the violet light as it expands. The golden light gets brighter and brighter. Doesn't invade; simply expands with it. Now, a pinpoint of pink light appears at the center of the violet light. The pink light begins to expand, pulsating, consuming, and blending with the violet light. And now, the pink light takes over the violet light, and the golden light is there around the pink light. Fills the whole picture with beautiful pink light. Now, a pinpoint of white light appears in the center and expands rapidly; consumes the pink light and leaves behind magnificent, soft white light. The White Light is the All-Consuming Christ; the Light of Creation that fills the whole picture.

"Images are forming in the White Light. Beautiful butterflies. Magnificent butterflies. The butterflies are changing. Now, behind the butterflies appear a forest, slowly it appears. There aren't butterflies, they are little Angels. Beautiful small Angels. The forest appears; the stream, the

347

waterfall, the pool of water, the lowers in the field, the roses that grows everywhere. The lilacs that are growing on the shrubberies beneath the trees. The waterfall bubbles over the moss-covered rocks.

"On the White Rock appears a beautiful golden flame. A flame like a candle flame that flickers only at the top. It is very bright and very fulfilling as it grows in size and intensity. Now it begins to soften and diminish. Ashlem is standing that flame. Ashlem is wearing his beautiful white robe of simplicity. Expressing everything in life to become more simplified. Ashlem has that beautiful smile on his face, and his twinkle and the flame goes out.

"Ashlem stands and turns toward the waterfall. He bows his head and puts his hands in front of his face, like in prayer. A white dove comes out of the waterfall and flies around clearing quickly, and flies around Ashlem and lands on the White Rock. Instantly turns into an oval shape of beautiful White Light. A great energy. Now, an image is forming in that White Light. It is the Blessed Virgin Mary, once again, who has come forth so often. Mary is magnificent as comes as the Dove of Peace. Mary has in her hand the beautiful, White Rose. Ashlem is bowing in his meditation to the Blessed Virgin Mary.

"Mary begins to speak in golden words come forth and the words say, **"Here, my friend, Ashlem, is Tracey's beautiful White Rose of her Creation of the Christ, that you may know the peace within. I give it to thee, please return it to I, when you are finished. I will plant it in my garden."**

She turns sideways and says, **"Unto the Light of Light, let love come into your heart through desire of** *existence, through this and that of life, find the peace within. When the peace is found, the doors open wider and wider. One may find the greater experience. Love is a secret word of all things. When love is found, it abounds greatly. Unto thee, I give to thee this beautiful White Rose. Cherish it, for I do love thee. Peace be upon thee."*

"Mary fades and Ashlem smiles, and he has in his hand that beautiful White Rose. He sits in a lotus position on the White Rock. I have noticed there are little animals coming out of the forest; kit foxes, bunny rabbits, and polecats coming out. They sit around the White Rock looking at Ashlem, as he summoned them with energy. He smiles and smells the White Rose. Ashlem bows his head and wishes to speak through. I give my permission."

"I am Ashlem, known as Golden Image, I say to thee hail. The blessedness of life come forth for they who decide what the purpose of life is most important. One walks down their pathway of Light, looking hither to there, sometimes ignore the flowers along the way. When they stop to smell the flowers, they may find a honeybee busy at work there, of that time. We have summoned forth the Angels of Light that they may bring of that time goodness and grace for thee. The devas of the garden and the devas of life have come forth as they have grown forth into larger sizes of this time. And now they sing celestial sounds of beauty and grace in perfect harmony. Harmony is that which a person would seek on the Earth's Plane,

but often not find, for they look into different directions of that harmony.

"When one seeks the harmony of truth of being, they find within themselves the greater being. Unto this time of life, as you walk upon the Earth's Plane of grace and understanding, you have to find your own self of this time. But, you will be shown a pathway very soon to come forth as we have spoken to you before. I understand that you are disturbed over these existences of Earth. There is nothing you can do about it of this time. But you will find your niche of life at this time. That things have been altered and changed for thee, of course. But we will begin to open a new door for thee to venture into. You must step forward to find of it.

"Now, there are many questions you have. Please begin."

"Ashlem, I wanted to ask you about the beginning of the reading. I wanted to ask about the lights. Bob said he saw a pinpoint of violet light with golden light surrounding it. Then a pinpoint of pink light took over, but the golden light stayed. I don't understand that."

"What does a violet light mean to thee?"

"Service. Spirituality."

"What is a golden light?"

"Wisdom and knowledge."

"If you use the wisdom and knowledge of golden light to blend together the violet light of spirituality, would it not be an impression of life for thee? We are *telling thee to do of this time. Then what came forward?"*

"*A pink light came forward and consumed the violet light.*"

"What is on your mind of this time?"
"*Love.*"
"Is pink not only a presentation of love?"
"*Yes.*"
"Then what happened to the pink light? Did it not invade the violet light?"
"*Yes*"
"Then would you say that the pink of love invades the violet of spirit that is governed by the golden light of wisdom and knowledge? Is it not a pathway of life for thee? Then you begin to understand what the colors mean. Our goal is to raise your inner Consciousness of this time. You are looking for a loved one, are you not? And you have been dissatisfied with what you have found. You have been you have marking time with a person who does not give thee the time. And I said that it is a possible chance that he may give thee more time. I cannot say to him, 'Go ahead. Do this with her.' For he taken, is he not?"

"*No.... is he?*"

"After this life force of this period of experience for thee, to realize of the precious life of this time, he has not come forward to commit to thee. Is he committed to another?"

"*From before, yes.*"

"Aye. And do you think it is all over?"

"They are divorced."

"Of course, they are divorced. What does freedom mean to thee?"

"Freedom means to me, in a loved relationship, that you don't love that person anymore. And you have allowed your heart and mind to be open to another."

"Freedom to him means, don't do that again. So, you can see his apprehension of this time. But I have said to thee, he is not free. That disturbed thee, did it not?"

"Because he hasn't said goodbye to his ex-wife."

"Aye."

"So, he still cares for her?"

"Of course. In time, he may find his lonely state to be with someone who cares for him. You may wear your heart upon your sleeve more if ye wish. I would look for another butterfly.

"Is there more question?"

"So, you would give me advice not to wait for him anymore?"

"Very good. You have learned."

"That doesn't make it any easier."

"I did not say I was to be easy, my dear. When a female gives her heart, it is fully. We say, my love, I want to be loved in the greatest way, and walk upon this Earth's Plane, that you were supposed to be together and loved in time coming forth. Yet he has not committed, even though he has been divorced. But a divorce does not always mean freedom. So, it complicates matters. As I have said, now you have a

choice, and you have had a hard time making that choice. You can either spend more time waiting, or you can look forward to another adventure. Is it not time to look around for another lifemate? As we have said before, if he is on his course of destiny, then he will be your lifemate. If he is not on his course of destiny, you may pass like two ships in the night. But he has only put one foot on his course of destiny. He has not found freedom. And his other foot is not placed upon his pathway. He is still holding on to the other pathway. And he is only given to thee a small portion. He may come to thee, I do not know. I understand your feeling of love. But you have not really felt it from him. Is it not better to have loved and lost than never have loved at all?"

"That is what they say."

"Are there more questions?"

"Ashlem, please give me a minute. I have to gather myself right now. I cannot speak at the moment. My tears and heartbreak...

"What do the animals mean? You were also talking about the devas?"

"They were called forth to pay homage to thee. You love animals, is it not so? They came forth to give honor to thee at this time. They do not do this with everyone."

"They never did that before."

"At this period of time of life, they know and feel sorrow in your heart. The animals come forth to say, 'We are still with thee.' Do not give up."

"It's extremely difficult with my life and family drama, and a lack of job, and now Gary." (I say this through my tears and my voice breaking.)

"They say you are overqualified. So don't be overqualified."

"How do you do that?"

"You say, 'I am not overqualified to work. Would a wise person turn away someone like you, or would they work with thee to find out and understand what wisdom ye have? Then maybe a greater position yet further to come. Then, an employer look at thee and say, 'Maybe ye are right.' You have to work towards your employment. We have said to thee that there is a position you will fulfill. You have to search it out. If you do not search it out, then you do not care anymore. Do not give up. Mary said this to thee, has she not?"

"Yes."

"Then do not give up. Place your feet firmly upon the pathway of righteousness of grace and understanding and then go for it. Apply your knowledge and abilities, but do not overextend them."

"I have applied for positions that I am qualified for and did not get the job. I applied for positions that I am overqualified for because it would be easier to go to school and have a full-time job. But that doesn't work out either. I am frustrated."

"Then talk to them. Remember, the squeaky wheel always gets the oil first."

"Ok. I wrote down that these last few months have been very hard and I am losing my faith."

"If you lose your faith, you lose everything."

"So much so, that I say to myself, 'I don't want to be here on Earth anymore."

"My dear, you MUST remain on Earth until you complete your course of destiny. A long time ago, we outlined your course of destiny. You must still work upon it. Are you doing herbs still?"

"Yes."

"Very good. Have you dried of them and stored of them?"

"I didn't have the money to do it this year."

"Very good. But you have to live. You cannot live on your looks. We will try to put that force of energy into that direction. But you must be loving and caring, and sincere and dress properly for that position. Be kind. Always remember who is boss. That is good for his ego."

"Because I have not done very well with my faith these past couple of months, is this what we are going to go through when the Earth starts changing. All of these trials and tribulations?"

"Of course, it is so. That is the way life is; it is a pendulum. It swings this way, and it goes to pot. It swings back the other way, and it is good. What you need to do is figure out the mediumship of the pendulum. Where are you at that period of time? Then make sure that the swing is shorter."

"How do you recognize you are in the middle?

"When it is flowing you are in the middle. Remember that."

"So, the one side is your highest highs and the other is your lowest lows?"

"Aye. You must work upon this attitude in friendships. Don't be too pushy with friendships. Be a little aloof. But still show interest. We are talking about love affairs. Be interested into it and have an enjoyment. You may find a gentleman say, 'I would like to go out with thee?' And you say, 'What is on your mind?' If he say, 'Maybe we can go to a movie or something of that order.' Then you may say to him, 'That is nice. What else?' If he say, 'We may have dinner together.' Then you say, 'That would be nice also.' If he says, 'You come to my house.' Then you say, 'I am sorry.' Do you understand? If thee want physical enjoyment only, then that is ok. But if ye want love, then you make a person respect thee. That is how to attract a male: respect with interest. Then you will have good times of life. But ye will not have good times of life; you are getting older. And you are going to attract has-beens. Remember this always: all has-beens are coming forth readily. You have to find one that is not going to be a has-been for me. You must ask him questions and listen to the answers to those questions. Always talk about them and not yourself."

"One of the things I wrote down is that I feel I need to fight against the injustices of the world like, the greedy corporations, the interpretations being handed down from the

courts, how disrespectful and not nice people are to one another."

"You are making a judgment. You cannot make those judgments, my dear. When you do that, you have already begun to lose. You make a judgment about what is right or fair for thee and others. You cannot make that judgment. But that produces an attitude of superiority. Companies and governments make those rules for a reason. When you accept a job or a service or the country you live in, you accept their rules. If you do not like it, go to another business or job. You cannot say, 'You are wrong.' Because that produces an unhappy thought, which creates more negativity. So, that is where the thought of superiority comes in. You say, 'That is alright.' And you go somewhere else. Once enough customers or employees have left, they may change their attitude.

"You are here to survive this existence, help people with their spirituality, their love, and their health. That is what your mission is. You are not here to change the world. For it cannot be done. If a person voices their opinion, that is ok. But if a person insists, they are right, then they become in trouble."

"Sometimes I do not understand the parables you give me. For instance, when I asked you about my past lifetime with Gary, we were together at the Great Wall of China, and we were lovers. Is that what is going to happen in this lifetime, or is it only the past, and what did happen?"

"You were lovers. Were ye married?"

"I don't know; I never asked."

357

"Nay. You were lovers, and you both perished in the Great Wall. Is it not so that your love is perishing because of a barrier?"

"Yes."

"Then you begin to understand the significance of it in this attitude of life. What is the old saying? You can lead a horse to water, but you cannot make it drink. But if you learn to make him thirsty, then he may want to take a drink. The question to answer is: Is he looking for someone to love and for someone to love him for the rest of his life or does he just want to be a free playboy now?"

"I don't know... sometimes I see the free playboy and then others I see he wants a relationship."

"He wants the security. And he will demand that you be faithful to him, while he plays the field."

"I'm not going to do that. That's not going to happen."

"I know that ye are not going to do that. But that is where he is at. I'm not saying that is what he wants. It is how he is acting of this time. So, you are with him and love him, what you need to figure out is how much he loves me."

"He doesn't love me as much as he loves himself."

"Then there is a problem."

"Then I won't come back. Once I leave, I won't open that door again, and it will be his loss."

"I understand. Turn your face and walk away, my dear. Let him be the one that suffers, not thee. You will find another, but do not use him as a pattern. He has many traits that you do like, so find those in *another. So, sit down and write a list of what you want. Then, seek the man who fits the list. You will alter your life. Do you understand? It is a simple rule of understanding in your standing of life. It is right to have desires. But when your desires overrule your protection of your pathway, are you going to fulfill your mission? So, alter your course of destiny to coincide with the things that support your true mission. Change your desires so that you do not change your true course of destiny. It is normal to find someone and love someone. But after a while, you will ask yourself, 'What did I ever see in that person?' To grow in that wisdom and knowledge, the person is not pursuing thee, you are pursuing a person. You get tired of running after someone, or eager to do this or that for him. So, therefore, you stop, and you turn around, and go on another trail. On that trail, ye find another one. One that you do not have to chase, one that will chase thee. There is someone for thee. You don't have to over the rocks looking. Be the beautiful person you are. Understand?"*

"Yes."

"It's an interesting life for thee. Sit and watch the birds in the stream. You might see the little sparrows here and there. Male and Female. The female ignores the male. The male will stretch his wings after her, or around her. She continues to ignore him, and turns her face another way. Is she ignoring him or is she making him strut some more? She may like him, but she is making sure he likes her.

Is it not like that in human life? Should it be the male that comes and struts himself for the attention of the female? And the female should be the one who says, 'I will stay for a little while if you want.' Understand?"

"You know, when I walk into a restaurant or other place, I do not notice anyone. I don't."

"Very good. That is the way it should be. There is a difference between a woman and a lady. Be a lady. As I have said before, at your age, they are a lot of rejects out there. Married, divorced. But it is not always their fault. He may have high standards and was with a woman who cheated on him. You want to find a man with good standards. A man that suggests going to your place to hit the sack, does not have good standards. Unless, all you want is sexuality, then you say, 'Yea, lets go.' Remember, the birds. The female is the decider. She lets the male think he is."

"An older friend of mine always says, 'We have it. They want it.'"

"Exactly! It will always be that way. It was instilled in the animal kingdom, as well as the human kingdom. That is the universal law."

"Ok. Ashlem, I am turning 36 in a few weeks, and this is the 4th cycle of my nine years. What does it mean? What does the nine year mean, and what should I expect?

"9th year is your spirituality. We have shown to thee to increase your spirituality to be loving of God and to the forces within. To arrange your own Consciousness of Spirituality, it might be good to find a person of your order of spirituality. You may look

360

into your churches or organizations of that order. It is your ninth year; your fourth segment of your ninth."

"Is this where you learn more? Question more?"

"This is where you be yourself of that which you desire to be; a spiritual, loving person with pleasantry. It is important to be pleasant. To laugh or make jest whenever you can. Not overabundantly, but be pleasant. Not to be too forward, yet not to be too shy. It is a happy medium that ye must seek in this lifetime of this period of time of this year."

"Why would this be different than any other year?"

"Because thee are working on different segments of your course of destiny. You are not going to have any children. Don't use the mating with a man to have a child. That would be devastating. Other women want a child so desperately that they jump in bed with this man and that man. And pretty soon, the man has disappeared."

"People say it is the greatest thing to do."

"Not if you don't like little children or you do not want to put the effort into raising a child. It becomes a problem for the child."

"I have a lot more ambitions right now."

"Very good."

"Ashlem, when I went to bed last night, I almost felt like I was not part of this world. I don't know how else to describe it."

"It is because you are unhappy. You are despondent and not happy with yourself. You say, 'What am I living for?' Then you are in trouble. But

the thought should be, 'I am still beautiful, I am still wanting a person to need I. And I am still wanting to need a person. And these are the things in your life. You give up, you have lost. But look at the adventure you have already learned with all these experiences since thee were a young girl. Has it not brought wisdom to thee? Then is your wisdom over? Are you going to stop learning because you got older? Nay. What you have to do is start living and learning from those mistakes that you made. You learn from them and do not do them again. Go about your work into life. Changing here and changing there."

"Ok. Ashlem, I don't like living in Arizona."

"Where do you want to move?"

"Montana or Idaho."

"You like snow?"

"Well, I don't like heat. And it's been a while since I lived in the snow."

"Then which one do you like less?"

"Isn't it my course of destiny to live in Arizona?"

"Did I say it was your course of destiny to live here? I say to thee, 'Don't move to California.' Could thee live in the upper countries of Arizona? It is up to thee? What about Denver? What about Colorado Springs?"

"What is a bad move for me?"

"What is a good move, or bad move for thee? You cannot find a position of work here. Could that be a sign that you should go elsewhere? Think of your own self. Investigate it. You have to make up your

own mind. You have been in Arizona for 12.5 years. You've had good times, but mostly bad times So, it is saying to thee, 'This is not where I'm supposed to be. Then you have to say, 'Where is it that I should be?' And I said to thee, 'Think about other places that are not the harsh, cold Montana winters.'

"Take ye this hand. Place upon heart. For this force of life upon thee and through thee at this time, as we venture into life, we find the difficulties of living. We find that we wonder through the forest of life, and cannot see the pathway, because there are too many trees in the way. But here of this period of life, from our heart we find the greater aspect. So, the desires of the heart are very important for the force of life. I want thee to picture in my hand this beautiful White Rose for thee. Mary will take it back. See this beautiful White Rose, now repeat after I:

"I and the Father are One.

"I stand forth into the Light of the Christ.

"For I am Light. I am LIGHT.

"I AM THAT LIGHT.

"Breathe deeply, receiving the Christ into your body. The hand of the Father upon thee. Feel the energy of the vibration passing through your heart. Feel the power of God passing through your vascular system. Feel the energy rising forth.

"I am that I am, and all that I am, I am which I think I am. Which I think I am, is a beautiful, loving person. Believe I am. Go about being that, and that is

what it is all about of the force of life of thee and
through thee. Place hand upon forehead.

"We open your inner eye so that ye may see
greater wisdoms. Anger solidifies it. Do not become
angry anymore or despondent. We lift your Veil and
open your crown chakra, and one with the Christ
Consciousness of this time. Each time ye become angry
the Veil solidifies. To open it, takes happiness, the
opposite of anger. Then be happy. Remember the Holy
Covenant: That the Circle of the Father and the Son,
and of thee and thy Holy Spirit, that the circle of God
is eternal within, never beginning, never-ending, and
never to be separated from the whole and that is thee.
It is time to fly.

"Peace be unto thee. I take my leave."

If I left this Earth now, I would face serious
consequences. However, I could move to a place like Denver or
Colorado Springs to start fresh. I needed to escape Phoenix,
Gary, heartache, sorrow, and disappointment. I was looking for a
school where you learn how to create custom herbal formulas for
patients. If I were to become a herbologist, I don't feel I would
have the foundation to be successful.

I researched Traditional Chinese Medicine (TCM)
schools, and it seemed that the Pacific College of Oriental
Medicine had the most comprehensive program at the time.
They had campuses in San Diego, Chicago, and New York City
(Manhattan). I knew San Diego was not an option for me.
Ashlem repeatedly warned us not to move to California. I wasn't

excited about relocating to Chicago; the winters were extremely cold and snowy. That left Manhattan.

Whenever I visited New York, I loved spending the day there because there was so much to see and do. Each corner offered a new experience. I was hesitant about living in such a big city because it was overwhelming. I had some fears about my safety but knew I would be protected. If moving there was right for me, I would do it.

I started planning my future. I decided to live in Pennsylvania and commute by train to Manhattan for school. This way, I wouldn't have to deal with traffic or safety concerns, and I could enjoy living in a quiet, rural community. I felt it was best to keep some distance from my family because I didn't want to get caught up in the daily drama. I loved Pennsylvania and wanted to experience all four seasons again. I wondered if I could return and rekindle the love I once had for the city from lifetimes ago.

I researched living around Washington Crossing, New Hope, somewhere in Bucks County. I always felt at home there. It would be convenient to catch the train to NY, and it was near Philadelphia, Allentown, Bethlehem, and Easton for a job. When I told my parents about my plans, my mother was excited, but my father was hesitant; he didn't believe I would return home.

I decided to talk again with Ashlem to go over my plans. I hoped for his blessing and support. I needed a complete change. I thought heading back home might be the best option because nothing else felt right. Even this move didn't seem like the right choice, just the right option among my possibilities.

On October 19, I had another reading where I learned a lot about my past lives and how they affect my future. The insights caught me off guard; one of the most surprising surprises ever.

Ashlem October 19, 2006

"I see a pinpoint of golden light expanding in the center of the picture, a beautiful golden light. The golden light is below the horizon. It is expanding. It is the beautiful moon rising, for I can see stars in the sky, yet faintly. As the moon is rising up, it seems to have streaks across its face, like a harvest moon. How beautiful it is. Magnificent. Now, a streak across the face of the moon.

"First, it is white light, then it turns to a rainbow. And the initial cause of that streak of light has turned and is coming forth. It is a spaceship. It passes overhead and disappears from view. The moon is clear again. It has risen above the waters. Flickers its beams across the water. Now, it begins to rise rapidly. higher. Now, the darkness fades away. We are in a beautiful place. It has trees that seem to be something like weeping willows. But, they seem to be different, as their branches hang down with tiny leaves on them. Like we are on the edge of a great body of water. The moon has turned to the sun, lighting everything. Night has become daylight.

"There is a pathway. I seem to be moving up this pathway from the body of water and the beach there. Up a hillside pass these beautiful trees. It seems to level off over the hillside and down a little valley. I seem to be moving in that direction. It is a man-made pathway. We enter something that looks like a grotto, an oriental grotto. Crossing an arched bridge with oriental rails of the similar design.

366

"Now the pathway enters into a beautiful horseshoe-shaped wall. Looks man-made. Beautiful stones are paved upon each other. I do not see any mortar between the stones. From above, a beautiful spring of water falls down upon the pool, and there are lily pads growing on this pool of water. There seems to be places, here and down there around this pool, a person could sit on a stone or concrete bench or chair.

"There at the head of the pool of water is the pedestal that raises up. The curvature on the edges are oriental in the design. On that pedestal appears a white area of rock, and the White Rock appears. A golden flame like a candle flame that grows in size and intensity and begins to soften and diminish. Ashlem is standing in that flame. Ashlem is wearing his beautiful white robe of simplicity.

"This is off to one side, a horseshoe-shaped pond. On the other side, the same thing occurs. A pedestal standing above turns beautifully, white; magnificently white. On it appears another image. It is Quan Yin, the Goddess. Now, spirits begin to appear around this small pool of water. The Brotherhood of Light is appearing. Confucius has come forth.

"And now walking down the pathway over that bridge, is the Blessed Virgin Mary. She's moving swiftly, but her feet are moving slowly. And she comes forth to an area, and comes next to Ashlem. Ashlem bows his head to Mary, and she has in her hand the beautiful White Rose. She smells the Rose and passes it to Ashlem. Then She sits on that bench next to Ashlem, smiles broadly. The Blessed Virgin Mary begins to speak, and golden words come forth, and they say, **'Ashlem, my friend, I have given to thee, Tracey's beautiful White Rose of her Christ. As I have said, I will always bring it forth.'**

367

*She turns sideways and says, '**Unto thee the blessedness of Angels of Light, as you have found your pathway, and we will monitor thee of this time. Be sure to understand all the goodness of life that will come forth soon, and these periods of time. As you're changing your pathway, we have brought to thee, of this beautiful scene of the Orient. It is not here, but in the Orient. I will not say where, but this is a place of existence. The waters of time flow directly from the Earth. Though man has created a monument to the water flow of life, as you find of life flowing through thee, you will begin to realize how this presence within your heart of this time. Continue your efforts. We stand with thee.**' Mary fades. Suddenly, Michael the Archangel has appeared and Gabriel. They stand on each side of Ashlem. Ashlem bows his head and wishes to speak through. I give my permission."*

"**To the blessedness of life of this time of Creation, you have come forth. We bring to thee this ancient place where the sages would sit here, at one time, to meditate upon the greater creation of Earth and the greater creation of the Heavens of time. Much wisdom and knowledge come forth here. Confucius is here, for he has sat into this place that I sit many times. But I say to thee, into the waters of this time, you may look and see the fishes swimming as we have shown before. But worry not about this experience; everything is relative to the present time of life. As a person changes their course of destiny, into the avenue, and the energy of healing. It is wonderful! It is**

368

a celebration that we bring to thee of this time of life. For they who believe into thee come forth of this time to pay homage into your experience. We are pleased of your direction. Now, there are many questions that I will answer for thee, please begin."

"Thank you Ashlem. I do have a question about the beginning, the harvest moon was rising and turned into day. Does that mean my life in the darkness is changing into goodness?"

"Aye."

"I decided to move back to Philadelphia to finish my schooling. My first question is, is this a beneficial move for me to move back?"

"Not beneficial for what would you call personal life."

"Not beneficial for my personal life? It would be more beneficial to stay here in Phoenix for my personal life?"

"My dear, it is your choice. Your personal life brings back old memories of Pennsylvania of heartache and sorrow?"

"Yes."

"You wish to renew it?"

"No."

"Your sister lives there? Your mother and father? So, the chicken comes back to roost."

"Is that a good thing?

"Never. It is never a good thing. It does not show progress, it only shows retreat. You must make your decisions. The school you wish to apply to is an accredited school into oriental medicine, so, that is

why we would say to thee, 'Go for it.' But not much happiness in your love life there."

"So, good for school but not good for my love life?"

"Old happenings there, my dear."

"But I haven't been happy in my personal life here either."

"That is what I am saying. You have always had work here, have you not?"

"Yes."

"Yet you're changing your profession into the healing existence. Then ye must look forward to a place where you can do your most work. I would suggest you check into Philadelphia and see how it is accepted by the communities."

"Some of it is. The largest western medical centers are in Philadelphia."

"Aye."

"The training of oriental medicine seems to be stronger than it is at my school here in Phoenix. Or I can go to San Diego?"

"Do not go to San Diego."

"And then there's also Chicago."

"Do not go to Chicago."

"So, you're saying to me, it is my choice. I understand. But, you say that it would be more beneficial for me to stay here Because the energy is more..."

"No. I say go to Philadelphia to enhance your education, into oriental medicines. You have the intellect to do this, and the wisdom to finish. There you will be helped by your parents, will ye not?"

370

"Yes."

"Very good. When you finish your schooling, then, you will move hither and there, to where it is necessary to practice the Oriental medicine. Remember the herbal existence as you understand. And learn of them into the Oriental medicines. Then you will find a place where thee are to go, and there you will find ability to gain your wisdom and knowledge to heal peoples with the energy that you already know, and consideration of your new doctrine of life. You will find this medicine will help thee immensely. Then you must remember to pay back your parents."

"So, I'm confused. You said personal life. Do you mean as a love life or do you mean with my parents and my sister?"

"I mean with both of them."

"So, if I go back to Philly, I will do well with school, but I will have a difficult time with my family and finding a loved one?"

"Are you planning to live with your parents?"

"No."

"Very good. Live upon yourself where you can visit, but not every day."

"Now, if I were to stay here in Phoenix, would be beneficial for me to stay here in Phoenix for school?"

"I believe the school that you're going, that into the region you have spoken of, in New York, is a better school. You need to get the best of your education. The certificate will be important for thee later on into your life as you begin a new life right now. It will be very

important for thee as ye continue on your course of destiny. Not into the area of Manhattan. Do not get involved with people who work around that school, for they speak with forked-tongue. They do not speak the truth. You have to be careful. No one can assure your safety. Only thee of this period of lifetime for thee."

"Ok. Then I will need to sell my house, and that was an issue the last time I tried to sell it."

"Did thee put a statue of Saint Joseph in the ground?"

"Yes?"

"Was it facing your house?"

"Yes. Tell me what the secret is for the Saint Joseph statue?"

"Plant it upside down, facing your front door in the ground. The Devas will work with that energies around there, cleansing the energies of negativity, for there is still negativity surrounding that house that has been brought over by others before."

"The ones from my sister and her family?"

"Aye. So, now, when you put the smile upon your face, others will come and say, 'Your house is too expensive.' If a person wishes to sell their rapidly, they must put a price on it that can sell, or else it will stand for years."

"Can AIDS can be treated by herbs?"

"Herbs can be cured AIDS. My dear, I do not know everything, but I say to thee, you are on the right track of exploration and discovery. You understand? You find the other things do coincide with

372

it in a combination of herbal extractions. Then, thee will discover a way that it can lessen the effects of HIV."

"And you say it can be cured, is that if it is caught early?"

"Aye."

"Ok. I keep seeing a vision of a farm, and a pond where I have my practice, and where people would come to the farm and relax and get their treatment there."

"It is called Oriental Spa."

"Is that something that I should be working towards? Is it already in existence?"

"Nay, it is in your mind. You will see in time. It will have therapeutic horses, and there will be therapeutic of herbal gardens. And there will be water."

"I read about a cancer treatment in addition to the chaparral, called Essiac Formula."

"Aye."

"I read that chaparral can be toxic."

"Of course, it can be toxic. Anything taken in overabundance can be toxic."

"How do you prepare chaparral?"

"You make a tea out of it. Then have your patients drink the tea; it shrinks tumors. If there is any reaction, cut down the dosage. But if you want pure. Then you must, pick it yourself like the natives. You pick just the leaf and the stem of the leaf. You understand? It is a tedious job. You may dry it or not. If you pick it, you pick it when the essential oils are

based upon it, which will be approximately this time, and spring before it flowers. You look at the chaparral bush you're taking, if it is shiny, it has the essential oils upon it. Then you pick the sprigs and take the leaf off of it, putting it into a jar. Not the stem of the plant, as it is not chaparral. It is creosote, which is very harmful. You have to be very patient getting it this way, so that you get the most benefit from it, the purest. Then you let it dry. And then you take it and put it into the metal teaball, two teaspoons to half gallon of hot water. And it let steep for at least 20 minutes. Keep it refrigerated. Experiment with sweetening it with honey."

"What about stevia?"

"They might have a different reaction to the chapparal and lessen its power."

"I have a friend who is suffering with arthritis. Is there anything to help them?"

"Arthritis? Pectin with sweet juice. It is a slow process for healing. The time frame is usually around two months but, it really just depends on the person.

"You still must make your own decisions, my dear. I am suggesting to thee, only, according to your course of destiny that you have just altered in your mind to fulfill your destiny, to find the values of healing. You have come forth this far along the Earth's Plane. Now, it is time to raise to the higher vibration of the Christ Consciousness within thee. As you do working with people in healing, you will learn many new things yet to come.

"There may be upon this pathway, you will meet that loved one we have spoken of. But again, do not turn over rocks looking. Be patient. It will pay off.

"You are here into Arizona where chaparral grows freely. Go to the regions of an area where there is not a lot of automobile traffic. In the desert. Because there you can choose the chaparral that is the purest. Then it will take thee many hours of collecting to get a gallon jar of chapparal dried. Put it into brown paper bag. Close the paper bag to keep insects out. Hang into a dry place where it will be warm, you understand? In a shed or place where it is hot. It will dry. Then you take the paper bag, and you open it up, and then put it into glass jar and seal it closed to help it. If the moisture does cause it to become mildewed. Then it should be dry enough. You put it in the glass jar. You close it tightly and put it into the sun. If moisture bubbles on the inside of the jar. It was not dry enough. Sometimes a week, sometimes two weeks. If depends on where it is and how much to be dried.

"When you're sealing your jars, warm the jar up with dry heat not with hot water. That would be the best. Pour the leaves into it and let it cool. That will keep any moisture out of it. Any more questions.

"You have changed your course of destiny by your thought pattern. You have been thinking about Oriental Medicine. And you had to make a decision, and you made your decision in that order, which changed your course of destiny. But I will say to thee, *you are upon your course of destiny, because now you are reaching a higher plateau of that course."*

"What about acupuncture?"

"Then work upon it with your schooling and see what occurs and how proficient you can be with it. You have the mind to know about it. You have the mind to practice it. You do what you need to do. It has a great, powerful energy. I have said unto thee for consideration of acupressure. And each one has similar healing properties. Acupuncture is more powerful than acupressure. Working with the meridians.

"Take ye this hand and press it upon thy heart. For the fulfillment of grace of the Christ Consciousness within, you see even the Orientals know of the Christ. They called it the Qi. So, of this medicine of life, all things, are the delivered By the Christ. Mary bring to thee your Christ Rose. I will return it to her. We sit at the Fountain of Life, here. a place into the Orient and yet etherical. Let this image of this place that Robert has described to thee, put into your mind and go there for meditations and sit where I Ashlem are.

"Meditate upon the greater consciousness of mankind. It will help thee to remember. Now, the White Rose, envision it. Now, repeat I, Ashlem:

"I and the Father are One.

"I stand forth into the Light of the Christ.

"For I am Light. I am LIGHT.

"I AM THAT LIGHT.

"Breathe deeply. Let the Christ flow through your body. Feel the energy rising forth through your heart. The muscle that pumps over through your body. Feel the expansion of it and the creation of it. as it passes through every meridian of your body and begins to open up the Christ Consciousness there. And that energy flows freely. By your proclamation, you bring this energy to yourself. Then continue to do the White Rose each morning. Breathe this energy into your body every day. When you feel negativity around thee, repeat your dedication to the Christ. Your Light will shine brightly, and those not of the Christ, will pass away from thee without any incidents. It is important to protect yourself at all times in your new adventure.

"Place hand upon forehead. We open your Veil greater. The greater Christ Consciousness descends upon thee in your crown chakra of this energy, one with the qi. Remember, Quan Yin, goddess, has come forth to pay homage also.

"I give to thee my Covenant of Peace. That the Circle of the Father, and the Son, and of thee and thy Holy Spirit, that the circle of God is eternal within. Never beginning, never-ending, and never to be separated from the whole, and that is thee.

"The old saying of America, 'Go for it.'

"Fly beautiful Angel, fly."

To be continued...

Lessons Learned

These are the lessons I learned from Ashlem that anyone can apply to their life journey. I hope my experiences will illuminate your path and make it easier to navigate.

1. **Stay true to your Self.** Everyone has heard the old saying, "To thine own self, be true." But no words are more important than these.

    Whether you're a parent, child, friend, spouse, worker, boss, or caregiver, always prioritize what's best for yourself. This isn't selfish; we've been conditioned to think it's selfish if we don't follow others' wishes. It's not. Each day, you're alive to recognize your self-worth and stand confidently in that conviction.

    Live the life you want to live. Experience what you want to experience—all with love and in a loving way.

    You are here to serve your Self, which is the knowledge that you are one with God, never separated from the whole. Sometimes, you need to set aside your desires because the decisions you made earlier must come to completion first. However, that does not exclude your desires; it only delays them for a period.

    If you serve others, remember not to compromise your dignity. Do not let the pressures of others influence your life decisions. Allow the person to make their own decisions. You cannot force them to do anything, and if you continually do what you think is best for them, you have not allowed their free will.

    Do not let life's experiences define you. Those experiences are not who you are. They are only what happened to you. Your way of thinking and acting beyond the grasp of the situation is what matters the most.

In love, remember that it is a partnership – a give-and-take. Do not always put others' needs ahead of yours. Observe how they treat you. If you notice that you are always giving or your wants and desires are ignored, that person may not be the right one for you.

And finally, don't judge yourself for your mistakes. They are opportunities to learn. If you've learned from them, then they aren't really mistakes. If you haven't, you'll be given chances to learn until you do.

2. **Don't judge others.** Everyone has their own journey in life, and their choices might not be yours. They have lessons to learn, and through those experiences, they will gain their own knowledge. Sometimes, the people in your life will do things that cause a separation or push you in a direction you never expected. And that's okay because it was meant to happen. When we judge others, we often claim to know better than they do. Remember: you know better for your Self, and they know better for their Self.

3. **Everything happens for a reason.** Great events happen in our lives for a reason, and traumatic events also happen for a reason. We cannot judge those events. There are things beyond our comprehension and understanding. We may not understand at the time, but they do happen for a reason.

If you're struggling to accomplish a goal, consider that it might not align with your life's purpose. If it is beneficial for your life, it could simply be a matter of timing. Keep moving forward and see where it leads you. The truth about whether it's not good for you or just a matter of timing will become clear.

4. **Put your anger aside.** Anger is one of the most dangerous emotions we can experience. When we're

angry, we lose perspective and stop loving ourselves and others. Yes, anger can be a temporary and understandable emotion because we are human. However, long-term anger has a profound impact on our lives, health, minds, and future.

We lose the ability to create, and creation is the reason for our existence. Creation brings peace, happiness, success, love, and fulfillment. When you experience moments of anger, remember the prayer:

Father, forgive them for they know not what they do. Father, I forgive them for they know what they do. Father, forgive me for I know not what I do.

5. **Be as loving as you can—universal and impersonal.** Universal and Impersonal Love is the goal for all of us. What does that mean? It means respecting each other as divine beings living on this Earth and allowing everyone to live accordingly, without judgment or attachment. There will be a time when people in your life will have attitudes that differ from yours. Let them have those opinions. They should not affect you, and your opinions should not affect them. When discussing differences in attitudes, be respectful and try to understand where the other person is coming from. If you are steadfast in your beliefs that you are better or more correct than others, you become judgmental and break the impersonal aspect. Remember the Law of Attraction: good thoughts bring good things.

6. **Don't rush along your path of life.** Every experience is necessary, whether you see it as good or bad. There is a time for everything, and sometimes the lesson is learning how to have faith and patience. You will be guided and will have the experiences needed for your life. Trust in that process. It's not easy. If you were given the tools or the people in your life that you want and need before you're ready, it would lead to disaster.

7. **Spirit recognizes both Spirit and other past lives.** You may experience déjà vu and feel an inexplicable connection with someone. You might be drawn to or repelled by a particular place or time in history. Don't doubt their validity. These memories could be lessons or reminders of who you truly are. Be cautious not to let them take control of your life. Remember, they are just memories. Sometimes they need healing because you carried them into this lifetime. It's not something to fear, but something to understand.

8. **Grow your own food and herbs, and start storing food.** The Earth is changing, making it increasingly difficult and expensive to find or purchase food. Try to buy a little extra each time you're at the grocery store. Stock up on dried foods, such as beans, rice, and pasta. Learn to grow your own food—this is possible no matter where you live. Start with containers and grow your own food. As resources become scarcer, people may resort to desperate measures, including wandering and committing crimes, out of hunger. Share your food with them and ask for help in growing your own. Show them how to grow food. Save your seeds—especially the organic ones. They will reproduce, whereas conventionally grown vegetables may be modified and won't grow. This will be a time to help your neighbor, not a time for chaos; there will be enough in the world during this period.

9. **And finally, you are a part of God/Creation, not separate from it.** You are one with Creation. You are not a servant to God or Creation. It lives within you. You chose to come into human form on Earth, but that does not separate you from the whole. You are a spark in the Greater Consciousness of Being. And you are worth it.

Glossary

ANIMALS:

> **Eagles:** Leaders who have great wisdom, great insight and foresight, and strength. Gatherers.
>
> **Doves**: Christdom, Truth, Teachers, Peacemakers, and are of Love.
>
> **Squirrel:** if is running up and down a tree hiding nuts, you need to start saving for the future.
>
> **Deer:** A doe deer and a buck are mates if they go down the life stream together. If they nuzzle, and one goes away, they will not pair up.

ASHLEM'S ROBE: The robe that Ashlem wears around him is your personal aspect. That is what you should be producing from yourself today.

BIRDS: Birds circling, or circling around Ashlem, are cycles of time.

- One revolution is one year
- Half a revolution is six months

COVENANT OF PEACE: *The Circle of the Father, and the Son, and of thee and thy Holy Spirit, that the circle of God is eternal within. Never beginning, never-ending, and never to be separated from the whole, and that is thee.*

COLORS: All colors have meaning.

> **Pink**: Love
>
> **Blue:** Emotions, Balancing of Emotions, Peace
>
> **White**: Truth and Purity
>
> **Gold**: Wisdom and Knowledge
>
> **Silver:** Cleansing. Cleansing of the Mind, Body
>
> **Orange**: Intellect
>
> **Green:** Healing
>
> **Brown**: Depression

Red: Sorrows and Negative Karma

Purple: Spirituality. The lighter the shade, the greater the Spirituality

Violet: Greatest of the Spirituality

CORD OR SASH: Cords or sashes around his waist are what binds that robe to you. In other words, it is how to do it. If he wears an orange robe, blue sash, and comes in a golden flame, he is telling you to balance your emotions to increase your Intellect, then stand in Wisdom and Knowledge. He is showing you how you should be living your life.

COVENANT OF PEACE PRAYER: *Of the Father and the Son, and of thee and thy Holy Spirit, that the circle of God is eternal; never beginning, never-ending, and never to be separated from the whole and that is thee. And the force of Being be upon thee at this time.*

FLAME: Ashlem comes in a flame. He is telling you to surround yourself with that kind of existence.

FLOWERS: The abundance of life

THE FOREST: Represents Past Lives

HARMONIC CONVERGENCE: It was the world's first synchronized global peace meditation on August 16–17, 1987. There was an extraordinary alignment of the Solar System: the Sun, the Moon, and six planets. During the peace meditation, the forgiveness of karma was granted to Earth's human race, so that each soul would have a chance to live in the Seventh Day.

I AM PRAYER: This prayer is an affirmation prayer that you and Christ are the same.

I, and the Father, are One.

I stand forth into the Light of the Christ.
For I am Light.
I am LIGHT.
I AM THAT LIGHT.

Essential to say each morning. Hold your hand over your heart and breathe in your Christ Light, and your oedic life force will be rejuvenated. This is very important to help your health and nervous system as the Earth continues its cleansing period, by exposing the negativity to the Light.

LITTLE STREAM OF WATER: Your destined course of your life today.

POOL OF WATER: The sum of all your life experiences. If the stream zigzags sharply, you are going through tough times. If your life's stream flows back into the forest, you are continuing life. A new path. If Ashlem turns around three times, then your life may change three times. If a new pathway opens before Ashlem, then a new path is opening for you in your life.

ROCKS: Bumps in your life that either the water flows over or goes around, just as you would do.

RAINBOW: A Rainbow is Higher Intellect, Higher Consciousness
> **Blue:** Balancing Emotions, Peace
> **Pink:** Love
> **Gold:** Wisdom and Knowledge
> **Brown:** Depression
> **Orange:** Intellect
> **Red:** Heartaches and Sorrows
> **White:** Truth and Purity
> **Silver:** Cleansing
> **Violet and Purple:** Spirituality. The lighter the color, the higher the Spirituality.

ROSES: Pay attention to the color of the roses.

386

White Roses: Represent your Christdom, Truth, and Purity. The greater the number of white roses you have, the older your soul is. Twelve is the maximum number of white roses, including the white rosebud. If the white bud begins to open, you are gaining wisdom and knowledge as it fully blooms. The White Rose symbolizes you and is for you.

Pink Roses: Universal, Impersonal Love

Gold Roses: Wisdom and Knowledge for Life

Purple Roses: Service and Spirituality

The pink and gold roses should eventually match the number of white roses in your life. So, if you have ten white roses but only six pink roses and five golden roses, it means you need to focus on love and work to bring the pink and golden roses closer to the white roses. That's what Ashlem is asking you to do: pay attention to yourself.

SIXTH DAY: The period we are living through on Earth. In the Torah and the Bible, in Genesis, the eras of Earth's existence are described in terms of days. Light was created, then Earth, followed by the waters to support life. Birds, animals, trees, and finally humans were then created. Each day ended when the Earth experienced a pole shift, which is when the Earth's poles moved from their current North and South positions. The rapture will occur in the last days of the Sixth Day.

SEVENTH DAY: After the Earth completes its cleansing and the poles shift back to North and South, the Spirits who have fulfilled their karma will come to Earth for 1,000 days of peace and love. There will be no negativity on Earth. A touch of love from another will be greater than any touch felt on Earth today.

TREES: Each Past Life

    Trees with Brown Leaves: Lives of Depression

    Barren Trees: Lives of Negative Attitude

    Trees with Purple or Violet Foliage: Lives lived in servitude of Spirituality

Trees with Green Leaves: Lives lived to the fullest expression
Trees with Pink Leaves: Loves of those lives lived by you

WATER FLOWING: The days

WATERFALL: Life. What happens in the water relates to you. If a beaver is building a dam, you will put in much effort to sustain your existence.

www.ingramcontent.com/pod-product-compliance
Lightning Source LLC
Chambersburg PA
CBHW070906130626
46555CB00001B/18